« C’était bien à l’époque mais l’avenir iko sombre »

Africa Multiple

CONTRIBUTIONS TO THE STUDY OF AFRICA AND ITS DIASPORAS

VOLUME 5

The titles published in this series are listed at *brill.com/afmu*

« C'était bien à l'époque mais l'avenir iko sombre »

Negotiating Nostalgia with and among Ex-Mineworkers in Lubumbashi (DRC)

By

Daniela Waldburger

BRILL

LEIDEN | BOSTON

Research results from: the Austrian Science Fund (FWF): Employment-tied Housing in (post)colonial Africa / Grant-DOI: 10.55776/P29566

Published with the support of the Austrian Science Fund (FWF): Grant-DOI: 10.55776/PUB1186

FWF Österreichischer Wissenschaftsfonds

Cover illustration: Lubumbashi, Cité Gécamines, July 2019, © Carl-Philipp Bodenstein (used with permission)

The Library of Congress Cataloging-in-Publication Data is available online at https://catalog.loc.gov

Typeface for the Latin, Greek, and Cyrillic scripts: "Brill". See and download: brill.com/brill-typeface.

ISSN 2772-7157
ISBN 978-90-04-72489-1 (hardback)
ISBN 978-90-04-72490-7 (e-book)
DOI 10.1163/9789004724907

This book is printed on acid-free paper and produced in a sustainable manner.

For all so-called Départs Volontaires

Contents

Acknowledgements

I was able to conduct the research for this monograph thanks to the support of various individuals and institutions. The Austrian Science Fund (FWF) provided the funds for research in the archives in Brussels, research trips to Lubumbashi, organisation of and participation in workshops and conferences, publication of this monograph, articles and a co-edited monograph as part of the project "Employment-tied Housing in (Post)colonial Africa" (Project no. P29566-G28). I would like to thank the project manager of the umbrella project, Prof. Kirsten Rüther, for her interest in my topic and her trust in me, which allowed me to design my case study according to my ideas. I am also grateful to the other two project members, Martina Barker-Ciganikova and Carl-Philipp Bodenstein, for their academic companionship and all the fruitful discussions we have had in the course of the project.

Patrick Mudekereza and Sari Middernacht from the Waza Arts Centre in Lubumbashi were essential for the implementation of the *baraza*, a council for co-generating knowledge, which is a core theme of this monograph. I thank them both for their enthusiasm, for sharing their experiences and for their support.

Prof. Donatien Dibwe dia Mwembu from the University of Lubumbashi deserves my heartfelt thanks for his support on the ground and his expertise. I was always very happy to receive his invitations to his offices: the office for "work", as he called his research office, and the "political office", as he called the dean's office. He offered debriefings and valuable exchanges and, as an unexpected mentor, he constantly asked about my research progress.

Without Marc (his name remains anonymous to ensure privacy), the research would not have been possible. He was my guide through challenging times in Lubumbashi, but above all he was the facilitator and mediator between the Départs Volontaires, who are at the heart of this research, and me. He solved the small and big problems that were often invisible to me. In the end, he became a great friend. The evenings with him and his wife remain unforgettable.

My biggest thanks go to all the members of the Départs Volontaires, especially to the president and the secretary. I thank them for their support, their openness, their curiosity, their concerns and their patience. Each conversation with each member of the Départs Volontaires was a privilege. We have created knowledge together and I hope that I do not disappoint them with the "academic book" that gives their voices a prominent space.

Many people have been instrumental during the research and writing process by supporting me in various ways. I am very grateful to all my companions. Very special thanks go to Walter Schicho and *mon petit frère*, Rémi Armand Tchokothe, for their helpful suggestions and constructive feedback on the first draft of the manuscript. All discrepancies, inaccuracies and errors are solely my responsibility.

Figures

CHAPTER 1

Introduction

How much value do words and voices from the archive still have when the person you are talking to, who lived through those events or suffers from their aftermath, is tearfully contesting the record? I have often thought about this question, because I am interested in the limits of the archive when the information in it is compared with the reality on the ground and with oral testimony. My emotional experiences led to this thought, which accompanied me throughout the entire research process on which this monograph is based. The question still preoccupies me.

This monograph is the result of archival and empirical research that relates to two topics. One is the narratives of former mineworkers of one of the most important players in the DRC's mining sector in Katanga, the Union Minière du Haut-Katanga (UMHK). Their stories tell of a glorious past and of hopes for the future. The relevance of their nostalgia for this past in managing their life today, the triggers of that nostalgia and the longing for what they have lost were of interest to me.

The second topic is knowledge production and the communicative processes involved that lead to it, which are essential to the analysis of nostalgia. The language used in communication reproduces inequalities by privileging some actors and marginalising others. In a communication process between people of unequal status – the dominant and the dominated – there is a constant process of negotiation, which depends on the specific goals of the participants at any given time. Furthermore, every event, and therefore any knowledge being produced at that very moment, has a performativity. The language used in concrete situations ultimately maps a person's reality and reveals that person's experience as part of a larger, complex social network. Communication is therefore fundamental to society and the formation of communities and individuals.

My study is a linguistic endeavour, in that I was exploring how meaning was made in the communication between the members of the focus group and me, and between themselves, and in the documentation of events in archival material by particular individuals or by a group such as the mining company. It is an analysis of language in a particular context.

Broadly, linguistics analyses language as a system, especially at the phonological, morphological, syntactic, pragmatic or semantic level. It includes lexicography and the numerous subfields of applied linguistics, such as forensic linguistics and psycholinguistics, to name a few. I position my approach within the areas of sociolinguistics and discourse analysis. The benefit of this disciplinary approach in the context of my research lies in revealing the ways in which meaning has been created in the continuum of language, history and the present.

I approach my endeavour on two levels. First, I explore the nostalgia of the former miners as a strategy to make sense of their current life situation; second, I consider their communication methods within the research setting as their way of giving voice to their wishes and concerns. I am using "voice" in the sense of Couldry[1] and Hymes,[2] who understand voice as a process we use to represent ourselves, our worlds and the worlds we inhabit. For them, voice is the capacity to make ourselves understood in our own terms and thus to produce meanings under conditions of empowerment. It was important for me not only to carefully consider the interplay between my role as a researcher and the role of the research partners and their influence on the collection and interpretation of the data, but also to show that power relations within a research setting need to be examined constantly. The connection between the researcher and the research partners thus also came into focus.

1 Into Interdisciplinarity

I conducted the research for this study in the context of an interdisciplinary project that looked at employment-tied housing in (post)colonial Africa,[3] during the so-called "development era" from the 1940s to the 1970s. Employment-tied housing refers to a system of accommodation provision, which was planned, designed and implemented by the state, municipalities and/or employers for a skilled and semi-skilled labour force in various employment settings. The overall objective of the project was to explore how this housing system controlled the private and social issues and relations of the inhabitants and residents. Housing was thus the lens through which we examined the exertion of power and domination to discipline colonial subjects and later citizens,

1 Nick Couldry, *Why Voice Matters: Culture and Politics After Neoliberalism* (Los Angeles, CA: Sage, 2010).

2 Dell Hymes, *Ethnography, Linguistics, Narrative Inequality: Toward an Understanding of Voice* (London, Bristol, PA: Taylor & Francis, 1996).

3 "Employment-tied Housing in (Post)colonial Africa" (Project no. P29566-G28, Department of African Studies, University of Vienna) funded by the Austrian Science Fund.

in three individual yet interlinked case studies: Livingstone (Zambia),[4] Thika (Kenya) and Lubumbashi (DRC). Each city represented a different economy, related to the most widespread forms of employment during the research period: mining, agriculture and public administration.

Interdisciplinary approaches in academia are very much in vogue. At the same time, researchers are occasionally forced to identify with one discipline to be able to argue for – and, more often, defend – an interdisciplinary approach. I am a linguist. This raises questions – from others, but most of all from myself – of the value I could add to our adventure of working on a project on housing, which is more commonly associated with questions of materiality and accessibility and the skills of an architect or urbanist. The period in focus, the years roughly from the 1940s to the 1970s, might demand a historian working on social history. So what could I contribute as a linguist? What more was there to offer that would enable me to work on and in Lubumbashi, other than my linguistic repertoire? How would I read the material in the archives? What kind of material would get my attention at all? In addition, how would I fill the gap between the data in the archives and the present? This topic has been of utmost importance to me since the beginning of the research project in 2017.

I came into the interdisciplinary project as a linguist (?)[5] from a discipline that is as diverse as any other. Four fields of application in this discipline characterise my main interests, as well as my teaching and research experiences. First, the field of sociolinguistics, which covers questions of language regarding all aspects of society. Second, the discourse analytical approach, which studies language production in relation to its social context. Third, my language repertoire. Swahili and its varieties have been my topic since I started studying and therefore are among my main research and working languages; equally French, with the difference that I do not teach it. Fourth, my interest in and awareness of the importance of methodological questions that cover not only the choice of a specific set of approaches but likewise the need to adapt to changing conditions during the research process. For instance, my unhappy experience with the police (see chapter two) was productive in sensitising myself to my impact on others and initiated behavioural methodological reflections and (re)actions, such as accepting silence, submitting to the research contact's

4 See, for example, Kirsten Rüther, "Asking Appropriate Questions, Reconsidering Research Agendas: Moving between London and Lusaka, in- and outside the Archive", *Administory*, 4 (2019).

5 I inserted a question mark here to emphasise that the notion of what linguistics is, how linguistics has to be and, therefore, what a linguist is interested in is a hegemonic idea.

experience and knowledge, or keeping silent to protect research partners and their network.

Reflecting critically on my methodological choices and their impact made me discover how important my background in social anthropology was. Working for 15 years mainly in a philological field, I realised that I needed to open up again to methods that are more usually situated within the disciplines of linguistic anthropology. For example, the description of the setting, especially of the *baraza* (a Swahili term for a discussion forum open to anyone), required participatory observation beyond the (usually) more restrictive concepts by linguists.[6]

By engaging with the biographies of the mineworkers, I entered the disciplines of social biographies studies and social historiography. Working with the material in the archives was on the one hand a discourse analytical endeavour and on the other demanded approaches from historiography in general.

This multidisciplinary methodological package allowed me to handle research that was characterised by constant change: my linguistic repertoire was the prerequisite for communicating with the mineworkers and adapting to my research partners' changes in language (whether by coincidence or as strategic choices); my experience with and knowledge of related discipline approaches enabled me to expand my actions when required. Most importantly, I experienced the differing concepts and vocabularies for similar topics as most insightful, and thus my study greatly benefited from this assemblage of disciplines.

Furthermore, issues of differences between my social position and power and that of my research partners persisted throughout the research process. I consider my positionality and that of my research partners as THE characteristic feature of our shared research path, the basic requirement of which was to gain mutual respect and trust.

2 The Lubumbashi Case Study

The mineworkers of the DRC had caught my attention years before, mainly for linguistic reasons. The Swahili that developed in that labour migration context, in that part of Africa, had different characteristics from the Swahili of the coastal and inland areas of Tanzania and Kenya where research on this language is usually focused.

6 Of course, that depends on the usual perception of the discipline of linguistics.

For this study, I intended to use a discourse analytical approach, which I understand as a method to evaluate discourses systematically. It deals with discourses in their individual historical moment and proceeds from the existence of different semiotic levels in the texts of its corpus.[7] From the archives,[8] I tried to understand how members of a former miners' association, the Collectif des ex-agents de la Gécamines (they refer to themselves as ODVs – members of Opération Départ Volontaire), presented topics and how they interpreted and explained the world.

In the sense of Foucault's discourse theory, discourse analysis serves to understand the collective knowledge of an era and the claims associated with owning the truth and asserting one's own interests.[9] Discourse theory thus recognises that certain people or groups of people are able to influence the body of knowledge more easily than others. It is usually people in perceived positions of power who can change and influence what we believe to be "true". Several factors, such as socioeconomic status, occupation, educational level and gender, affect a person's perceived power. As will be shown, the members of Collectif des ex-agents de la Gécamines (ODVs) also have a position of power in presenting their views and thus can define the reading of the master narrative. By "master narrative", I mean the ODVs' recurring themes, even slogans, in our conversations.

I recognise discourse as a set of constructed statements that are organised systematically. This recognition is linked to the question of how and why these statements are constructed in this way, or considerations of which things are allowed to be communicated and which are not. The analysis, although always related to signs and strings of signs as material, inscribes itself in the framework of a more comprehensive epistemology that transcends linguistics.[10] In the context of this study, I therefore consider language as a means of acting in and shaping the world.

---

7 For a discussion of the theoretical positions and methodological possibilities of discourse analysis, see, for example, Andreas Gardt, "Diskursanalyse – Aktueller Theoretischer Ort und Methodische Möglichkeiten", in *Diskurslinguistik nach Foucault*, ed. Ingo H. Warnke (Berlin, Boston: De Gruyter, 2007), 27–52.

8 The footnoted references to the archives are given in abbreviated form. The full references are found after the Bibliography, in Archival Sources.

9 Michel Foucault, *Dispositive der Macht: Über Sexualität, Wissen und Wahrheit* (Berlin: Merve Verlag, 1978); Michel Foucault, *Die Ordnung des Diskurses* (Frankfurt am Main: Fischer-Taschenbuch-Verlag, 1991); Michel Foucault and Daniel Defert, *Analytik der Macht* (Frankfurt am Main: Suhrkamp, 2005).

10 Dietrich Busse, "Diskurslinguistik als Kontextualisierung – Sprachwissenschaftliche Überlegungen zur Analyse Gesellschaftlichen Wissens", in *Diskurslinguistik nach Foucault*, ed. Ingo H. Warnke (Berlin, Boston: De Gruyter, 2007), 81.

The theme of this monograph, the ODVs' perception of a glorious past and its meaning as a practice to manage the challenges of current daily life, is the result of a research process that was characterised by changes and adaptations to new questions. The long journey between the original research idea and the current outcome started in the archives. Soon after research began, it became obvious that Lubumbashi's entangled history with the UMHK and its successor Gécamines, the mining company that provided housing to its workforce, were key pillars on which to build the questions on housing. Furthermore, housing was one of the main measures used by the (post)colonial state and mining company to control the workforce. I had been reading countless pages of annual reports of the UMHK, which detailed complaints by workers: from flimsy doors in the houses to the lack of postal delivery to their homes, from embarrassing treatment in the hospitals to the lack of hearses and shortages of meat. I was therefore convinced that the company's attempts to shape and control the mindset of the workers – during the colonial and postcolonial period – must have left traces. In that context, workers' resentment against the company would have been understandable. To talk to ex-workers who had actually lived in the houses provided by the company, or had grown up in these houses as the children of workers, seemed only appropriate. We spoke in interviews during my three research trips to Lubumbashi – in 2017, 2018 and 2019.

Two aspects of the interviews[11] I conducted with the ex-mineworkers in Lubumbashi were of utmost importance to me as a researcher and for the result of this work: irritation and involvement. A perplexity sprang up soon after I started my first interviews in 2017. My interview partners talked about their past experiences with immense nostalgia. I had expected antipathy towards the company or the Belgian colonial state that was the backbone of the company. On the contrary. "*C'était bien à l'époque!*" (In the past it was all good!) was the sentence I heard most frequently, and it did not change in 2018. In 2019, even though the narrative of the glorious past was repeated, it started to weaken here and there. What would be the right way to approach this contradiction? How could it be that exploitative living and working conditions were remembered with nostalgic feelings?

After I started research in Lubumbashi, I was challenged on an emotional level. How could I ignore the current social problems of the ex-mineworkers that I met? Could I think exclusively about housing after an interview partner told me, when I offered sandwiches and drinks during a gathering in Cité Gécamines, that his last meal had been two days earlier? Could I ever forget

11 The interviews are discussed in more detail from a methodological point of view in chapter three.

my first encounter with the ex-mineworkers of UMHK/Gécamines, when they were very close to attacking me because they thought I was a member of the World Bank and actively involved in the decision for or against the compensation they had been fighting for? Could I ever wipe from my mind the image of scars that one interview partner showed me, all over his upper body, the result of a lack of healthcare? Could I ever not remember my interview partners' warm welcome into their houses and their willingness to share the most intimate corners of their private rooms as well as their thoughts? Or the moments when Mama Helene,[12] blind after years of hard work, touched my face and scanned the outline of my body to welcome me back? Or the gifts I received? Would I ever want to forget? Absolutely not. However, there was a problem in that: establishing the necessary distance to ensure an objective approach. But reflecting on these questions cemented the tracks that I then followed.

Hearing the narratives of the workers, about the glorious past and their hopes for the future, offered a unique opportunity to trace their perspective of that point of reference, "*à l'époque*". Until then, my only source of information about that time had been documents I found in the archives produced by those who had controlled all aspects of the workers' lives, including housing. The central issue therefore became a conceptual elaboration of the "object of loss",[13] based on the question not only of what is expressed but also how the "what" is communicated. What was the object – a product of imagination and memory – the workers pined for? How did they describe it? And how did the UMHK/Gécamines present this object itself? What effect did the measures taken in early times have in shaping this object?

This approach allowed the frictions and intersections of the imagined past among the workers to be highlighted against the perspective of the company and the colonial state. And it allowed me to answer the question I posed at the start of the introduction: Do the words read in the archives still matter when the one you are talking to you is crying because she or he lived through those events or suffers from the decisions of those times? Yes, they do, and they gain greater importance because they contextualise the object of loss from another point of view.

I shared the archive materials, such as the propaganda movie and excerpts of annual reports, with my interview partners who showed an interest in them. Often, they gave me papers from the past, for instance promotion documents

12 All names have been changed to ensure interviewees' privacy.

13 Eric Worby and Shireen Ally, "The Disappointment of Nostalgia: Conceptualising Cultures of Memory in Contemporary South Africa", *Social Dynamics: A Journal of African Studies* 39, no. 3 (2013): 468.

or awards received for excellent service or for sports competitions. Jointly reflecting on this material was rewarding, because it not only allowed me to witness my interviewees' perception but also gave them an opportunity to access information from which they were usually excluded. In addition, focusing on the ODVs' nostalgia allowed me to comply with a wish they expressed – to make their voices heard without involving myself in their political agenda.

As a linguist, I work on a textual basis. Texts, however, exist not only in written form as documents found in the archives; the words of a speaker are equally conceived of as texts, though presented in oral form. Even the written documents in the archives often had an oral text as a basis – minutes of UMHK board meetings, for instance. In presenting the discourse on specific topics in a linear and classified order, the minute-taker decided what to note and what to leave out, and on the hierarchy of the information. Regarding the interviews, I have selected appropriate quotations. My emotional involvement may have left its traces in my choice of quotations, but I am convinced that any research activity, for instance in the archives, is equally biased by personal preferences and choices.

3 The Collectif des ex-agents de la Gécamines

While I was writing these words, I looked at a copper rooster standing on my bookshelf. It was a gift from the board members of the Collectif des ex-agents de la Gécamines at the end of my second stay in Lubumbashi in August 2018. The rooster is the symbol of their association, as the president explained to me after one joint photo session, which they insisted on holding each time I arrived and left. The rooster crows every morning; he does not stop as long as he lives. Likewise, the president of the Collectif claimed that the members would not stop fighting for their compensation as long as they existed. The association was founded in 2003 with the main aim of taking on the World Bank. So, who were the members of this association and why did they become important for my research?

The mining business in the DRC had gone into a steep decline in the 1990s, and by the early 2000s, Gécamines was "a shadow of the former mining and industrial empire of the Union minière [sic] du Haut-Katanga".[14] Then, in

14 Benjamin Rubbers, "Towards a Life of Poverty and Uncertainty? The Livelihood Strategies of Gécamines Workers After Retrenchment in the DRC", *Review of African Political Economy* 44, no. 152 (2017): 190.

2001, Joseph Kabila came to power, and two urgent reasons led the DRC and the World Bank to co-operate once more. The first was to support the peace process and the second to revive the national economy. Within this context, the liberalisation of the mining sector was paramount for the World Bank: the political elites were blamed for poor governance, while the mining company was expected to attract foreign private investors to bring back its former glory and success.[15] The World Bank started a reform programme with the aim of giving the company a fresh start – Operation Départ Volontaire (ODV). This initiative sought to cut the number of employees from roughly 24,000 to 14,000. Thus, "voluntary redundancy would be available to all employees with more than 25 years' service on 31 December 2002. In return for accepting the termination of their contract of employment by 'mutual agreement', all those who took redundancy would receive 'in full settlement' a lump sum lower than the legal minimum".[16] Because the workers had not been paid salaries since October 2001, they were financially depleted at that moment and therefore 10,655 workers accepted to "depart voluntarily". Workers received between USD 2,000 and USD 4,000.[17]

Against the backdrop of this retrenchment programme, former employees established the Collectif des ex-agents de la Gécamines with the aim of demanding the full payment of all wage arrears and other benefits in kind. The association worked with two trade unions and demonstrated in Kinshasa. An NGO supported the World Bank panel and long negotiations followed. However, in 2011, "when the World Bank published its final answer, it became clear that ex-Gécamines workers would not receive full payment of all wage arrears and other benefits in kind".[18]

The Collectif des ex-agents de la Gécamines is organised into several sub groups; the Lubumbashi group is the focus of this study. Its members hold weekly meetings at their gathering place in Cité Gécamines, to report on the progress of their claims and to report on the dead. Whenever I was there, one or two new names had to be added to the list of the deceased.

15 Benjamin Rubbers, "Claiming Workers' Rights in the Democratic Republic of Congo: The Case of the Collectif Des Ex-Agents De La Gécamines", *Review of African Political Economy* 37, no. 125 (2010): 330.

16 Rubbers, "Claiming", 331.

17 Managers received between USD 8,000 and USD 15,000, directors between USD 20,000 and USD 70,000 (Rubbers, "Claiming", 331).

18 Rubbers, "Towards", 192.

4 C'était bien à l'époque/UMHK njo baba njo mama

At the start of the research process, the nostalgia of the Collectif members (ODVs)[19] was an unexpected finding for me because, as Ferguson puts it when discussing an article by an anonymous Zambian journalist, "[o]ne places the blame for African poverty and suffering squarely on the neocolonial exploiter; the other praises 'Europe' and appeals pathetically for paternalistic neocolonial benevolence. One rouses us in our accustomed anthropological anti-imperialism; the other makes us squirm".[20]

The UMHK had dominated and shaped workers' lives in a profound way, by providing not only an income but also a moral script for them. The ex-workers regarded the company as a parental figure, and it seems that without this figure and the attendant working life it offered, they were lost. The loss of work "was experienced as a form of betrayal since the company had reneged on its implicit colonial social contract to be 'baba', 'father', and 'mama', 'mother', to its workers".[21] My difficulties in understanding the ODVs' glorification of the company as a parental figure, while at the same time being aware of the company's domination of the workers, led me to conceptualise these contradictory positions under the single common denominator of nostalgia, which I would even describe as a master narrative about the "good old days". The master narrative was and had to be maintained in order to endure today's life situation. Moreover, nostalgia is the ODVs' strongest argument for their struggle for compensation.

The effects of mining companies on society on the Zambian side of the Copperbelt are described by James Ferguson.[22] He argues that there, too, mining companies had to provide housing, medical care, schools and so on, and that the mining business therefore involved more than just mining: it was a large and long-term social project, which he describes as "socially thick". The lack of provision of this infrastructure therefore offered a "socially thin" situation. Ferguson's description fits the status of former mineworkers in Lubumbashi well.

---

19 I hereafter refer to the members of the Collectif des ex-agents de la Gécamines as "ODVs", a terminology they themselves use in reference to the World Bank's programme.

20 James Ferguson, *Global Shadows: Africa in the Neoliberal World Order* (Durham, NC: Duke University Press, 2006), 172.

21 Timothy M. Makori, "Artisanal Mines, Governance and Historical Generations in the Congo Copperbelt" (PhD dissertation: University of Toronto, 2019), 120.

22 James Ferguson, *Expectations of Modernity: Myths and Meanings of Urban Life on the Zambian Copperbelt,* Perspectives on Southern Africa 57 (Berkeley, CA: University of California Press, 1999); Ferguson, *Global Shadows*, 36.

For the ODVs, the loss of work meant a "socially thin" situation that no longer allowed the same life as before. The longing for the lost was omnipresent.

The nostalgia for past experiences and the shared sense of today's suffering have created a common bond between the ODVs. In all interviews and group discussions, they eventually referred to themselves as *un/une départ volontaire* or *gécaminois*. The first phrase describes a person affected by the World Bank scheme, conveying the cynical attitude that no one left the company voluntarily, but rather signed the contract because they had no other choice while waiting for unpaid wages.[23] All ODVs use the term introduced by the World Bank, as a marker of their joint struggle. *Être gécaminois* (to be a [worker of] Gécamines) refers to a situation of the past. It is a concise way of expressing the life they have lost and the memories they share. In this context, they explained what differentiates a *départ volontaire* from a *gécaminois*: *hakuna heshima* (there is no [more] respect). To be respected by others is one of the key aspects of identity with a social group, as I discuss in chapter four.

Petit and Mulumbwa Mutambwa described the crucial value of the UMHK and Gécamines for workers.[24] The company defined the life of a worker and equally offered a group he or she could identify with.

> [T]he town lived according to the rhythm of the Union Minière/Gecamines, which regulated the lives of its personnel from birth to death: the company housed and fed them, sent missions to the country side to seek spouses for the worker, educated their children, planned their leisure and so on (Dibwe 2001a). A proverb stated that "the Union Minière [or alternatively: salaried work] is the father and the mother (Union Minière [*kaji*] *njo baba, njo mama*)".[25]

The metaphor of the father, however, was not invented by the workers but had been used in earlier times by the Belgians, as the following extract from an eyewitness description of the strike in December 1941 illustrates:

> Those people refused to work – they wanted some more money. M. Maron was a governor here. He said "when a child asks his father for something

23 On average, wages had not been paid for 21 months (Benjamin Rubbers, "When Women Support the Patriarchal Family: The Dynamics of Marriage in a Gécamines Mining Camp (Katanga Province, DR Congo)", *Journal of Historical Sociology* 28, no. 2 (2015): 214).

24 Pierre Petit and Georges Mulumbwa Mutambwa, "'LA CRISE': Lexicon and the Ethos of the Second Economy in Lubumbashi", *Africa* 75, no. 4 (2005): 470.

25 Petit and Mutambwa, "LA CRISE", 470.

> to eat his father never refuses, so I won't refuse to give you what you want. But what I ask is that by tomorrow morning you resume your work".[26]

During one of the group discussions, the reference to *baba* and *mama* became an emotionally charged topic in the context of feeling abandoned. Moreover, feeling abandoned had an enormous effect on everyday life. Men had lost their central role as the breadwinner.[27] Cuvelier illustrates the situation of a worker who had lost his job, referring to a play by the Lubumbashi based theatre group, Mufwankolo. The worker is obliged to tell his wife about his situation and the wife responds as follows:

Eeeh! Mina kufwa	Eeeh! I'm dying
Na hii muzululu ya batoto	With this long train of children
Tuta ishi je?	How will we be able to survive?
Nyumba ya kuripiya, mayi	A house to pay, water to pay
ya kuripiya	Electricity to pay
Moto ya kuripiya	What are we going to do with our
Batoto masomo paka kule campus	children at the university?
Uyu mwingine njo mwaka	And with the one who is in the
ya mwisho	graduation year of secondary school
Ya kupata nini diplôme Ni …	It is … Mufwa, how are we going to
Mufwa wangu, tuta ishi je ?[28]	live?

The wife lists the obligations she and her husband have as parents, but most of all the loss of her husband's role as breadwinner. Now, without a job, he will not be able to meet his obligations.

Dibwe dia Mwembu interviewed ODVs in 2005, two years after the association was established.[29] What he reports reads very like what I heard roughly

26 Charles Perrings, *Black Mineworkers in Central Africa: Industrial Strategies and the Evolution of an African Proletariat in the Copperbelt, 1911–1941* (New York: Africana Publishing Corporation, 1979), 227.

27 Donatien Dibwe dia Mwembu, *Bana Shaba abandonnés par leur* père: *Structures de l'autorité et histoire sociale de la famille ouvrière au Katanga, 1910–1997,* Mémoires lieux de savoir. Archive congolaise (Paris: L'Harmattan, 2001); Petit and Mutambwa, "LA CRISE".

28 Jeroen Cuvelier, "Work and Masculinity in Katanga's Artisanal Mines", *Africa Spectrum* 49, no. 2 (2014): 9; Jeroen Cuvelier, "Men, Mines and Masculinities: The Lives and Practices of Artisanal Miners in Lwambo (Katanga province, DR Congo)", (Ghent: Instituut voor Antropologie in Afrika, Ghent University, 2011), 289. The play "Mambo ina nipita" is available online: https://lpca.socsci.uva.nl/aps/vol6/mufwankoloentretiensketch.html#sketch

29 Donatien Dibwe dia Mwembu, *Faire de l'histoire orale dans une ville africaine*: *La méthode de Jan Vansina appliquée à Lubumbashi, R-D Congo,* Mémoires lieux de savoir, Archive congolaise (Paris: L'Harmattan, 2008).

15 years later, that "*à l'époque c'était bien*". Dibwe cites one of his interviewees, whose statement matches the overall master narrative that emerged from my interviews as well. Dibwe's interviewee emphasises not only that the workers were well taken care of but equally that nobody would have left the company voluntarily:

> À l'époque de l'Union minière la vie était bonne parce que chaque le 15 du mois, chaque travailleur avait droit à son salaire. Nous avions deux "posho" chaque semaine, nous avions bien vécu. Nous avons vu que l'UMHK était bonne. De tout ceci, il y a deux choses que je dois te dire : la nourriture et l'argent étaient donnés. […] À l'approche de noël, nous avions droit à une gratification qui était un signe de reconnaissance après un semestre de travail. Chaque année nous avions droit à un congé légal, au salaire et aux frais de congé. Après chaque trois ans de travail, nous recevions les frais de mobilier. Et si cela coïncide avec la gratification, nous avions droit à toutes les trois perceptions (salaire, gratification et frais de mobilier). À cause de tous ces avantages, nous ne pensions jamais qu'un jour nous quitterions la GCM.[30]
>
> At the time of the Union Minière, life was good because every 15th of the month every worker was entitled to his salary. We had two "posho" (food rations) every week, we lived well. We saw that the UMHK was good. Of all this, there are two things I have to tell you: food and money were given. […] As Christmas approached, we were entitled to a gratuity that was a sign of recognition after a semester of work. Every year we were entitled to statutory leave, salary and holiday expenses. After every three years of work, we received the furniture costs. And if this coincided with the bonus, we were entitled to all three payments (salary, bonus and furniture costs). Because of all these benefits, we never thought that one day we would leave the CMG.[31]

The topics emphasised by Dibwe's interviewee on the one hand refer to material objects (salary, food rations, right to holidays, gratuity and furniture) and thus to benefits all workers were entitled to. On the other hand, the interviewee also mentions that he understands the gratuity as a sign of appreciation for the work he did and thus points to the immaterial aspects, such as being a valued and respected worker, which was equally important.

30 Dibwe dia Mwembu, *L'histoire*, 120–21.

31 Unless otherwise indicated, all translations are mine.

The "[a]bjection for the pensioners of *Gécamines* elicited colonial nostalgia, a sense of loss, but also self-reliance", Makori argues.[32] The ex-mineworkers' loss of benefits forced them to find other means to meet their daily needs, while at the same time, this loss fostered their nostalgia. Also, Larmer et al. point out that after the economic decline, a nostalgia for the past was prevalent among the ex-mineworkers in the whole Copperbelt region:

> While in the 1950s and 1960s the rural past served as a negative counterpoint to hopes for modernisation and development in the urban Copperbelt, since the 1980s economic decline and political discontent – and in DR Congo, political violence – have fuelled nostalgia for a late-colonial/postcolonial "golden age" when authoritarian one-party states and paternalist mine companies provided stability and social welfare. Analysts of the contemporary Copperbelt are constantly confronted with the potency of this historical memory, while historians must be aware of how this nostalgia, and the current state of the region, shape residents' recall of the past.[33]

The authors point out the need to accept that the interview partners' recall of the past is shaped by sentimental memories. I read this less as a call to be "cautious" as an academic with the evaluation of interviewees' statements, and more as a supporting argument that the ex-mineworkers' nostalgia is indeed worth studying carefully. This nostalgia, which was my first finding after the initial interviews, serves as my starting point to discuss nostalgia as a productive sentiment that helps to endure today's situation and to imagine an alternative future nourished by the images of the good old days. The ODVs construct this nostalgia against the backdrop of a glorification of the mining company after losing their employment and their present economically precarious situation. The conceptualisation of their master narrative later serves as the conceptual background to discuss their objects of loss.

5 Inspiring Thoughts

From a historical and spatial perspective, the mining companies in the Copperbelt in general, the UMHK/Gécamines in Lubumbashi, the mineworkers

32 Makori, "Artisanal Mines", 42.

33 Miles Larmer, Enid Guene and Benoît Henriet, eds., *Across the Copperbelt: Urban & Social Change in Central Africa's Borderland Communities* (Suffolk, Rochester, NY: James Currey, 2021), 12.

and ex-mineworkers, and the city of Lubumbashi, have attracted interest from many scholars. So have issues regarding the inhabitants of Katanga and inhabitants in colonies in general, especially those related to (imposed) modernity. Similarly, and importantly, the Swahili variety from Lubumbashi and the general linguistic singularities in Lubumbashi during the colonial period and today have garnered attention. In addition to these perspectives, I consider the sociolinguistic reality. Finally, the communicative aspect, whether written or spoken, as a basic prerequisite for knowledge to be created, is reflected in a rich repertoire of studies from different disciplines.

At this point, I refer to some works that inspired me and triggered productive thoughts. I therefore consider them relevant for the further understanding of my approach and its different disciplinary perspectives. I have arranged these "inspiring thoughts" into nine clusters of ideas.

5.1 *Cluster One: Lubumbashi's Social History*

To contextualise the archival material and the situation of the UMHK and its workers in Lubumbashi in general, the following works were particularly helpful: Vanthemsche covers the general history of the Belgian Congo over a period of roughly 100 years.[34] Young writes about the history of the Belgian Congo 50 years earlier, shortly after independence, with a strong focus on political issues.[35] Cooper also takes on the question of decolonisation, looking at labour and comparing it in the context of French and British colonialism.[36] Questions of modernity in general are discussed by Ferguson[37] (who also discusses them in relation to the Zambian Copperbelt)[38] and Mantuba-Ngoma and Zana Etambal,[39] while Vellut[40] focuses on modernity in the Belgian Congo. Dumett looks into the role of resource extraction during the Second World War.[41]

---

34 Guy Vanthemsche, *Belgium and the Congo, 1885–1980* (New York: Cambridge University Press, 2012).

35 Crawford Young, *Politics in the Congo: Decolonisation and Independence* (Princeton, NJ: Princeton University Press, 1965).

36 Frederick Cooper, *Decolonisation and African Society: The Labour Question in French and British Africa* (Cambridge: Cambridge University Press, 1996).

37 Ferguson, *Global Shadows.*

38 Ferguson, *Expectations.*

39 Mabiala Mantuba-Ngoma and Mathieu Zana Etambala, eds., *La société congolaise face à la modernité (1700–2010): Mélanges eurafricains offerts à Jean-Luc Vellut,* Cahiers africains, no. 89 (Paris: L'Harmattan, 2017).

40 Jean-Luc Vellut, ed., *Itinéraires croisés de la modernité Congo belge (1920–1950)*, Cahiers africains / Afrika Studies (Paris, Tervuren: L'Harmattan, Institut Africain – Cedaf / Afrika Instituut-Asdoc, 2001).

41 Raymond E. Dumett, "Africa's Strategic Minerals During the Second World War", *The Journal of African History* 26, no. 4 (1985).

The history of the UMHK and its workers is described by Dibwe dia Mwembu[42] and Fetter,[43] for instance. The mineworkers' protests and strikes in that period are examined by Higginson[44] and Seibert,[45] while the same authors also provide insightful thoughts on a working class that was forged in the Belgian Congo.[46] Perrings takes a broader focus and looks at the issue of mineworkers in Central Africa.[47] Vellut not only discusses the mining sector in the Belgian Congo[48] but also its economic history in general.[49] A comparative approach to the Zambian Copperbelt is taken by Larmer et al.[50] and Larmer[51] and in relation to mining and governance by Makori.[52] Hunt[53] has a narrower thematic focus, discussing domesticity and colonialism, and Malevez[54] writes about domesticity through male architecture. Masandi looks into female education in the Belgian Congo.[55] The formation of the social class of the *evolués*

---

42 Donatien Dibwe dia Mwembu, *Histoire des conditions de vie de travailleurs de L'Union Minière Du Haut-Katanga/Gécamines (1910–1999)* (Lubumbashi: Presses universitaires de Lubumbashi, 2001).

43 Bruce Fetter, *L'Union Minière Du Haut Katanga, 1920–1940. La naissance d'une sousculture totalitaire,* (Brussels: Centre d'études et de documentation africaines, 1973).

44 John Higginson, "Bringing the Workers Back in: Worker Protest and Popular Intervention in Katanga, 1931–1941", *Canadian Journal of African Studies / Revue Canadienne des Études Africaines* 22, no. 2 (1988); John Higginson, "Steam Without a Piston Box: Strikes and Popular Unrest in Katanga, 1943–1945", *The International Journal of African Historical Studies* 21, no. 1 (1988).

45 Julia Seibert, ""Wind of Change": Worker's Unrest and the Transformation of Colonial Capital in Katanga – Belgian Kongo", in *Work and Culture in a Globalized World. From Africa to Latin America*, ed. Babacar Fall, Ineke Phaf-Rheinberger and Andreas Eckert (Berlin, Paris: Karthala, 2015).

46 John Higginson, *A Working Class in the Making. Belgian Colonial Labor Policy, Private Enterprise, and the African Mineworker, 1907–1951* (Madison, WI: University of Wisconsin Press, 1989); Julia Seibert, *In die Globale Wirtschaft Gezwungen: Arbeit und Kolonialer Kapitalismus im Kongo (1885–1960)* (Frankfurt, New York: Campus Verlag, 2016).

47 Perrings, *Black Mineworkers.*

48 Jean-Luc Vellut, "Mining in the Belgian Congo", in *History of Central Africa*, ed. David Birmingham and Phyllis M. Martin, 4th imp. (London, New York: Longman, 1993).

49 Jean-Luc Vellut, *Les bassins miniers de l'ancien Congo belge. Essai d'histoire économique et sociale (1900–1960)* (Brussels: CEDAF, 1981).

50 Larmer, Guene and Henriet, *Across.*

51 Larmer, Guene and Henriet, *Across;* Miles Larmer, *Living for the City* (Cambridge: Cambridge University Press, 2021).

52 Makori, "Artisanal Mines".

53 Nancy R. Hunt, "Domesticity and Colonialism in Belgian Africa: Usumbura's Foyer Social, 1946–1960", *Signs: Journal of Women in Culture and Society* 15, no. 31 (1990).

54 Apolline Malevez, "'Les Douceurs De L'intimité': Men and the Making of Domesticity in Belgian Architecture Magazines (1890–1914)", *Dix-Neuf,* 2021.

55 Pierre K. Masandi, "L'éducation féminine au Congo belge", *Paedagogica Historica* 40, no. 4 (2004).

is taken up by Kadima-Tshimanga[56] and Mutamba Makombo.[57] I consider the work on oral history to be equally significant, such as Dibwe dia Mwembu's thoughts on doing oral history in Lubumbashi.[58] Linked to that topic, Kerr's[59] considerations in oral history for a collaborative analysis are revealing; equally so is the discussion of the oral interview in relation to dialogue and experience by Portelli.[60]

5.2 *Cluster Two: Ethnographic and Social Studies*

Various ethnographic and social studies related to the mineworkers in Katanga exist: Cuvelier discusses the question of masculinity among artisanal miners.[61] Quaretta looks at contemporary masculinities in relation to beer consumption.[62] Dibwe dia Mwembu's compilation includes manifold contributions to the question of urban identities.[63] Dibwe dia Mwembu also discusses the family structure of the working-class family.[64] *Kazi* (work) is addressed by Dibwe dia Mwembu[65] and Fabian.[66] Rubbers offers several interesting contributions, such as on the question of paternalism and liberalisation of the mining sector,[67]

56 Bajana Kadima-Tshimanga, "La société sous le vocabulaire blancs, noirs et evolués dans l'ancien Congo belge (1955–1959)", *Mots* 5, no. 1 (1982).

57 Jean-Marie Mutamba Makombo, *Du Congo belge au Congo indépendant, 1940–1960 : Émergence des* évolués et genèse du na*tionalisme* (Kinshasa, 1998).

58 Dibwe dia Mwembu, *L'histoire*.

59 Daniel Kerr, ""We Know What the Problem Is": Using Oral History to Develop a Collaborative Analysis of Homelessness from the Bottom up", *Oral History Review* 30, no. 1 (2003).

60 Alessandro Portelli, "Living Voices: The Oral History Interview as Dialogue and Experience", *The Oral History Review* 45, no. 2 (2018).

61 Cuvelier, "Men".

62 Edoardo Quaretta, "Apprendre à « prendre la bière ». Masculinité, distinction sociale et rapports de couple dans la Lubumbashi contemporaine", in *Lubumbashi aujourd'hui: Langues, arts et société,* eds. Flavia Aiello and Roberto Gaudioso (Paris: L'Harmattan, 2021).

63 Donatien Dibwe dia Mwembu, ed., *Les identités urbaines en Afrique. Le cas de Lubumbashi (R.D. Congo)*, coll. Mémoires lieux de savoir (Paris: L'Harmattan, 2009).

64 Donatien Dibwe dia Mwembu, "La structure de la famille ouvrière de Lubumbashi (1910–2010)", in Amuri Mpala-Lutebele, *Lubumbashi, cent ans* (Paris: L'Harmattan, 2013).

65 Donatien Dibwe dia Mwembu, "La perception du kazi (travail salarié) par les travailleurs de la Gécamines (1910–2010)", in *La société congolaise face à la modernité (1700–2010): Mélanges eurafricains offerts à Jean-Luc Vellut*, eds. Mabiala Mantuba-Ngoma and Mathieu Zana Etambala, Cahiers africains No 89 (Paris: L'Harmattan, 2017).

66 Johannes Fabian, "Kazi: Conceptualizations of Labor in a Charismatic Movement Among Swahili-Speaking Workers", *Cahiers d'études africaines* 50 (1973).

67 Benjamin Rubbers, *Le paternalisme en question: Les anciens ouvriers de la Gécamines face à la libéralisation du secteur minier katangais* (RD *Congo*), Cahiers africains (Paris: L'Harmattan, 2013).

on women who support the patriarchal family system,[68] and on the livelihood strategies of ex-mineworkers.[69]

The following case studies, inherently linked to the existence of gainful employment, inspired my subchapter on leisure and motivated me to think in comparative terms: Akyeampong and Ambler as well as Thomas[70] contribute general thoughts on the topic; Odhiambo's[71] considerations are helpful to think about the gendered discourse on leisure; Chipande's[72] explanations on football in the Zambian Copperbelt; and Martin's[73] account of leisure in colonial Brazzaville.

5.3 *Cluster Three: Urban History and Space*

Spatial considerations are important in the context of this study, because I understand space as the underlying condition of nostalgia. The history of the city of Lubumbashi is discussed by Chapelier[74] and Fetter.[75] Dibwe dia Mwembu links the city's history with memory.[76] Many aspects of Lubumbashi's history are addressed in Jewsiewicki et al.'s anthology on the occasion of the 100th anniversary of the city.[77] Population and land use in Lubumbashi are discussed by Dibwe dia Mwembu and Kayembe wa Kayembe.[78] The retell-

68 Rubbers, "Women".

69 Rubbers, "Towards".

70 Emmanuel Akyeampong and Charles Ambler, "Leisure in African History: An Introduction", *International Journal of African Historical Studies* 35, no. 1 (2002); Keith Thomas, "Work and Leisure", *Past & Present* 29 (1964).

71 E.S.A. Odhiambo, "Kula Raha: Gendered Discourses and the Contours of Leisure in Nairobi, 1946–63", *Azania: Archaeological Research in Africa* 36–37, no. 1 (2001), 1.

72 Hikabwa D. Chipande, "Football on the Zambian and Katangese Copperbelts: Leisure and Fan Culture from the 1930s to the Present", in *Across the Copperbelt: Urban & Social Change in Central Africa's Borderland Communities*, eds. Miles Larmer, Enid Guene and Benoît Henriet (Suffolk, Rochester, NY: James Currey, 2021).

73 Phyllis Martin, *Leisure and Society in Colonial Brazzaville* (Cambridge: Cambridge University Press, 2009).

74 Alice Chapelier, *Elisabethville – Essai de géographie urbaine* (Brussels, 1957).

75 Bruce Fetter, *The Creation of Elisabethville, 1910–1940* (Stanford, CA: Hoover Institution Press, 1976).

76 Donatien Dibwe dia Mwembu, "Lubumbashi: Histoire et mémoire d'une ville industrielle», in *Itinéraires croisés de la modernité Congo belge (1920–1950)*, ed. Jean-Luc Vellut (Paris: L'Harmattan, 2001).

77 Bogumil Jewsiewicki, Donatien Dibwe dia Mwembu and Rosario Giordano, eds., *Lubumbashi 1910–2010. Mémoire d'une ville industrielle – Ukumbusho Wa Mukini Wa Komponi* (Paris: L'Harmattan, 2010).

78 Donatien Dibwe dia Mwembu and Matthieu Kayembe wa Kayembe, *"La ville de Lubumbashi. Population et consommation de l'espace, 2000 à 2017", in Lubumbashi aujourd'hui: Langues, arts et société,* eds. Flavia Aiello and Roberto Gaudioso (Paris: L'Harmattan, 2021).

ing of Lubumbashi's story from the perspective of a former domestic worker is particularly significant to me because in it the voices of the colonised are heard. The publication itself was by Fabian,[79] while works referencing it are discussed by Schicho[80] and Pauni and Dibwe dia Mwembu.[81]

The general question of belonging in a place is discussed by Bennett and inspired me to think about space in relation to nostalgia.[82] Questions of urbanity are also linked to place. Thus, Coquery-Vidrovitch's[83] writing on urbanisation in Africa was helpful, equally Vellut's[84] examination of the urban history of Africa. Since the workers' camps and houses were of particular importance to the overall project, publications on Lubumbashi's architectural history were of great interest. The history of the labour camp is reviewed by Dibwe dia Mwembu[85] and Rubbers.[86] Viewed from the discipline of architecture, Lagae and also Boonen discuss aspects such as the ideal colonial house,[87] post-war domestic practices,[88] colonial built heritage,[89] the early urban development

79 Johannes Fabian, ed., *History from Below: The "Vocabulary of Elisabethville" by André Yav, Text, Translations, and Interpretive Essay* (Amsterdam, Philadelphia, PA: John Benjamins Publishing Company, 1990).

80 Walter Schicho, "Linguistic Notes on the 'Vocabulary of Elisabethville', in *History from Below: The 'Vocabulary of Elisabethville' by André Yav, Text, Translations, and Interpretive Essay*, ed. Johannes Fabian (Amsterdam, Philadelphia, PA: John Benjamins Publishing Company, 1990).

81 Pierre K. Pauni and Donatien Dibwe dia Mwembu, "Vocabulaire de ville de Elisabethville, rédigé par André Yav, traduit et commenté», in *Lubumbashi 1910–2010. Mémoire d'une ville industrielle – Ukumbusho Wa Mukini Wa Komponi,* eds. Bogumil Jewsiewicki, Donatien Dibwe dia Mwembu and Rosario Giordano (Paris: L'Harmattan, 2010).

82 Julia Bennett, "Gifted Places: The Inalienable Nature of Belonging in Place", *Environment and Planning D: Society and Space* 32, no. 4 (2014).

83 Catherine Coquery-Vidrovitch, "The Process of Urbanization in Africa (From the Origins to the Beginning of Independence)", *African Studies Review* 34, no. 1 (1991).

84 Jean-Luc Vellut, ed., *Villes d'Afrique: Explorations en histoire urbaine,* Cahiers africains (Paris: L'Harmattan, 2007).

85 Donatien Dibwe dia Mwembu, "A History of the Gécamines Labour Camp, Lubumbashi, 1912 to Present Day", in VANSA/Centre d'Art Waza, *Revolution Room.*

86 Benjamin Rubbers, "Mining Towns, Enclaves and Spaces: A Genealogy of Worker Camps in the Congolese Copperbelt", *Geoforum* 98 (2019).

87 Johan Lagae, "In Search of a 'Comme Chez Soi'. The Ideal Colonial House in Congo, 1885–1960", in *Itinéraires croisés de la modernité congo belge (1920–1950)*, ed. Jean-Luc Vellut (Paris, Tervuren: L'Harmattan, 2001).

88 Johan Lagae, "Modern Living in the Congo: The 1958 Colonial Housing Exhibit and Postwar Domestic Practices in the Belgian Colony", *The Journal of Architecture* 9, no. 4 (2004).

89 Johan Lagae, "Rewriting Congo's Colonial Past: History, Memory, and Colonial Built Heritage in Lubumbashi, Democratic Republic of the Congo", in *Repenser les limites: L'architecture à travers l'espace, le temps et les disciplines*, eds. Alice Thomine-Berrada and Barry Bergdol (Paris: Publications de l'Institut national d'histoire de l'art, 2005).

of the city,[90] the transformation of the neighbourhood Ruashi[91] and the local memory in connection to toponymy.[92]

5.4 *Cluster Four: Nostalgia*

Writings on nostalgia were of crucial importance in framing my research about the ODVs' glorification of the past. I have been inspired by publications on mineworkers in Lubumbashi, especially those by Rubbers.[93] He, too, picks up the thread of nostalgia. He focuses not only on nostalgia of the workers but also of the (ex-)colonisers and for instance argues that

> If the nostalgia of the former colonialists and the former colonised express in both cases a feeling of unhappiness in the present, they also refer to two different imaginaries. While the Congolese nostalgia is mainly about material benefits, the European nostalgia seems to be mainly about the neo-aristocratic way of life that flees from the colonisers in the style of the film *Out of Africa*.[94]

In his view, the Congolese nostalgia "is mainly about material benefits". However, it was important for my research endeavour to get an idea of what else nostalgia can mean, and a nuanced description of what is missing, including the non-material, thus seemed advisable. In addition, Donatien Dibwe dia Mwembu offers us extensive literature about Lubumbashi's social history. He

90 Johan Lagae and Sofie Boonen, "A City Constructed by 'Des Gens D'ailleurs': Urban Development and Migration Policies in Colonial Lubumbashi, 1910–1930", *Comparativ: Zeitschrift für Globalgeschichte und vergleichende Gesellschaftsforschung*, 25, no. 4 (2015); Johan Lagae and Sofie Boonen, "Scenes from a Changing Colonial 'Far West': Picturing the Early Urban Landscape and Colonial Society of Cosmopolitan Lubumbashi, 1910–1931", *Stichproben* 28 (2015).

91 Johan Lagae and Sofie Boonen, "Ruashi, a Pessac in Congo? On the Design, Inhabitation, and Transformation of a 1950s Neighborhood in Lubumbashi, Democratic Republic of the Congo", in *The Politics of Housing in (Post)Colonial Africa*, eds. Kirsten Rüther, Martina Berker-Ciganikova and Daniela Waldburger (Berlin: De Gruyter, 2020).

92 Johan Lagae, Sofie Boonen, and Donatien Dibwe dia Mwembu, "M(G)R. De Hemptin(N)E, I Presume? Transforming Local Memory Through Toponymy in Colonial/Post-Colonial Lubumbashi, DR Congo", in *Place Names in Africa: Colonial Urban Legacies, Entangled Histories*, ed. Liora Bigon (Cham: Springer International Publishing, 2016).

93 Benjamin Rubbers, "The Story of a Tragedy: How People in Haut-Katanga Interpret the Post-Colonial History of Congo", *The Journal of Modern African Studies* 47, no. 2 (2009); Rubbers, "Claiming".

94 Benjamin Rubbers, "Au temps béni de la colonie. Le Congo belge dans la mémoire des anciens coloniaux et des anciens colonisés", in *Autour de la mémoire. La Belgique, Le Congo cassé Colonial*, ed. Rosario Giordano (Paris, Turin: L'Harmattan, 2008), 128.

also held interviews in the 1990s and early 2000s and writes about nostalgia.[95] On a more general level, Angé and Berliner as well as Pickering and Keightley[96] offer essential thoughts on the debate. It was probably Dlamini's well-known work on "native" nostalgia of those living in townships in apartheid South Africa that triggered most of my ideas related to that topic.[97] Nostalgia is discussed from various other points of view: colonial nostalgia by Bissell,[98] imperialist nostalgia by Rosaldo[99] and nostalgia for the future by Boym[100] and Piot.[101] A somewhat different approach is taken by Strangleman who focuses on the nostalgia of organisations.[102]

For the conceptualisation of the objects of loss in relation to nostalgia, I am grateful to have discovered Worby and Ally's contribution.[103] Seen from another angle, nostalgia is associated with remembering. This is discussed by Blokland,[104] for instance, in relation to collective acts of remembering and by Brichet[105] in relation to heritage work.

5.5 *Cluster Five: Social Identity*

Issues related to identity were important, in order to conceptualise ODVs on the one hand as a community[106] and to analyse the different levels associated with identity on the other. In terms of construction of social identity, the works by Ochs[107] and Ochs and Capps[108] were helpful, as was the work by Bucholtz

95 Dibwe dia Mwembu, *Bana Shaba*.

96 Olivia Angé and David Berliner, eds., *Anthropology and Nostalgia*, 1st ed. (New York, Oxford: Berghahn Books, 2015), Michael Pickering and Emily Keightley, "The Modalities of Nostalgia", *Current Sociology* 54, no. 6 (2006).

97 Jacob Dlamini, *Native Nostalgia* (Johannesburg: Jacana, 2009).

98 William C. Bissell, "Engaging Colonial Nostalgia", *Cultural Anthropology* 20, no. 2 (2005).

99 Renato Rosaldo, "Imperialist Nostalgia", *Representations* 26 (1989); Special Issue: Memory and Counter-Memory.

100 Svetlana Boym, *The Future of Nostalgia* (New York: Basic Books, 2001).

101 Charles Piot, *Nostalgia for the Future* (Chicago, IL: University of Chicago Press, 2010).

102 Tim Strangleman, "The Nostalgia of Organisations and the Organisation of Nostalgia: Past and Present in the Contemporary Railway Industry", *Sociology* 33, no. 4 (1999).

103 Worby and Ally, "Disappointment".

104 Talja Blokland, "Bricks, Mortar, Memories: Neighbourhood and Networks in Collective Acts of Remembering", *International Journal of Urban and Regional Research* 25, no. 2 (2001).

105 Nathalia Brichet, *An Anthropology of Common Ground: Awkward Encounters in Heritage Work* (Manchester: Mattering Press, 2018).

106 Mike Savage, "Histories, Belongings, Communities", *International Journal of Social Research Methodology* 11, no. 2 (2008).

107 Elinor Ochs, "Constructing Social Identity: A Language Socialization Perspective", *Research on Language and Social Interaction* 26, no. 3 (1993).

108 Elinor Ochs and Lisa Capps, "Narrating the Self", *Annual Review of Anthropology* 25 (1996).

and Hall[109] in terms of interactions. More specific to my research setting is the publication by Dunn[110] on Mobutu's undertakings to create a Zairian identity. Strangleman discusses mineworkers' identity perceptions, though against the background of the setting in Great Britain.[111]

5.6 *Cluster Six: Languages of Research*

Very general thoughts on the connection between language and power are offered by Fairclough.[112] In relation to the Belgian Congo, the works by Fabian[113] on missions and the colonisation of African languages, by Kadima-Tshimanga[114] on the language used to describe different members of society, and of course Ngalasso's[115] essay on the status of languages and state languages in Zaire must be mentioned. The status, role and form of contemporary Swahili is discussed by Ferrari et al.,[116] Gysels[117] and Mulumbwa Mutambwa,[118] while Kasombo Tshibanda et al.[119] work on the linguistic traces that mining left on Swahili in Katanga. Fabian[120] focuses on Swahili in the former Belgian Congo

109 Mary Bucholtz and Kira Hall, "Language and Identity", in *A Companion to Linguistic Anthropology*, ed. Alessandro Duranti (Oxford: Basil Blackwell, 2004); Mary Bucholtz and Kira Hall, "Identity and Interaction: A Sociocultural Linguistic Approach", *Discourse Studies* 7, nos. 4–5 (2005).

110 Kevin C. Dunn, "Imagining Mobutu's Zaïre: The Production and Consumption of Identity in International Relations", *Millennium – Journal of International Studies* 30 (2001).

111 Tim Strangleman, "Networks, Place and Identities in Post- Industrial Mining Communities", *International Journal of Urban and Regional Research* 25, no. 2 (2001).

112 Norman Fairclough, *Language and Power* (London: Longman, 1989).

113 Johannes Fabian, "Missions and the Colonization of African Languages: Developments in the Former Belgian Congo", *Canadian Journal of African Studies / Revue Canadienne des Études Africaines* 17, no. 2 (1983).

114 Kadima-Tshimanga, "La société".

115 M.M. Ngalasso, "Etat des langues et langues de l'etat au Zaire", *Politique Africaine* 23 (1986).

116 Aurélia Ferrari, Marcel Kalunga and Georges Mulumbwa, *Le Swahili de Lubumbashi: Grammaire, textes, lexique,* Dictionnaires et langues (Paris: Éditions Karthala, 2014).

117 Marjolein Gysels, "French in Urban Lubumbashi Swahili: Codeswitching, Borrowing, or Both", *Journal of Multilingual and Multicultural Development* 13, nos. 1–2 (1992).

118 Georges Mulumbwa Mutambwa, "Kiswahili Kya Mu Lubumbashi, un dialecte ou une langue ? Une contribution au débat", in *Lubumbashi aujourd'hui: Langues, arts et société*, eds. Flavia Aiello and Roberto Gaudioso (Paris: L'Harmattan, 2021).

119 Kasombo Tshibanda, Michaël, Agnès Mwamba Chomba, and Diane Kabedy' a Sombw, "Traces du kiswahili dans l'exploitation minière au Katanga", in *La société de la copperbelt katangaise. Une autopsie de la situation socio-économique, politique et culturelle*, ed. Donatien Dibwe dia Mwembu (Paris: L'Harmattan, 2021).

120 Johannes Fabian, *Language and Colonial Power: The Appropriation of Swahili in the Former Belgian Congo 1880–1938,* African studies series 48 (London, New York, Melbourne: Cambridge University Press, 1986); Johannes Fabian, "Simplicity on Command: On Pidginization of Swahili in Shaba (Zaïre)", in *The Fergusonian Impact, in Honor of Charles A.*

and Meeuwis[121] examines questions of different languages in the Belgian Congo. The "Vocabulary of Elisabethville" by André Yav is also discussed from a linguistic point of view, for example by Kasombo Tshibanda[122] and Schicho.[123] Specifically related to the text genre of theatre regarding the question of power and performance is Fabian's publication.[124] Petit and Mutambwa examine the lexicon of Swahili used in Lubumbashi within the domain of the second economy.[125] The language of the letter to the editors of UMHK's company magazine *Mwana Shaba* is the focal point of De Rooij's paper.[126]

5.7 *Cluster Seven: Artistic Expression*

Various forms of artistic expression in Lubumbashi have interested scholars. Paintings are discussed by Jewsiewicki[127] as are questions on collective imaginary[128] or on explorations of past and present.[129] The theatre group of Mufwankolo in Lubumbashi is the focus of Schicho's monograph.[130] The role of art for Mobutu's campaign of authenticity is closely examined by Van Beurden.[131]

Ferguson on the Occasion of His 65th Birthday. Vol. 1: From Phonology to Society, eds. Joshua A. Fishman et al. (Berlin: Mouton de Gruyter, 1986).

121 Michael Meeuwis, "Bilingual Inequality: Linguistic Rights and Disenfranchisement in Late Belgian Colonization", *Journal of Pragmatics* 43, no. 5 (2011).

122 Michaël Kasombo Tshibanda, "«Vocabulaire de ville de Elisabethville': Commentaire d'un point de vue sociolinguistique", in *Lubumbashi 1910–2010. Mémoire d'une ville industrielle – Ukumbusho Wa Mukini Wa Komponi*, eds. Bogumil Jewsiewicki, Donatien Dibwe dia Mwembu and Rosario Giordano (Paris: L'Harmattan, 2010).

123 Schicho, "Linguistic Notes".

124 Johannes Fabian, *Power and Performance: Ethnographic Explorations Through Proverbial Wisdom and Theater in Shaba, Zaire / Johannes Fabian,* New directions in anthropological writing (Madison, WI and London: University of Wisconsin Press, 1990).

125 Petit and Mutambwa, "LA CRISE".

126 Vincent A. de Rooij, "Letters to the Editor from the Section Habari Za Kwetu in Mwana Shaba (Journal D'entreprise de L'U.M.H.K)", *Archives of Popular Swahili* 1 (1998),

127 Bogumil Jewsiewicki, "Peintures de cases, imagiers et savants populaires du Congo, 1900–1960", *Cahiers d'études africaines* XXXI, 3, no. 123 (1991); Bogumil Jewsiewicki, *Mami Wata. La peinture urbaine au Congo* (Paris: Gallimard, 2003).

128 Bogumil Jewsiewicki, "Imaginaire collectif des katangais au temps de la désindustrialisation. Regard du dedans et regard d'en dehors", *Cahiers d'études africaines* 50, nos. 198-199-200 (2010).

129 Bogumil Jewsiewicki, "Leaving Ruins: Explorations of Present Pasts by Sammy Baloji, Freddy Tsimba, and Steve Bandoma", *African Arts* 49, no. 1 (2016).

130 Walter Schicho, *Le Groupe Mufwankolo. Textes enregistrés et édités par Walter Schicho en collaboration avec Mbayabo Ndala* (Vienna: Afro Pub, 1981).

131 Sarah van Beurden, *Authentically African: Arts and the Transnational Politics of Congolese Culture* (Athens, OH: Ohio University Press, 2015).

5.8 *Cluster Eight: Reflexivity and Shared Authority*

Methodological considerations were certainly important to me in taking the first steps in pursuing a "shared authority" approach. I was first inspired by Linda Tuhiwai Smith's statements on decolonising methodologies.[132] Bhattacharya's work goes in a similar direction, namely towards decolonising approaches to qualitative research with a special focus on questions of Othering.[133] For thinking about my actions and their effects, Coghlan's essay was important, which comes from the strand of action research I had used especially for the evaluation of my teaching performance.[134]

At the heart of all research is the wish to produce knowledge, and thinking about who is involved in this production and who is heard and represented was important to me. From the discipline of literary studies, the reflections of Meizoz were helpful, as he addresses the question of the plurality of authors.[135] Thoughts on the multiplicity of voices in the field and in the academic text production that follows them are discussed by Segall.[136] Not only the plurality of voices, but also the multiplicity of worlds is argued by Blaser and De la Cadena.[137] A plurality and diversity of voices and words ultimately requires us as researchers to relate things to each other and look for connections. Strathern's reflections were very enlightening on this subject.[138] My wish to include my research partner's perceptions as equally valuable was inspired by essays on shared authority by Frisch,[139]

---

132 Linda Tuhiwai Smith, *Decolonizing Methodologies: Research and Indigenous Peoples*, 2nd ed. (London, New York: Zed Books, 2012).

133 Kakali Bhattacharya, "Othering Research, Researching the Other: De/Colonizing Approaches to Qualitative Inquiry", in *Higher Education: Handbook of Theory and Research*, ed. John C. Smart, (Dordrecht: Springer Netherlands, 2009), 24.

134 David Coghlan, "What Will I Do? Toward an Existential Ethics for First Person Action Research Practice", *International Journal of Action Research* 9, no. 3 (2013).

135 Jérôme Meizoz, *Postures littéraires: Mises en scène modernes de l'auteur* (Geneva: Slatkine Érudition, 2007); Jérôme Meizoz, "Sociocritique, ethnologie et sociologie de la littérature", *Romantisme* 145, no. 3 (2009).

136 Avner Segall, "Critical Ethnography and the Invocation of Voice: From the Field/in the Field – Single Exposure, Double Standard?", *International Journal of Qualitative Studies in Education* 14, no. 4 (2001).

137 Mario Blaser and Marisol de la Cadena, "Pluriverse: Proposals for a World of Many Worlds", in *A World of Many Worlds*, eds. Marisol de la Cadena and Mario Blaser (Durham, NC: Duke University Press, 2018).

138 Marilyn Strathern, "Opening up Relations", in *A World of Many Worlds*, eds. Marisol de la Cadena and Mario Blaser (Durham, NC: Duke University Press, 2018).

139 Michael H. Frisch, *A Shared Authority: Essays on the Craft and Meaning of Oral and Public History*, SUNY series in oral and public history (Albany, NY: State University of New York Press, 1990); Michael H. Frisch, "Commentary – Sharing Authority: Oral History and the Collaborative Process", *The Oral History Review* 30, no. 1 (2003).

High,[140] Rouverol,[141] Shopes[142] and Sitzia.[143] For this to be possible at all, I needed to think about not only my research but my positionality. Reflexivity in general is addressed by Hertz[144] and with a focus on the issue of confession or catharsis by Pillow.[145] Patai's reflections on positionality were particularly helpful.[146] In terms of the intertwined connections between researcher and people I prefer to call "research partners", given their agency, Jiménez's contribution was most insightful.[147] In relation to Lubumbashi and with regard to the *baraza*, Middernacht's experiences with collective curating were particularly valuable.[148]

5.9 *Cluster Nine: Voices in the Archive*

My reading of the documents from the archives has benefited greatly from the following readings: Alexander's reflections on the question of historical absence, evidences that are often peripheral, and how to preserve the dynamics of culture that often remain undocumented.[149] Battley focuses on the archive and record-keeping and the challenge of keeping authenticity of collective memories.[150] Ketelaar approaches the archive as a space of memory.[151]

140 Steven High, "Sharing Authority: An Introduction", *Journal of Canadian Studies/Revue d'études canadiennes* 43, no. 1 (2009).

141 Alicia J. Rouverol, "Collaborative Oral History in a Correctional Setting: Promise and Pitfalls", *Oral History Review* 30, no. 1 (2003).

142 Linda Shopes, "Commentary – Shared Authority", *The Oral History Review* 30, no. 1 (2003).

143 Lorraine Sitzia, "A Shared Authority: An Impossible Goal?", *Oral History Review* 30, no. 1 (2003).

144 Rosanna Hertz, *Reflexivity & Voice* (Thousand Oaks, CA: Sage, 1997).

145 Wanda Pillow, "Confession, Catharsis, or Cure? Rethinking the Uses of Reflexivity as Methodological Power in Qualitative Research", *International Journal of Qualitative Studies in Education* 16, no. 2 (2003).

146 Daphne Patai, "(Response) When Method Becomes Power", in *Power and Method: Political Activism and Educational Research*, ed. Andrew D. Gitlin, Critical social thought (New York: Routledge, 1994).

147 Alberto C. Jiménez, "Spiderweb Anthropologies: Ecologies, Infrastructures, Entanglements", in *A World of Many Worlds*, eds. Marisol de la Cadena and Mario Blaser (Durham, NC: Duke University Press).

148 Sari Middernacht, *From Collective Curating to Sharing Curatorial Authority: Collaborative Practices as Strategies of Democratisation in Exhibition Making in Lubumbashi, Democratic Republic of Congo*, (Unpublished MA thesis: University of Witwatersrand, Johannesburg, 2018).

149 Ben Alexander, "Excluding Archival Silences: Oral History and Historical Absence", *Archival Science* 6, no. 1 (2006).

150 Belinda Battley, "Authenticity in Places of Belonging: Community Collective Memory as a Complex, Adaptive Recordkeeping System", *Archives and Manuscripts* 48, no. 1 (2020).

151 Eric Ketelaar, "Archives as Spaces of Memory", *Journal of the Society of Archivists* 29, no. 1 (2008).

I found Harris very inspiring, particularly on silenced voices and ghostly voices in the archive.[152]

I called this section "inspiring thoughts" instead of the more common "literature review". The idea was to highlight different streams that accompanied my journey. In chapter three, I show how I developed my approach, built on the realities of the field, the nature of interaction I had with my research partners and my concern with coming up with context-relevant and updated methods regarding the creation of new alternative archives and the inclusion of silenced voices.

6 Structure of the Book

In the Introduction, I give the general background of the research project: the interdisciplinary and collaborative research project within which the case study of Lubumbashi is to be understood; the narrative by the Collectif des ex-agents de la Gécamines, "*C'était bien à l'époque/UMHK njo baba njo mama*" [In the past it was all good/the UMHK is the father and the mother]; and a grouping of inspiring literature categorised into nine clusters, which clarifies the context of my contribution's originality.

In chapter two, I deal with questions of positionality, because these influenced and potentially biased my understanding of and outlook on the world. I have paid special attention to how I may have influenced my environment. I consider these reflections of utmost importance for this monograph because they disclose my (re)actions and decisions transparently.

I discuss methodological and theoretical premises in chapter three, explaining why I chose a triangulation of methods, how I approached the archive, why the interviews were important and, above all, why the development of the *barazaweb* as my new method to respond to the realities of the context was so important. I also outline why and how the languages involved in the research process are important. These steps prepare the setting for engaging with the conceptual background against which I analyse what the ex-mineworkers longed for in their nostalgic memories.

The ODVs' recurring slogan of "*C'était bien à l'époque!*" (In the past it was all good!) is understood as the scope of daily experiences to which former

152 Verne Harris, "Hauntology, Archivy and Banditry: An Engagement with Derrida and Zapiro", *Critical Arts* 29, sup1 (2015); Verne Harris, *Ghosts of Archive* (Abingdon, NY: Routledge, 2020).

mineworkers refer. Therefore, in chapter four, I group their social and emotional objects of loss into three categories: stability, respect (*heshima*) and identities.

The question of (performing) identities is relevant in chapter five, which touches on the communication between the ODVs and myself, the reading and the interpretation of themes that came up during our talks and the different roles at play. I first analyse the ODVs' report on my stay in 2019 and then describe and discuss the *baraza* with the ODVs, to which the shared production of knowledge that strengthens my idea of the *barazaweb* was central.

Chapter six concludes the book and opens up to future research perspectives.

CHAPTER 2

Positionality

In her book, *Decolonizing Methodologies* (2012), the New Zealand researcher on decolonising education, Linda Tuhiwai Smith, states that methodology refers less to the selection of a specific technique but more to "the context in which research problems are conceptualised and designed and with the implications of research for its participants and their communities" as well as to questions of the power of the institution of research.[1] I am guided by this approach. However, Smith writes from the perspective of being a person "within", addressing "researchers who work with, alongside and for communities who have chosen to identify themselves as indigenous".[2] My research endeavour differs in at least two ways. First, I do not write from a perspective from within but as a researcher who comes from outside. Second, I do not define the members of the Collectif des ex-agents de la Gécamines as an "indigenous"[3] group, nor have they ever referred to themselves in ways other than as being a *départ volontaire* or *être gécaminois* (to be a [unremembered worker of] Gécamines). They do, however, share the experience of having worked for a company that was founded by the Belgian King Leopold II (along with a diamond-mining business and railway company),[4] whose legacy includes the gap between those in power and those who are kept powerless.

In her chapter, "Imperialism History, Writing and Theory", Smith discusses a point that inspired me, that history is not only about who is allowed to talk, who is heard and whose voice is valid; it is also about power. "In this sense, history is not important for indigenous peoples because a thousand accounts of the 'truth' will not alter the 'fact' that indigenous peoples are still marginal and do not possess the power to transform history into justice."[5] From my position as a researcher from the outside, writing from a privileged vantage point, I do not presume that members of the Collectif des ex-agents de la Gécamines need me to raise their voices to successfully get their compensation. But thinking about them not having the power to transform history into justice raised

1 Linda Tuhiwai Smith, *Decolonizing Methodologies: Research and Indigenous Peoples*, 2nd ed. (London, New York: Zed Books, 2012), IX.

2 Smith, *Decolonizing*, 5.

3 I use Smith's terminology. For her discussion of the term, see Smith, *Decolonizing*, 6–7.

4 See, for example, Smith, *Decolonizing*, 23.

5 Smith, *Decolonizing*, 35.

 | DOI:10.1163/9789004724907_003

my awareness of the research approach and process. In addition, I did not want to consider the members of the collective as paralysed. They have their strategies to talk about the past and to claim their compensation, even though these strategies have (not yet?) been successful. As a researcher, I was one of their strategies to make their voices heard.

1 Facing the Ghost(s)

> Ich habe eben auf dem Balkon eine Zigarette geraucht, plötzlich sah ich ihn unten auf der Strasse, ich war so geschockt, dass ich mich hinter der Balkonmauer versteckt habe. Ich erinnere mich genau an diese goldene Uhr, sie hat in der Abendsonne geblendet, und an die Kofia, das sieht man sonst selten hier. Ich weiss, dass kann nicht sein und doch sah ich ihn eben. Ich zittere gerade, hoffentlich geht das wieder vorbei.
>
> [I was just smoking a cigarette on the balcony when suddenly I saw him down on the street, I was so shocked that I hid behind the balcony wall. I remember that gold watch clearly, it was dazzling in the evening sun, and that *kofia*, you rarely see that here. I know it can't be, and yet I saw him just now. I'm shaking right now; I hope it will pass.]
>
> Notes in my research diary, 17 August 2018

I was haunted by a ghost for some days in August 2018. I knew my mind was playing tricks on me. Still, the ghost felt real then, and I was forced to confront my fears. And one way to do this was to think about my personality and positionality, not as a researcher (I come to that further below), but as a white[6] woman in Lubumbashi. Let me approach the topic of positionality in a roundabout way, based on an encounter that is not even directly linked to the relationship between the researcher and research partners but which took place in the larger setting of everyday life in Lubumbashi. At the same time, I consider the researcher's willingness to immerge into the community at large as crucial to understanding wider social dynamics.

One day, I travelled to Kipushi, a mining city 35 kilometres from Lubumbashi. Some members of the ODVs I knew from the meetings in Lubumbashi had invited me to visit Cité Gécamines in Kipushi and to interview them in

6 I understand the terms "white" and "black" as sociocultural constructs.

their homes. I happily accepted. I was advised not to travel by bus, which they judged not to be safe enough for me, but instead to take a trustworthy taxi driver. Marc (my local research contact and son of an ODV) organised this with a friend of a friend, Albert, and I knew that I would be safe in their company. And I was. They saved me from severe harassment by a bunch of corrupt police officers, not without getting into an uncomfortable situation themselves – because of me.

On the way to Kipushi, a roadblock by the police forced us to stop, and one of the well-known strategies to seek a bribe was played by staging a breathalyser test. Albert had to take a test that "proved" he was driving while drunk; the only way out was to pay a fine. The police did not notice me and Marc sitting in the back and the process of paying the fine moved quickly and discreetly. All parties involved seemed to be familiar with the process. Some hours later on our way back, the police stopped us once more for the same purpose. The driver was not happy to be forced to do the alcohol test again, and uttered some words of complaint.

Immediately, we were surrounded by several policemen, and the policewoman who had stopped us disappeared. One officer asked the driver for his papers, went away with them and then returned and asked the driver to get out of the car. Several policemen, I cannot remember how many, surrounded our car. Marc told me that now we would be in trouble and he urged me to be quiet, to stay calm, not to show fear and simply to trust him. A policeman appeared at the rear window on Marc's side and asked him to get out of the car as well. Alone, I could see Albert and Marc in the rear-view mirror, in heated discussion with the policemen but out of earshot.

Then a policeman came to the front window of the car. He wanted to see my passport. I gave him a copy of it and told him that the passport itself was at the place where I was staying. He was not happy and told me that by travelling without the original passport I was violating the law. He waved at someone who had been out of my sight before. The man was big, his wrist was adorned with a huge gold watch and he was wearing a *kofia* and civilian clothes. He smiled at me and told me that if I could not produce my passport, I would spend the night in a cell at the police station in Lubumbashi because it was too late to go to my accommodation to fetch it. I did not say anything. He looked at me in an insinuating way and stressed again that I would spend the night at the police station. He opened his jacket to make sure that I would see the pistol holstered on the right side of his chest. He took it out and pointed it at me, very discreetly. He repeated his threat a few more times. I kept my mouth shut as Marc had instructed earlier.

The big man called a policeman who was close by and told him to stay at the window while he went to join the group discussion behind the car. The policeman leaned against the car, looking at me, playing with his handcuffs where I could see them constantly. I cannot recall how much time passed until Marc came back to the car and told me that they were negotiating a price. I asked what for exactly, and suggested that he agree to it and that I would pay. He asked me for a few *francs congolais,* but said that I would certainly not have enough money on me. He assured me that all would be well, but that it would take some more time to solve the "problem" and went away. The following hour felt endless; it was hot in the car, and I dared to sip from my water bottle only once in a while, the handcuffs always in sight. Now and then, the big man came to the car and leered. I said nothing.

At some point Albert and Marc came back to the car and off we went. Only then did I started to tremble, relieved that it was all over. My companions seemed to be happy with the outcome. Marc told me that the supervisor had asked for 500 dollars because I did not have a passport, plus a fine for Albert, for complaining about the alcohol test. In the end, they were able to bargain down to 10 dollars. Plus, he added, there was a second negotiation going on with the supervisor – the price for a night with me, that white woman just perfect for fulfilling his sexual fantasy. The discussions had taken so long because of this second negotiation. Although Marc and Albert were familiar with the usual harassments by the police and well-practised in dealing with these challenges, Marc stressed that negotiating that I was not for sale was a new thing for him.

We still had quite a way to go to Lubumbashi and on our journey Marc and Albert went over the details again and again. Unfortunately, they concluded, we could not lay a charge with the police, for obvious reasons. I fully understood. I commented, rather to myself than to my company, that it was indeed incredible that such incidents with the police could not be reported and that people experiencing this kind of harassment were silenced. I am not used to not being heard. My voice has always mattered. However, remaining silent before the supervisor and his colleagues was probably a way of speaking, too – my only way to contribute and avoid the situation escalating at a cost to myself and my companions.

Some days after that I noted in my diary that I had learned three important lessons from this experience. First, even by doing nothing other than sitting in a car, I had put the people with me in an uncomfortable situation, simply by being a white woman. My existence was a challenge for those around me, for those willing to support my research, for those trusting me and in whom I trusted. Even though I thought of myself as a reflexive researcher with a sensitive approach, thanks to prior research experience, after this experience I self-scrutinised and determined that some attributes of my identity probably mattered more than I had ever thought. If, without doing anything, I had such an impact on those around me what were the implications when I was acting? Furthermore, thinking about one's positionality should go beyond the simple dichotomy between researcher and research partners. The research partners are entangled in a net of relations to others – family, partners, friends, enemies, colleagues, etc. – who might be affected indirectly by the researcher's presence. And there are people, as in the case of Albert, who might be affected coincidentally. I therefore argue that it is also important to keep the research partners' entanglements in mind when acting during research.

Second, it was a strange and frightening feeling to have no voice and no place or institution where we could lodge a complaint (apart from the debriefing with Marc over many days, which was important to both of us). The reasons for no place to go with the complaint might be manifold, but there is one thing that was obvious to me: we were the ones without power. Being powerless – having no agency – is something I was and am not used to. I therefore consider that this experience increased my awareness of those who are silenced and whose voices are usually unheard. It thus heightened my sensitivity to the ODVs' voices and the research methodology.

Third, the experience triggered more thoughts on silence – silence as a choice and as a strategy. First, it was my choice to follow Marc's suggestion to remain silent, which seems to have been a successful way to deal with the harassment by the police officers' supervisor. Second, I realise there must have been many topics that the ODVs preferred not to talk about, that they did not want to discuss or elaborate on. Silence as a strategy thus became something to keep in mind during the interviews.

My positionality is significant to the research process and my general approach that went along with this study. The following two questions guided my reflections: How do I assess my effect(s) on my research partners? (And I am aware that I will describe these thoughts based on my, and not my research partners', perspective(s).) And, from which points of view, which are shaped by my experiences, do I start and base my assumptions?

2 Trust and (re)gaining Mutual Respect

I came to Lubumbashi as a white person, a female and scholar from the global North. The expectations I held about the first meeting with the ODVs were based on a misunderstanding.

They were eagerly waiting for a person from the World Bank when I happened to show up to introduce myself at the voluntary, weekly outdoor meeting of the ODVs. The president, however, was aware of my visit, thanks to Marc, who had put us in contact and briefly informed the president about my research and intentions. The president had invited me via Marc to come to the weekly meeting to present myself after it concluded. We were a bit early, so we decided to join the big gathering that takes place in the open air close to the meeting room where we were supposed to have our rendezvous a bit later. As we approached the group, the president figured out that I must be the researcher. He waved to invite me closer. Suddenly, I was encircled by people who started shouting at me. The ODVs saw a white person, a person they probably had not been expecting that day but had been waiting for over the years in which they had been fighting for compensation. Even though I took the opportunity to briefly introduce myself as invited to do so by the president, I was not listened to and my voice was inaudible in the turmoil. I was shouted at; I was a surface for projection: a white face that had finally showed up. And I do not blame them.

The president tried to calm down the group and concluded the meeting instantly. He invited me, Marc and the ODV board members to their meeting room. There, the president officially welcomed us and a chair was placed for me and Marc in the middle of the room, the members of the board around us. The president introduced the members of the board, the vice president, secretary, treasurer, the lay priest and other board members without a specific assigned function. As per the communicative norms that setting required, Marc, whom the ODVs knew as the son of an ODV who had passed away, introduced me to those present before I was invited to speak. I chose to do so in French, because the president had spoken to me in French. I pointed out that French was not my first language; I explained where I was born, where I worked, what intentions had brought me there. This allowed me to present myself as non-Belgian, which I considered to be significant information for them against the backdrop of the DRC's colonial history. Furthermore, I assumed that talking about my nationality (Swiss) and my country of residence (Austria) was helpful to underline the intention of my research interests. Both countries are equally unimportant in terms of (geo)politics – at least at first sight.[7] I thus assumed

7 Looking deeper, the question of dictators such as Mobutu keeping their nation's wealth in Swiss bank accounts might of course be relevant. But, although I am Swiss, I have no clue about the complex banking systems that cover dictators. Happily, it was never a topic we discussed.

that I was considered not to have come from or work in a country against which these people held specific reservations.

For the second part of my presentation, I switched to Swahili because that vocabulary came to mind, whereas French failed me. I cannot recall all the details of that first conversation. But I do remember that I felt not unwelcome anymore, and that there was some vague sense that they were interested in my research. And it was during this very first meeting that I first heard the master narrative "*C'était bien à l'époque!*". In the following weeks (and of course during my later stays in Lubumbashi), attending the board meetings became a central part of my routine, and the living room of Mama Helene became the spatial locus of my research (see chapter five for the importance of during the *baraza*).

This first meeting was the start – as I perceive it now – of a mutual trust and respect that steadily grew stronger. What had begun as a verbal (and nearly physical) attack developed into a research situation in which people wanted to talk to me, asked why I had not interviewed them yet, and were interested in participating in the *baraza* (public forum). I observed their shift from justified anxiety to trust, a trust I later concluded was also the basis for their strategy to see in me a potential conveyer of their master narrative.

What makes me assume that there was trust and respect? There were some occurrences, which I discuss next, related to requests to be interviewed, mutual risk management and dealing with emotions.

3 Change of Perspective: from Near Attack to Registering for the *Baraza*

During my first stay, all the ODVs I asked accepted my request to talk with them, and during the following weeks the interest in participating grew. We met regularly during their weekly gatherings, but the interviews during the first year usually took place in Marc's home in Cité Gécamines. Despite the fact that I wished to visit their homes (housing, after all, was the entry point into this research), I did not want to intrude into their private space before being invited in. Marc's home was a stone's throw away from the place where the weekly gatherings took place.

The following weeks were filled with interviews. The first days were scheduled with one or two interviews a day, but other ODVs contacted Marc, having suggested that he be the one responsible for scheduling the interviews, and asked to be interviewed as well. Thus, towards the end of that first stay, several interviews had to be planned per day. I did not want to reject anybody who wished to share and was just happy about the positive attitude towards my request to talk to the ODVs. And many of them invited me to visit them at home the next time I was in Lubumbashi.

That I should come back the following year so that we could proceed was requested by the members and board members of the ODVs several times during the weekly gatherings, especially at the last meeting before I travelled back. Somehow we had managed to improve our relationship, from one of suspicion to an agreement that we would continue the exchange once I returned. Back in Vienna, I called the president three or four times just to pass on my greetings to everybody.

At the beginning of the second trip to Lubumbashi, during my first attendance of the weekly meetings, the good relationship was explicitly confirmed. That I had remained in contact while I was away and came back to "support" them and their fight for compensation, as the president described it, was appreciated, they told me. The start of the second stay was thus characterised by mutual respect and trust, by the ODVs' wish that I support their fight and by my wish to continue the planned interviews. "Supporting" them was an important matter during the first meeting.

I had stated during my first stay, and wanted to clearly state this time, that I would not be able to fight the World Bank, but that my contribution would be "my academic book", as I described my planned dissemination, where their voices would matter. They assured me of their understanding and agreed that a book would be a good thing. Reflecting about the fact that both sides – the researcher and the research partners – had their own agendas also came as a relief.

Having "opposite parties" with their own ideas took away my feeling of being only a petitioner. Until that moment it had felt as if I was pursuing a research interest that was of interest to me but without any benefit to "them", a position that is somehow immanent in research "about" others.

Thoughts on how I could work more in the direction of research "with" others started during those first days of my second stay. However, I realised that to capture "their" voices was not the only problem: "research informed by Western imperialistic discourses conducted on/with non-Western participants and packaged and represented in the Western academic world carries within it some inherent impossibilities of capturing the voices of people".[8] But also, "their" voices wouldn't fit into what Bhattacharya[9] and Chow[10] describe

8 Bhattacharya, "Othering", 107.

9 Bhattacharya, "Othering".

10 Rey Chow, *Writing Diaspora: Tactics of Intervention in Contemporary Cultural Studies* (Bloomington, IN: Indiana University Press, 1993), 38.

as "third world experience", and therefore wouldn't fit into the imperialist discourse of the "first world".

I discussed my first thoughts about my concerns, that I was the one producing knowledge about others, with Sari Middernacht of the Waza Art Centre. What I felt would be right would be to produce knowledge with others to overcome the outlined incompatibility of "third world experience" – even if their experience was only voiced. She then told me about the Art Centre's former project working with the ODVs for an exhibition, where objects from their lives found their way into an exhibition together with their voices.

Those thoughts about methodology accompanied me during the packed weeks of my second stay. Many former interviewees invited me to their home, and there we continued our interviews that had started the previous year. New interviews were set up at interviewees' homes and I even received queries from some ODVs asking why I had not (yet) interviewed them. I realised that I had another role to play that year. Despite having clearly stated that I wouldn't have the power to fight against the World Bank, I was still seen as a kind of ambassador for their worries, expected to channel their concerns to higher institutions via my "academic book".

I was also seen as a researcher who came back because I was interested in them.[11] Mama Mariam explained this to me when she took my hand and showed me through her house, to a bedroom that was filled from top to bottom with belongings that did not fit into the living room, which had to stay clean and tidy for welcoming visitors. While we were in the bedroom, she told me about her health issues and the difficulties she faced in accessing medical care. I remember trying to orient myself in that lightless room, listening to what she wanted to share, where nobody could see us and her tears. During this second stay, I experienced many tearful outbursts by women in dark bedrooms, a space safe from the others, from men, and heard accounts of challenging life situations. These women were taking a moment to involve me in their private issues, issues I often did not know how to deal with, except by being there and listening.

Two or three times, these were the moments when I was asked for money. Whether this was because by then they considered me to be a person close enough to help, or because I was seen as the privileged researcher, I cannot determine and it is not important. I took it as proof of trust, that they counted on me not to tell the other ODVs – and I did not. I decided that I would not help

11 Mama Mariam and others I talked to had experiences with researchers whose research was obviously planned as a single visit, and who did not pay much attention to their voices and their knowledge agency.

them as a private person, to avoid any further expectations. However, I stopped by some days later with an envelope, explaining that I had a small amount from the research budget to thank them for the time they had dedicated for the interview. I counted on the fact that they would not tell the other ODVs – and they did not.

That I had a camera with me was well known throughout my stays. I was explicitly asked to take pictures. During the first stay, I was asked to take portraits of the interviewees; on the second stay, while visiting them in their homes, the whole family was usually called over for family portraits. I ordered paper copies of all the pictures, from a copy shop in the city centre. The president asked me to hand the copies to him so that he could distribute them. I followed his advice and trusted that he knew best as to why the distribution needed to be done this way. However, picture prints were much in demand throughout the third stay, a year later. Some ODVs asked me for more copies or for new pictures. I did what time allowed – knowing that these copies were basically the only material objects I was able to offer.

During the third stay, for which the *baraza* were planned, the ODVs showed me how much they appreciated that I came back again. They made me understand that they wanted to continue our discussions. This is discussed in chapter three, in the section on 'Shared authority/*barazaweb*'.

Unlike the mineworkers discussed in the previous section, some ODVs were former senior staff and lived in Makomeno, the neighbourhood where the UMHK and later Gécamines housed the senior staff members. Lubumbashi was planned according to the ideology of segregation, like many other colonial cities. Thus, the question of gaining trust in the neighbourhood of Makomeno, especially with those interviewees who were not ODVs, had to be evaluated from a slightly different angle, even though they too had lost their jobs in 2003. It was thanks to Marc's connections that I was able to conduct several interviews with former senior staff members who were not members of the ODV. They were not informed about my research endeavour via the weekly gatherings but through Marc, who explained my aims. All those who Marc contacted invited me to visit them.

Our first contact took place in their homes. All ex-senior staff lived either in bigger homes than the ex-blue-collar workers in Cité Gécamines or in an annex or the *boyerie*[12] so as to rent their homes to make a living. In most cases, my first visit was to introduce myself and describe my research. Marc accompanied me

---

12 The *boyerie* was the modest accommodation for the domestic servants and gardeners who were housed in the garden, next to the garage or storage areas of the house that was inhabited by a senior staff member.

and officially introduced me to the people we visited. In all cases, I was invited to visit again and conduct the official interview. Unlike with the ODVs in Cité Gécamines, the first encounter was very personal but equally characterised by restraint in the beginning. The restraint, I evaluated in discussions with Marc, emanated from the fact that I had started my research in Cité Gécamines with blue-collar workers, who were worse off after 2003 than the former senior staff. The senior staff in Makomeno lived in bigger houses and often found employment again; they were aware that their economic loss was not as drastic as for the ODVs in Cité Gécamines.

Weighing heavier, though, was the loss of prestige (see chapter four, on *Heshima*). So, it was up to me to assure them that their biographies and voices were equally valuable for me. I visited many interviewees several times, and with every visit interviewees opened up more, invited me to look at photographs from the "good old times", showed me certificates, and shared thoughts that they did not dare to share in the beginning. However, with two exceptions, they insisted that I should not take any photos and that I had to make sure they would remain anonymous.

4 Mutual Risk Management – *On se voit sous Kabila*

Whenever I went to Cité Gécamines, I first took a *taxi partagé* (shared taxi) to the city centre, where Marc was often waiting for me. Our meeting point was under a huge billboard showing a portrait of President Joseph Kabila. "*On se voit sous Kabila*" (Let's meet under Kabila), was Marc's suggestion to make sure that I would be recognised and thus be safe, he argued. He was worried about me, because even though it was one of the most crowded places, I stood out. Therefore, he concluded, for me to be safe I had to be recognised. The billboard stood above a central square with numerous stalls, at a point where most taxis and buses stopped. Indeed, after a few days, the policemen working at that corner knew me, grinned at me with their ever-demanding expression. However, they let me be. Once in a while, the police even shouted at taxi drivers who were offering their services to me too vehemently – in their opinion. I observed how the police officers discreetly demanded money from the taxi drivers who stopped at the square to get passengers on board. The owners of the small shops got used to me too. As a result, Marc concluded after some days during my first stay in Lubumbashi that it was safe enough for me to travel to Cité Gécamines on my own.

From that square I had to take either a taxi or a bus. Most often, I took the bus. First, because I did not have to negotiate the fare, something I never got used to and never will. Second, I thought it would be more appropriate to travel to the ODVs by an inexpensive means of transport. Whenever I arrived at the house where the gatherings took place, by foot and with shoes dirty[13] from the dust, the president and the secretary welcomed me and asked me about my trip. Although the means of transport was not questioned during my first stay, it became a problem during my second stay. They were not happy about me travelling by bus; it would be too dangerous for me as *une femme blanche* (a white woman). I read their concern for my safety as a sign of their trust and also hope in me (after all, I had to write that "academic book") and thus followed their advice of travelling by taxi to visit them.

Those weeks in the summer of 2018 were tricky in terms of safety, for everyone and not only for me as a foreign researcher. Political riots resulted in some days of curfew; communication during those days was difficult, because services such as WhatsApp were interrupted, and Marc and the members of the ODVs preferred to know that I was safely ensconced in the guesthouse. Once the situation improved, we continued with the interviews in Cité Gécamines. During the gatherings, we discussed who I would visit, and when and where I would interview them. As an aside, I was told that just recently two killings had taken place in Cité Gécamines – both poisonings. Even though there was no risk that anybody would poison me, they assured me, it would still be much safer if I were accompanied at all times. Thus, a masterplan was set up. Marc and one of the members of the ODVs, very often the secretary, would walk me to the home of the interviewee. Often, the interviewee would come to the meeting place and accompany all of us to his home.

I learned at this time, when we talked about the safety issues, that the decision to hold the meeting at Marc's house the previous year had been taken because the members of the board thought it would be safer for me to not walk around. I consider their concerns, and Marc's, about my wellbeing as one aspect of our mutual risk management. We gained each other's trust, and we all wanted the other not to worry about any problems that could result from being seen together. I was under surveillance – for better or for worse.

Safety was a worry not only in relation to me and my routes from A to B in Cité Gécamines; it was often a topic that was brought up, for example, when people described the security system that operated in Cité Gécamines in "the good old days", as I explain in chapter four.

---

13 Marc always carried a cloth to wipe off the dust before we entered a home. Only white people would arrive with dirty shoes, he commented one day, while looking at my appearance. I then started to also carry a cloth to always clean my shoes.

The concern about my safety was underpinned by the demography of Cité Gécamines. "All kinds of people" were living in Cité Gécamines then. Therefore, unlike in the "good old times", one could not trust all neighbours – there was theft, there were attacks, "those people" would not know who I was.

I was not a novice to fieldwork when I went to Lubumbashi. Experience thus helped me manage and evaluate unanticipated risks that resulted from "a variety of factors that related both to the conditions in the field site and to researcher characteristics", as Sampson wrote about her research experience aboard ships.[14] She argues that many situations require a continuous evaluation. There is the internal struggle between the wish to continue research, within reason, having invested in it, and the recognition that some undertakings could be too risky. Sampson describes this ambivalence, when she decided to talk to the captain of a ship first before climbing up the side of the ship in the way that experienced staff must do, via a combination ladder:

> Ignoring all of my instincts and my own personal risk assessment I knew with certainty that at this stage in the trip, after all the investment of time and money, I would not abandon the research opportunity. It was fortunate that previous experience and confidence (as an older researcher), knowledge of ships and shipping companies – their procedures and their safety policies – provided me with the wherewithal to resist the agent's attempts to get me to do something which I felt was probably [but not certainly] beyond my capability.[15]

I felt comfortable with the ODVs, and I was confident that our shared research endeavour would be characterised by a willingness to understand each other's concerns. In retrospect, I think about the factors that were crucial for this trust. And my conclusion is that the management of emotions was one of the key factors.

5 Emotions/Weakness/Strength

"[W]ho we are as individuals and as academics, cannot but influence the conclusions we are able to draw."[16]

---

14 Helen Sampson, "'Fluid Fields' and the Dynamics of Risk in Social Research", *Qualitative Research* 19, no. 2 (2019): 137.

15 Sampson, "Fluid Fields", 136.

16 Simon Down, Karin Garrety, and Richard Badham, "Fear and Loathing in the Field: Emotional Dissonance and Identity Work in Ethnographic Research," *M@n@gement* 9, no. 3 (2006): 97.

As a researcher, I am also a private human being with a backpack full of experiences and tools to deal with emotions – at least I had assumed this. Experience had taught me very personal strategies to handle emotions, as did the societal norms with which I grew up. And this backpack was and still is important for the research process, its influences and, as Down et al. point out, the conclusions I draw. Down et al. emphasise that "the questions – what are the messy and contested feeling rules inherent in research situations and how do researchers wrestle with these? – often remain unasked and unanswered".[17] The authors reinforced my decision to address the question of emotions and the strategies related to expressing them, such as verbal and non-verbal expressions of emotionality, as well as silence.

One moment that sticks in my mind is when, during a group discussion, one of the participants lifted his shirt to show me scars all over his upper chest. Upset about the current lack of health services, he explained how this had affected his health condition. His voice was loud; he addressed me directly as "Mama Daniela" and asked me to look at him, his eyes filled with tears. I later watched that scene on the video shot by Gulda and Carl.[18] I could not remember how I had reacted, although I knew that I had been close to tears. The video proof was unambiguous. My eyes were brimming; I looked straight into his eyes after having looked at the scars; I obviously could not find the appropriate words to say. I sat there, touched, and I remained silent. There was a rather long pause, which the video shows, in which nobody said anything. And the video showed something else: all the participants were looking at me, while I was looking at the man who had just shared his difficult health condition with all of us, but mostly with me. I will never be able to know if a different reaction was expected from me. However, I assess that my silence was not the wrong way to react. After the pause, the man with the scars thanked me for listening and looking at the scars. Silence, this time, was not the wrong strategy. This time it was not a strategy to save me and others from further trouble, as with the police officers, but a non-verbal expression of my sympathy in a situation where I could not find the appropriate words.

It was also a moment where the closeness/distance dynamic came into play and the question of whether I was an insider or outsider at this particular moment. How can one judge own's position in an emotional moment, or of the research partners? Do these emotions interfere with my ability to be the researcher? Down et al. write about the contradictory position, the inherent

17 Down, Garrety and Badham, "Fear", 96.

18 Gulda El Magambo is a Congolese artist based in Lubumbashi. He filmed the *baraza* together with my colleague Carl-Philipp Bodenstein for the "Mitaani #mapping Moments" project that is described in the next chapter.

moral ambiguity of the researcher in managing the nexus of closeness and distance: being a friend, an emancipator, a judge, emotionally engaged or emotionally detached.[19] What I take from these reflections is that all of us experienced emotional moments during our research project, and that we accepted them, gave them space, were silent when words were missing or found another strategy to deal with them in what we conceived to be an appropriate way.

Let me illustrate the last point with an example. When my second stay in Lubumbashi came to an end, I discussed with Marc my wish to thank the board members of the ODVs, those who attended regularly and those who had welcomed me for an interview in an appropriate way. We concluded that an invitation for lunch after my last visit of their regular meeting would be reasonable. A small restaurant next door operated by two ladies was thus the choice and a reservation was made. I informed the president, who was pleased to announce this invitation to the ODVs for the upcoming Friday. That day we enjoyed a cheerful get-together and I was glad to know that at least I could offer something.

A lunch was no matter of course for many of them, because of their precarious financial situation. One member came to me and offered me a necklace and bracelet made from malachite. I was surprised and touched, but at the same time felt uncomfortable accepting a gift, knowing how costly it must have been for him. That day, I wanted to be the one offering something, not receiving. However, I had to accept that it was equally his right to decide what was appropriate and to offer me something if it was his wish. After lunch, we went back to the house where the gatherings took place for the official farewell. There the president handed me not only the rooster made of copper that I mention in the Introduction but also a picture made from copper, showing the daily activities of a woman in the region. I was again very surprised and touched, but it was easier to accept these gifts from a group than the jewellery from an individual person. Receiving a gift is an emotional act, and it was easier for me to allow and show emotions towards a group than towards an individual, a man. The question in my mind was: why did he give it to me? What kind of expectations are connected with this gift, and what kind of damage would I perhaps cause by declining the expectations I imagined?

I am still unsure of how to evaluate and represent my emotions adequately in an academic publication, and probably will never find a satisfying solution. As Down et al point out:

> This narrative strategy in published work denies the emotional realities of life as much as it ignores the covertness we have discussed here. We are

---

19 Down, Garrety and Badham, "Fear", 98.

> aware today that all research positions, including objectivity, are social constructions, and as such, have moral and political consequences.[20]

Revealing too much of our identities and emotions can be dangerous, because it could let us assume that the knowledge we produce is more transparent and reliable than knowledge produced without these self-disclosures.[21] Pillow points out this danger:

> Prominent in much qualitative research is the idea that the researcher, through reflexivity, can transcend their own subjectivity and own cultural context in a way that releases them from the weight of (mis)representations. Self-reflexivity can perform a modernist seduction – promising release from your tension, voyeurism, ethnocentrism – a release from your discomfort with representation through a transcendent clarity.[22]

Pillow refers to Patai, who criticises those people "who stay up nights worrying about representation" as privileged academics engaged in the erotics of their own language games.[23] She also asks the "one question that the new methodological self-absorption seems not to ask … : Does all this self-reflexivity produce better research?"[24]

Could this research endeavour have been done better in a different way? I am not able to answer this question. I try to be as transparent as possible without claiming any moral high ground because I disclose my feelings and my identity(ies). Then, "we can still hope that doing so (or perhaps sometimes deciding not to) will help us to enhance our understanding of ourselves, those in the field, and ways in which we can work (together or apart) on improving the worlds that we live in".[25]

I drew on different methods, now understood in terms of techniques, changed my approach over time, adapted my approaches to what I thought

20 Down, Garrety and Badham, "Fear", 113.

21 Down, Garrety and Badham, "Fear"; Kari Lerum, "Subjects of Desire: Academic Armor, Intimate Ethnography, and the Production of Critical Knowledge", *Qualitative Inquiry* 4, no. 7 (2001); Wanda Pillow, "Confession, Catharsis, or Cure? Rethinking the Uses of Reflexivity as Methodological Power in Qualitative Research", *International Journal of Qualitative Studies in Education* 16, no. 2 (2003).

22 Pillow, "Confession", 186.

23 Daphne Patai, "(Response) When Method Becomes Power", in *Power and Method: Political Activism and Educational Research*, ed. Andrew D. Gitlin, Critical social thought (New York: Routledge, 1994), 64.

24 Pillow, "Confession", 176.

25 Down, Garrety and Badham, "Fear", 113.

the situation required. I made decisions, which I do not want to assess in terms of right or wrong but rather as moments during which my role as researcher influenced the outcome of the research in one way or another. I thus try to be as transparent as possible, because "[…] research is not an innocent or distant academic exercise but an activity that has something at stake and that occurs in a set of political and social conditions".[26]

And I take note that different ghosts have accompanied me: that of the man with the gold watch, that of my institutional and privileged background, that of the methods we are taught far from the field, and that of the false assumption that I was a World Bank envoy.

I am aware that positionality is part of methodological considerations, but I chose to single it out because the research topic and research context required particular attention to where I come from, institutionally speaking, which affected the way in which I navigated through the research context.

26 Smith, *Decolonizing*, 5.

CHAPTER 3

Methodological and Theoretical Considerations

1 Approaching the Archive

The first archival research brought me to the Africa Museum in Tervuren, Belgium, in particular the Archive of Colonial History, the Archive of Decolonisation and Independent Congo, and the Library of Contemporary History. The Archive of Colonial History holds a wide collection of writing on the (Belgian) Congo's history, covering different periods, from Leopold II's colonial expansion policy to the formation of the Congo Free State in 1885, to the Congo under Belgian colonial rule from 1908, to the Congo after independence in 1960. The collection was therefore the right place to read colonial publications and approach colonial policies.

The Archive of Decolonisation and Independent Congo is vast, with valuable accounts from private individuals who lived or worked in the Congo or who carried out research there. It is a veritable goldmine of information, but one in which I felt lost. However, in the Library of Contemporary History in Tervuren, I came across issues of the workers' magazine, *Mwana Shaba*, published by the Union Minière du Haut-Katanga. It immediately captured my attention because the articles in it implicitly disclosed the company's different strategies to shape its workforce, and sometimes even – though through the words of the editors – the voices of workers in the letters to the editors. *Mwana Shaba* thus became an important element of my corpus.

Mwana Shaba was not a unique publication of that mining company or in the Congo. Workers' magazines were commonly produced by bigger employers, by public and private firms alike. Callaci, for instance, discusses publications in Tanzania in the 1960s:

> Nurses, teachers, postal workers, doctors, police officers, diamond mine employees, electrical workers, and engineers all had their own magazines produced by and for employees. These publications contained discussions about the profession as well as portrayals of the social lives of the workers and their families. Some magazines also gave tips on urban life, instructing their readers on how to open a bank account and how to plan healthy, nutritional meals after work in the evenings.[1]

1 Emily Callaci, *Street Archives and City Life: Popular Intellectuals in Postcolonial Tanzania*, Radical Perspectives (Durham, NC: Duke University Press, 2017), 35.

Whereas in Tanzania these publications envisioned "an urban middle-class readership that would invest in the future of the modern city of Dar es Salaam", *Mwana Shaba*'s readership was the blue-collar worker and senior staff member, including his family members, and especially his wife.

The company archives of the UMHK/Gécamines/Umicore are located in the Joseph Cuvelier repository of the State Archives of Belgium, in Brussels. I spent several weeks there, browsing through minutes and annual reports. These documents proved to be another goldmine. All the topics about what were then called the "*main d'œuvre* ~~indigène~~" (MOI, meaning ~~native~~ workforce) (my deletions),[2] referring to Congolese and immigrant workers, were noted in detail: statistics on the demographic structure, school matters, the curriculum, housing, evening courses for the workers, organisation of leisure activities, health care, social problems in the settlement of the workers, demands by workers, and so on.

In my first readings of these annual reports, I was surprised that there was more material on social services (such as education, from kindergarten to evening courses for adults) than, for instance, statistics on workers employed in different kinds of services. Only after having engaged with my research topic for some months, and after the first stay in Lubumbashi, did it suddenly make sense to me that the UMHK was organising not only work-related matters but also the social life of the workers. Naturally, concerns for children and women found their way into the annual report of the Services d'Afrique, Département MOI, a company department principally intended to deal with matters related to work.

Thus, documents like these gave me an insight into the problems and perceptions of the company related to work, often in a context I initially would not have searched in for this specific kind of information. For instance, in the annual report of 1951, after a statistical overview of the number of children then enrolled in schools, numbers of African and European staff members, and so on, the report assesses the UMHK's general guidelines. The first point refers to the company's aim for education within the UMHK, which is followed by a detailed description of course content for all levels of education, from primary school to professional courses, language education and courses for adult women. The general guidelines are well hidden between statistical charts and curricula, but they offer an important view of UMHK's perception of male and female roles, which I had not expected to find there. Regarding men, the annual report said its aims were:

2 MOI = *main d'oeuvre indigène* (native workforce). I have struck out quoted words from which I dissociate myself, and indicate this with the insertion [DW] The term "indigène" often appears as part of names or in quotations. For the benefit of readability, it is later no longer struck out, even though I dissociate myself from its use.

[T]enter de faire progresser l'ensemble vers la civilisation par la diffusion des principes chrétiens, et des notions de sociologie occidentale (famille, cité, travail, etc.)[3]	To try to advance everything towards civilisation by the diffusion of Christian principles and notions of Western sociology (family, city, work, etc.)

The UMHKs plan for the female population was presented as follows:

1. Agir sur la majorité sinon sur la totalité des femmes adultes pour en faire de meilleures femmes de ménage. 2. Doter tous [sic] nos filles des connaissances, des habitudes, et de la volonté nécessaire pour devenir épouses et mères chrétiennes ; faire des meilleurs des exemples et des auxiliaires.[4]	1. To make sure that the majority, if not all, of adult women become better housekeepers. 2. Give all our daughters the knowledge, the habit and the will to become Christian wives and mothers; make them the best role models and auxiliaries.

These extracts show that even in an annual report the text that accompanied the lists indicated the UMHK's efforts to shape their workers' lives, down to the roles that men and women were expected to fulfil. A list showing the legally determined holidays of workers was presented as follows:

Nombre de travailleurs ayant bénéficié du congé.[5]	Number of workers who benefited from the leave.

The choice of wording, even for a statistical overview, tells us more than the numerical data does. In this example, the verb "to benefit" clearly presents the workers as beneficiaries of the company's generosity, granting them what was legally entitled to them anyway. Seventy-three pages later in the same annual report, another statistic on the "elements of the human coefficient per camp" again presents the company's perception of the workers:

3 AGR 2 – n°655–03047, Rapport Annuel 1951, 28.

4 AGR 2 – n°655–03047, Rapport Annuel 1951, 28.

5 AGR 2 – n°655–03047, Rapport Annuel 1951, 20.

Il est normal qu'un homme qui travaille régulièrement demande parfois un congé, qu'il soit parfois malade. Il est normal aussi que, malgré les congés et les repos qu'on lui accorde, il s'absente parfois. Enfin, pour faire régner la discipline, il est parfois nécessaire de recourir aux sanctions pénales.[6]	It is normal that a man who works regularly sometimes asks for leave or is sometimes ill. It is also normal that, in spite of the holidays and the rest granted to him, he is sometimes absent. After all, to make the discipline prevail, it is sometimes necessary to resort to penal sanctions.

In seemingly benevolent wording, the company comments on reasons workers do not report to work, with the added rationale that sometimes sanctions would be needed to ensure discipline. The chart that follows this statement is a numbered list of the reasons for absence from work. The sanctions, which become clear only when reading the chart itself, refer to prison, as used in the extract above. The indication that this punishment would be applied in extenuating circumstances reveals that the company must have been sensitive to "prison" at that time.

I read the annual reports of the UMHK with the following questions in mind: What was being said? Whose voice was it? Which topics were being discussed? And which discursive entanglements to other topics could be elicited?

It was clear that workers' voices were muted in the UMHK documents. Therefore, talking to workers who had actually experienced life in the company would be of utmost necessity, especially regarding those topics that seemed important to me during my archival research and which were later brought up by the ODVs during the interviews and group discussions. Speaking with the workers directly was doubly important because the archival material mainly covers the period of the 1940s and 1950s, rather than the 1960s to the 1980s when which most ODV members had worked for UMHK/Gécamines. Documents for the latter period are much more difficult to access, not having been systematically archived after the end of colonial rule.

The invisibility of workers' voices in the archival material does not mean that the voices did not exist. Harris discusses these ghosted voices and suggests that by reading sources in the archive in a spectral way these voices become visible. "[T]he work of archive is fundamentally spectral", he argues.[7]

Notwithstanding the fantasy of a comprehensive, complete archive, an archive is always an assemblage of fragments. In structuring an archive, no

6 AGR 2 – n°655–03047, Rapport Annuel 1951, 93.

7 Verne Harris, "Hauntology, Archivy and Banditry: An Engagement with Derrida and Zapiro", *Critical Arts* 29, sup1 (2015), 13.

matter how thorough the process might be, no matter how great the commitment to completeness, there are dynamics of inclusion and exclusion, and what has been excluded will whisper around the fragments. Ghostly voices.[8]

Harris's understanding of the term "archive" is insightful. He argues that the archive operates on three levels. First, there is a recording of a trace on or within a surface, the substrate.

> [Second,] the substrate has the quality of exteriority; it is external to the psychic apparatus of an individual. In this understanding, traces located only within the latter are the traces of memory rather than of archive. So that traces of memory shared with others, in for instance "collective memory" or "public discourse", because they have the quality of exteriority, can become archive.[9]

Third, such external traces must be considered worthy of protection, preservation and classification.

Harris argues that both the archive and the memory are best understood as belonging to the genre of traces. Neither should be anchored to notions of stability, durability and reliability because both are always already in the process of formation and both emerge out of the future.[10] Harris's thoughts encouraged me to think of the voices of the workers as a part of the archive and/or as an alternative archive. The archive's content does not sit only in buildings fronted by information boards that announce opening hours and access rules. The archive is open and an assemblage of fragments, including (and of course excluding) silenced voices that can be awakened through interviews and the *baraza*.[11]

2 Interviews

During my first two research stays, I conducted 63 qualitative interviews with members of the Collectif. They were born between 1930 and the 1960s, in most cases as children to workers at the UMHK, and thus grew up in the company's housing compounds. Approximately three-quarters of my interviewees, who

8 Verne Harris, *Ghosts of Archive* (Abingdon, NY: Routledge, 2020), 60.
9 Harris, "Hauntology", 15.
10 Harris, *Ghosts*, 10.
11 *Baraza* is a singular and plural noun.

were blue-collar workers or wives of workers, lived in Cité Gécamines; the rest were senior staff members who lived in the neighbourhood of Makomeno.[12]

The interviewees shared an immense amount of information, from childhood memories to their work life and all domains related to it through to their current situation. The members expressed great interest in participating. Towards the end of each stay in Lubumbashi, some addressed me and asked why I had not yet talked with them. In fact, the opportunity to conduct more interviews was limited by my time for these research visits. Furthermore, additional qualitative interviews would not have enhanced my insight. As Lepore states: "[H]owever singular a person's life may be, the value of examining it lies not in its uniqueness, but in its exemplariness, in how that individual's life serves as an allegory for broader issues affecting the culture as a whole".[13]

Some ODVs had been participating in a research project called *Ukumbusho* (memory), grounded in oral history practices.[14] This was the first iteration in 2000 of the oral history project "Mémoires de Lubumbashi". The aim was to present at the Museum of Lubumbashi the research conducted by Lubumbashi University (UNILU) on memories of recent history and daily urban life in the mining city of Lubumbashi. The exhibition displayed objects that the participants of the *Ukumbusho* project had brought into the museum with their testimony.[15]

I was lucky to make contact with UNILU early on, but also with people from the Waza Arts Centre who were involved in the *Ukumbusho* project as curators. They put me in touch with Marc,[16] who grew up in Cité Gécamines as a child of a blue-collar worker. He represents the new generation that is trying to overcome the situation of their parents, who he described as paralysed.[17] He was a useful observer of ODVs, on the one hand having a critical distance from them because of the generation gap, while on the other hand supporting the group through his close-knit network (of trade unions and NGOs).

Marc became my most important research partner and key reference person – and teacher in many ways. Right at the beginning of my first stay in

12 The segregation of the city is discussed in chapter 4 under the subheading *Space*.

13 Jill Lepore, "Historians Who Love Too Much: Reflections on Microhistory and Biography", *The Journal of American History* 88, no. 1 (2001): 133.

14 Sari Middernacht, "From Collective Curating to Sharing Curatorial Authority: Collaborative Practices as Strategies of Democratisation in Exhibition Making in Lubumbashi, Democratic Republic of Congo", (Unpublished MA thesis: University of Witwatersrand, Johannesburg, 2018).

15 Middernacht, "Collective Curating".

16 For reasons of security, I have changed his name.

17 The experiences of the ODVs' children were not the focus of this research.

Lubumbashi, he put me in contact with the president of the ODV branch in Lubumbashi.

The procedure of our meetings after the ODV weekly gatherings, to which I was then invited, was usually very formal, with the secretary taking notes on everything. I soon realised that I would not be able to operate in Cité Gécamines without this group. And at each of the many meetings I attended during the three stays in Lubumbashi, I had to explain what I intended to do. But at the same time, every member was extremely helpful and became interested in my research. They supported me in organising interviews, even putting interview lists together, and arranged for someone among them to accompany me every time I travelled to an interview.

They insisted on that point for my security. They explained that I would not be safe enough on my own, but if a member of the ODV accompanied me, I would be fine. Let me return to the hostility I faced on my first visit. The president explained to me that the people of the ODV were fighting for compensation, that they had been doing so for a long time, and that a representative of the World Bank was desperately expected. Even though most of them were aware that this representative would not come without advance notice, the long fight had exasperated some members, who had developed tunnel vision – the result being that any European showing up in the context of this meeting was likely to get into trouble. Rumours about the presence of the World Bank representative spread quickly, repeatedly, every time I was in Lubumbashi. It was thanks to the board members of the ODV that I was made aware of this and they put me under special surveillance now and then.

Shortly after my first meeting with the ODVs, I realised that an exclusive interest in the houses and the housing of workers would not make sense without taking into consideration the ODVs and their situation today. Being interested in a group that has a political agenda has its own challenges. The board members and I had several discussions on that point. I took time on several occasions to explain that, as a researcher, I would not be able to organise the money they were fighting for, nor would I personally interfere with the World Bank. However, it became important to me to make their voices heard. It was during the third stay in Lubumbashi, in July 2019, during the group discussions, that this effort was probably most apparent.

3 Shared Authority/*barazaweb*

I wondered how I could get closer to what is rightfully expected from any research based on qualitative methods, namely that "[t]he result of all of this reflexivity is to produce research that questions its own interpretations and is reflexive about its own knowledge production towards the goal of producing better, less distorted research accounts",[18] without running the risk of spending "too much time wading in the morass of our own positionings".[19]

My desire to talk about my understanding of the topics discussed during the interviews with my research partners became a must. It was *their* voices that were important to contextualise and recalibrate my initial findings. It is important to acknowledge that producing "better, less distorted research accounts" was (and still is) my ideal, but that there was a barrier, which had to be recognised – namely, the unequal power relations between the ODVs and me, whether I liked it or not. Therefore, it was essential to think about the recognition of the "other", and, as a consequence, it was indispensable to think about how to draw close(r) to my ideal of a more inclusive research approach, which included sharing authority(ies) over knowledge production.

Pillow points to the imbalance of power between the subject/author/academic and the communities of research. She reminds us that there is quite a lot of research methodology for sharing power between research partners: "This may include discussions of co-development of the research focus and analysis, use of extensive member checks, 'sharing the data' with the subjects, and co-writing".[20] But she rightly argues that "[A]s Trinh points out, this share of power is 'given' to the research subject, 'not taken'".[21] Thus, in our research we continually have to question the capacity of the subject to define themselves or even their desire to do so. Reflexivity, then, always occurs out of an unequal power relationship and, in fact, the act of reflexivity may perpetuate a colonial relationship while at the same time attempting to mask this power over the subject.[22]

My way out of this dilemma was to understand the ODVs' own interest in me as a mediator for passing on the master narrative I described earlier. It was a relief to know that they too had their own agenda. However, I was aware that they could be pinning some of their hopes on me only because I was initiating the research. As Pillow and Trinh asserted, I was still the one "giving" them this opportunity or, to put it differently, I was the one actively claiming their (re) actions.[23] Understanding our exchanges and negotiations as partners using

18 Hertz, "Reflexivity", cit. in Pillow, "Confession", 178.

19 Patai, "(Response)", cit. in Pillow, "Confession", 177.

20 Pillow, "Confession", 185.

21 Pillow, "Confession", 67.

22 Pillow, "Confession", 185; Minh-Ha Trinh, *When the Moon Waxes Red: Representation, Gender and Cultural Politics* (New York: Routledge, 1991).

23 Pillow, "Confession"; Trinh, *Moon*.

the imagery of a spider's web, where prey and predator constantly change roles, seemed a valid approach to me. I discuss this conceptualisation in more detail further on.

To recognise the "other" and thus consider the ODVs as equal partners, was important. I wanted to avoid being seen as "generous", one of the dangers that Pillow alerts us to: "This characterization of the research relationship maintains a colonial relationship of one person with power, the researcher, who will then demonstrate humility and generosity toward the research subject".[24]

The start would be, I assessed, to share my material with those who were the focus of the research, to – at least partially – offer them access to material they otherwise could not access. I tried to be transparent about how and where I got my information, and what kind of archival material I had collected so far, which served as my basis for the questions. Ideally, I hoped, the research partners would get an insight into how I gained the information that triggered the questions that guided the interviews.

A more inclusive research approach is sensitive to the questions of authority over knowledge production that challenge the generally accepted habitus in academia. The norm is to recognise the achievements of other academics by citing them, but we often ignore others who are equally important in the production of knowledge. They share their knowledge, their views, their perceptions, and we, as academics, evaluate them and sometimes cite them in excerpts when their statements help to underline our arguments. I am no exception. It is necessary to think about possibilities to "deconstruct the author's authority in the research and/or writing process".[25] I am aware that I am writing this monograph, I am the author, trapped in the constraints of our professional habitus. Thus, I am far from deconstructing my authority in the writing process. However, what I aimed for was to broaden the understanding of authority, at least during the research process, by asking my research partners to evaluate my reading of our interviews and discussions and to discuss their and my perceptions of the issues at hand.

Sharing authority has gained interest especially among scholars in museology working with artefacts in museums, and in literary studies. The debates in the latter discuss ideas of collective creation and the possibility of a plurality of authors. In literary studies and literary production, as Meizoz points out, author, publisher, printer-typographer, various institutions (patronage, scholarships), literary agents, critics and other agents are involved in the process

24 Pillow, "Confession", 185.

25 Pillow, "Confession", 179.

of creating an accessible text.[26] Taking all these actors into account, texts are subjected to a critique that then allows the ideologies of all participants to be uncovered:

> La sociocritique cherchait, au contraire, à décrire le social dans le texte, elle montrait comment la représentation littéraire (codes rhétoriques, narratifs, dispositifs axiologiques, clichés, etc.) construisait une 'idéologie'.
>
> [Sociocriticism, on the other hand, sought to describe the social in the text by showing how literary representation (rhetorical and narrative codes, axiological devices, clichés, etc.) constructed an 'ideology'.][27]

Sharing with the ODVs some of the archival material as well as my preliminary research results and my reading of the issues discussed during the interviews, was an idea that emerged in 2018 from discussions with Sari Middernacht and Patrick Mudekereza from the Waza Arts Centre in Lubumbashi. I was inspired by reading about the approach of *shared authority*,[28] which the Centre had been exploring in creative production and research projects, such as the *Ukumbusho* project. We decided to collaborate on a project called "Mitaani #mapping Moments", planned for July 2019. It would be a collaborative discussion of my research issues with the ODVs, with the Waza Arts Centre as a facilitator and as the space to exhibit the discussion results.[29] In their very insightful study on the role of digital technologies in memories in Nigeria, Yékú and Ojebode (2021) discuss reconstructing history with and among the public, sharing archival material and transmission of history through digital means. They discuss the historical voices of "digital subjects" who engage in conversations about the past. However, their focus is on interlocutors with access to digital platforms. In contrast, the ODVs' lack of access to digital technologies, lack of electricity and so on turns them into "digital subalterns" (Yékú and Ojebode, 2021: 500). Therefore, it would not have been possible to work with them on a collaborative analysis using digital technologies. But, what Yékú and Ojebode's

---

26 Meizoz, *Postures*, 41–42.

27 Jérôme Meizoz, "Sociocritique, Ethnologie Et Sociologie De La Littérature", *Romantisme* 145, no. 3 (2009), 100.

28 See, for example, Frisch, *Shared Authority*; Frisch, "Commentary"; High, "Sharing" ; Middernacht, "Collective"; Portelli, "Living"; Shopes, "Commentary"; Sitzia, "Shared Authority"; Alistair Thomson, "Introduction – Sharing Authority: Oral History and the Collaborative Process", *Oral History Review* 30, no. 1 (2003).

29 James Yékú and Ayobami Ojebode, "From Google Doodles to Facebook: Nostalgia and Visual Reconstructions of the Past in Nigeria", *African Studies Review* 64, no. 3 (2021).

study have in common with my research with the ODVs is that through commentary and discussion, fragments of history could be put together.

In addition, we wanted to explore the notion of *shared authority* with all its possibilities and limits. Moreover, the project aimed to make the research process transparent and the research results accessible through a creative act, by using shared videography, so that the product of this approach would enable a collective creative response to sociopolitical issues.[30]

My desire to discuss the preliminary results of my research in the archives and the research based on the interviews with those actually involved was twofold. First, I wanted to share with the workers concepts and their modifications as reflected in the interviews and archival sources. Second, I was aiming at a collaborative analysis of the changing conceptualisations of the topics addressed in the discourse. Two of these topics briefly illustrate this point – work and identity.[31]

Work: Employment and the loss of it are the basis of existence of the ODV. Work, or "*kazi*", as the term is used in Swahili and by the ODVs, is thus one of the central concepts from which everything else starts. Up until the 1940s, work in the mining industry could certainly be described as similar to slavery: the living conditions of contract workers were not very different from those of slaves. After the Second World War, *kazi* took on a positive connotation and stood for "a good life".[32] The change of connotation occurred against the backdrop of the UMHK's urgent need for a stable workforce. Then, the company provided everything the workers needed in order to become and remain a controllable and efficient source of labour: housing, leisure facilities, health services, and so on. The focus was on the establishment of a society of workers organised according to the Belgian idea of how this society was supposed to function.

This rationale did not change much after independence in 1960. From the 1960s, the Congolese were increasingly given better positions and many became members of the company's cadre. The workers' perception of *kazi* (work) changed in 2003, when they were forced to leave the company "voluntarily" in

30 Carl-Philipp Bodenstein and Daniela Waldburger, "'There Is a Fault Here! A Report on a More Inclusive Research Method in a Project in Lubumbashi (DR Congo)", *FIELD: A Journal of Socially-Engaged Art Criticism*, no. 17 (2021); Daniela Waldburger, "Il y a une erreur ici !" Rapport sur une méthode de recherche plus inclusive dans le cadre d'un projet impliquant d'anciens mineurs à Lubumbashi", in *Lubumbashi aujourd'hui: Langues, arts et société*, eds. Flavia Aiello and Roberto Gaudioso (Paris: L'Harmattan, 2021).

31 These concepts are related to each other and can include several sub-concepts.

32 Dibwe dia Mwembu, "History"; Fabian, "Kazi"; Petit and Mutambwa, "LA CRISE".

order to receive paltry compensation. Their house was the only material asset they still had, which is why it serves as a trigger and the locus of their nostalgia. The interpretation of *kazi* today is that of an object of loss. The non-existence of work has not only created a precarious economic situation, it has also deprived the ex-mineworkers of one of the core pieces of their identity.

Identity: Of course, a diverse range of anchor points to identity exists, including social categories such as a blue-collar worker or member of the cadre, place of origin of the first generation that moved to Lubumbashi, and gender-specific categories. But primarily, all the interviewees identified themselves with the company.[33] Promotion, for example, often entailed moving to a new house and changing work location, sometimes within Lubumbashi from Cité Gécamines to Makomeno. Thus, work had an impact on social and spatial mobility. Another identity-relevant topic was the pride in having been an agent of the company instead of merely a wheel in the system. This was revealed in statements such as "*J'étais très fière*" (I was very proud), "*Napenda kazi, utarespecté*" (I loved the work, you were respected), or even total identification as a part of a company already at birth, such as "*Je suis née dans le groupe sud*" (I was born into the southern group).[34] Others would say "I was born to my parents who were [names])". One interviewee in Makomeno was living in the *boyerie* and renting out his big house to earn some money. His living room was filled with objects of his past as a cadre of Gécamines, such as sports trophies, which he displayed with a great deal of pride and nostalgia.

The fact of having been a mineworker and identifying with that occupation manifested itself in different spheres of life – not only in those that related to the individual but also in the sphere of community. Strangleman describes mineworkers' identity perceptions in Great Britain, and reports that their occupational identity and community identity, and the norms and values linked to them, "are produced and reproduced within the context of workplace and community networks".[35] He points to the fact that stability and predictability

33 For the discursive analysis of concepts of identity, see for example, Bucholtz and Hall, "Identity"; Ochs, "Constructing"; Daniela Waldburger, *Komorisch im Transnationalen Kontext,* Grazer Plurilingualismus-Studien 3 (Graz: Karl-Franzens-Univ. Graz Treffpunkt Sprachen Forschungsbereich Plurilingualismus, 2015); Daniela Waldburger, "Social identity/identities among plurilingual Comorians in Marseille (France)", in *Mobility and Minorities in Africa – Nova Collectanea Africana,* ed. Michele Carboni (Cagliari: Nova Collectanea Africana Collana del Centro di Studi Africani in Sardegna, 2018), 193–214.

34 The UMHK and Gécamines had mining sites in different geographical locations.

35 Strangleman, "Networks", 259.

of life are valued by workers and that "acting accordingly is enabling identity through the achievement of one's role".[36] The ODVs' life plans were destroyed with the loss of work; predictability, stability, every aspect of what they identified with, were shattered in 2003.

Interviews with the former workers revealed the concerns that were most important to them. They disclosed not only individual perceptions of a specific topic at a specific time but also discursive links to other topics. Stråth argues that this temporality of "concepts" allows a translation of past experiences into futures. Moreover, "[t]the gap between the imageries of the past and those of the future is continuously revised".[37] The provision of housing was not only one of the main means of control over workers by UMHK and Gécamines; the house was also an object that belonged to the ODVs during their whole work life. The interviews revealed the workers' evaluation of these experiences.

Following the idea(l) of *shared authority* means first and foremost the willingness of all involved to talk to and listen to one another. Sharing authority, then, in its simplest version, "is shar[ing] in oral history by definition – in the dialogic nature of the interview, in the history-making offered by both interviewer and narrator".[38]

3.1 *Planning the* baraza

For the "Mitaani #mapping Moments" exhibition in July 2019, the Waza Arts Centre and I decided to organise the *baraza*. The conversation between the ODVs and myself at the *baraza* were expected to be a collaborative analysis of the changing conceptualisations of the topics that emerged after the interviews, based on my thoughts after the archival research. Although the ex-workers had shared their individual perceptions in the interviews, during the *baraza* we planned a collective analysis between all ex-workers present and the researcher. My intention was to elaborate on the analyses in collaboration with the ex-mineworkers, and as a consequence to value their voices as equally important in the knowledge production process. Despite the challenges, it allowed all of us to communicate under the premise of being an important part of the project as a whole. We transgressed the borders of the sphere that our roles as either researcher or researched partner normally allowed and required.

36 Strangleman, "Networks", 259.

37 Bo Stråth, "Ujamaa – the Evasive Translation of an Elusive Concept", in *Doing Conceptual History in Africa*, eds. Axel Fleisch and Rhiannon Stephens, Making sense of history 25 (New York: Berghahn Books, 2016), 186.

38 Frisch, "Commentary", 113.

I associate transgressing borders with transdisciplinarity. Therefore, any approach under the label of shared authority I regard as transdisciplinary, an adjective that is often emphasised in academia. As Jahn et al. point out, independent from the definition of trans- and/or interdisciplinarity, "[c]ombining 'interdisciplinarity' and the 'participation' of extra-scientific actors seems to be the common recipe for defining transdisciplinarity".[39] I view the term "extra-scientific actors" as crucial because it acknowledges the ODVs' agency.

The same idea, but under a different term – "participatory transdisciplinarity" – is discussed by Mobjörk.[40] Societal actors are partners in a joint research process where their knowledge is "equally valuable to scientific knowledge".[41] Another layer in the discussion of the framework of transdisciplinarity is the question of the motives behind the research. Who has which interest to participate, assuming that the research endeavour is indeed a shared one? I argue that both the ODVs and myself had an interest in co-operation and our own agendas.

The goals of the "Mitaani #mapping Moments" project were threefold. First, as a researcher, I aimed at an analysis of the concepts related to the nexus of housing and nostalgia. In the process, the ex-workers' voice should be given equal value. Based on the principle of shared authority, new ideas and additional societal knowledge to which I might have been otherwise blind should be enabled. This in turn would increase public acceptance of the research results. In addition, the documented *baraza* should serve as data for the analysis of the negotiation process about nostalgia.

The second goal was to highlight that the ex-workers' voices were vital in a process of collaborative analysis, contributing equally to the different layers, changes and meanings of concepts. This approach would therefore democratise the production of knowledge. It would be a co-creation of scientific knowledge.

Third, the negotiation process itself and the objects linked to it (the filmed sessions and the cartoons of these discussions) would serve as curatorial material for the Waza Arts Centre, which would make them public and accessible to the ex-workers. It would allow critical examination of the research results by participants and the wider public.

---

39 Thomas Jahn, Matthias Bergmann and Florian Keil, "Transdisciplinarity: Between Mainstreaming and Marginalization", *Ecological Economics* 79 (2012): 2.

40 Malin Mobjörk, "Consulting Versus Participatory Transdisciplinarity: A Refined Classification of Transdisciplinary Research", *Futures* 42, no. 8 (2010): 867, 870.

41 Mobjörk, "Consulting", 870.

The first week started with a meeting at the Waza Arts Centre to discuss the fine-tuning of the project. We had discussions on, for instance, how to deal with nostalgia and its impact on the ODV members' current life dynamic. In a follow-up meeting with the ODV board members, we discussed our idea and were given their approval and support – and equally important – their interest in this collaboration. In a joint collaboration, we thus organised what we called the "trigger event" that took place three days later.

The aim of this event was to present and discuss the idea of the planned *baraza* with all members of the ODV who were interested in participating. The first challenge was to find a fitting location. With the ODV board members, we decided on a location in Cité Gécamines. Access needed to be as easy as possible, so that no bus fares and long journeys were necessary. We scheduled the trigger event for a Friday, after the meetings at which the members of the association usually assembled. The board members distributed the information for this scheduled meeting. On 12 July 2019, the interested audience was large; approximately 100 chairs were set out and nearly all of them were taken. Three tables provided space for a projector, a laptop and the equipment for the microphones. The board members suggested that I should welcome everyone personally at the entrance. Patrick Mudekereza of the Waza Arts Centre formally opened the event and explained the general idea of the *baraza*. Then, I reported on my research that had started two years earlier.

I showed, for instance, pictures of the files I had found in the archives and explained how I worked with the idea to reveal the (colonial) state's, and especially the UMHK's, strategies of implementing measures of control. I played a propaganda film by the UMHK, which was produced to celebrate the company's fiftieth anniversary in 1956 and which was a useful research source for me. This film showed the UMHK's different measures of organising and controlling the workers – at least that was how we critically reflected upon it. However, the vivid and emotional discussion that followed the screening was not what I had expected.

Those present did not criticise the measures of "control" made by the company at that time. On the contrary, they argued that they had been "well taken care of", as shown in the movie (for instance, the kind of benefits awaiting newly arrived workers were described in detail), whereas today they felt neglected and deprived of the benefits they had enjoyed before 2003. Many participants shared their memories of how those measures were beneficial.

Discussing this film was the first moment in which sharing thoughts helped me recalibrate my assumptions about the workers' positions. At another point during the trigger event, I explained to the audience the great importance to the research endeavour of the interviews that I had conducted earlier. Their voices allowed me to link their current perception to my reading of the archival material. I then suggested the topics for the *baraza*, derived from the interviews and archival sources: identity, health and hygiene; women's roles; and surveillance. No one objected to this procedure or the topics. We then invited ex-workers to sign up for discussions scheduled for the next week, according to their preference of topic, if they were interested in participating at all. To close the trigger event, the members of the Waza Arts Centre expressed our wish not only to give the ODVs a voice but also to preserve their voices, by taking them back to Europe and by presenting them in Lubumbashi.

We therefore suggested that these *baraza* could be filmed, if the individuals involved would give us permission to do so. The filming of these discussions and negotiations would be done by two pairs of eyes – those of the Congolese artist Gulda El Magambo and of my colleague, Carl-Philipp Bodenstein. Sharing in this layer of performance would then be extended to the editing suite afterwards, to combine the perspectives of the two observers. The feedback would finally be shared as a collaborative product. The benefit of this endeavour was not only to document the process of sharing authority but also to extend the concept of shared authority on different levels through form and content and finally synthesise the two layers of performance.

3.2 *Holding the* baraza

The group discussions followed the week after, in Cité Gécamines; the board members had invited us to use their meeting room. The advantage was obvious: the place was familiar to those attending. After the trigger event we had eight group discussions scheduled, two for each of the four topics. For reasons that are very common and comprehensible in the research setting, two group sessions did not take place. Nobody showed up. There were funerals to attend or other priorities that prevented people from being present.

The gathering started after the videographers had set up the technical equipment for filming. The *baraza* were set up in half-circles, in the middle of which a small wooden table served as a pedestal for the microphones. The videographers set up four cameras and field-recorders close to the entrance of the room, facing a corner of two window-less walls, to the right and left of which sat the participants of the *baraza*. Natural light came through a facing window and shone on the participants, eliminating the need for additional lightning. Two cameras them remained stationary and captured the entire scene. The other two were hand-held, operated by Carl-Philipp and Gulda. ODVs who had attended the trigger event had agreed to be filmed; however, we asked each participant for their consent again. There were no objections. On the contrary, they often stressed that it was important to them that their voice be recorded and seen.

After the welcome, the gathering started by addressing the language question. Would they prefer French or Swahili?[42] Each time, we agreed that both languages would be used to allow the conversation to develop naturally.

Patrick Mudekereza took notes in French and Swahili, often combining both languages in one sentence. Later, I compared how he formulated the utterances in terms of language choice and found that he used and mixed the two differently from the actual verbal utterances documented in the films. Thus, the interesting observation was that mixing codes (using different codes within a sentence or utterance) is the normal usage of a plurilingual repertoire.

To end the "Mitaani #mapping Moments", the final event (*le grand baraza*) was organised by the Waza Arts Centre for the Friday of the following week. As soon as the *baraza* were over, the videographers started to work together to edit and grade the footage for a film that was planned to be screened to the ODV. The film was characterised by the fact that in order to be able to understand it, one had to have participated in the *baraza*. It was thus a film produced solely for those who had actually taken part in the project.

The *grand baraza* was held in the facilities of the Waza Arts Centre. Outside in the courtyard, a stage and a screen were prepared and plastic chairs were set up for the ODVs and other guests, who arrived in vast numbers. Patrick Mudekereza welcomed everybody, and the event started with the artist DJ Spilulu presenting a performance based on the audio files recorded during the *baraza*. For instance, he alienated my voice and combined it with extracts from the interviews. The ODVs listened carefully (as we all did) and frequently pointed to the one whose statement was heard. This was then followed by the performances of four poetry slammers, whose works commented the current situation of the ODVs.

At the same time, the accompanying exhibition was presented in the building. Colby, a cartoon artist, used the notes taken by Patrick Mudekereza during the *baraza* and turned them into art pieces, big drawings of the statements with accompanying illustrations that covered the walls of the exhibition room of the Waza Arts Centre. Chairs were set up in the room where viewers could watch a TV playing the film made by the videographers. I observed the visitors

---

42 For a discussion of the role of Swahili in Lubumbashi, see, for example, Ferrari, Kalunga and Mulumbwa, *Le Swahili*, 127; Daniela Waldburger, "Swahili in Eastern Congo – from a Dominated to a Dominant Language or Vice Versa?", in *Pluricentric Languages and Non-Dominant Varieties Worldwide: Volume 1: Pluricentric Languages Across Continents – Features and Usage*, ed. Rudolf Muhr (Frankfurt, Vienna: Peter Lang, 2016), 149.

in the exhibition rooms and talked to them; often, they recognised the topics or statements they had made.

In one very moving moment, a participant addressed me and said: "*Mama Daniela, il y a une erreur ici, je ne l'ai pas dit comme ça*" (Daniela, there is a mistake here, I did not say it like that). Even though the error was not relevant for the overall argument (in my assessment) – the wrong type of machine had been depicted – it was important for the participant to clear up this inaccuracy. So, we took a red pen and corrected the art object. It was a moment when his voice indeed mattered.

During the screening of the film, after the poetry slam session, the participants went back and forth between the exhibition inside and the screening outside, not paying the careful attention we had hoped for. But they addressed us and expressed their view of the importance of this event. In the office, the participants who had attended the *baraza* could fetch an envelope containing prints of the pictures that Carl and Gulda had taken and money for the bus transport back to Cité Gécamines. It turned out that the screening had been planned at bit too late for the participants; for safety reasons they needed to return home before it got too late into the night. We had not considered this point, thinking only about the darkness we would need for an outdoor screening. This was another subtle lesson learned.

3.3 *After the* baraza

After the events, we brainstormed our approach. We concluded that perhaps it had not been the right decision to hold the exhibition in the gallery of the Waza Arts Centre and the screening of the movie in their courtyard. We had asked the ODVs to come to an art gallery because we considered it as the normative place for an exhibition. Maybe placing the representation of participants' voices in their own quartier would have been more appropriate. The question remained open.

Reviewing the group discussions of the *baraza* revealed many topics that had not popped up in the interviews I had led. The setting of the *baraza* had fostered discussions among the ODVs, whereas during the interviews my research partners had often waited for my questions and I was thus the leading voice. In the individual interviews, there was more criticism of the mining company or the supervision it exercised. Or introspective statements like "Maybe we were badly prepared because we were always given everything". During the *baraza*, the participants were more confident about taking the lead in the discussion than had been possible during the interviews, even though the interviews were more open than structured. Still, the discussions during the *baraza* allowed more associative thoughts to be communicated.

In retrospect, I realise that the setup of the *baraza* resembled a stage, a stage that demanded a performance and an audience. Looking again at the video, I discovered that the performative setting revealed two important aspects: first, that the master narrative in its overall dimensions was maintained strictly; second, the hierarchies among the participants influenced the adherence to the master narrative. The ODVs were acting within their network of hierarchies and I was equally a part of it. It is my understanding that we were all part of a network, manoeuvring between roles characterised by dependency and capacity for action at the same time.

3.4 *Leaving the Spider Web and Entering the* **barazaweb**

I conceptualise the *baraza* as a *barazaweb*, a methodological contribution to describe a research situation in which the participants constantly adapt to each other and to the situation. The *barazaweb* is especially important because it evolved from the field, showing how important it is to pay attention to how the field can nourish the theory and not necessarily the other way round. In speaking with the Nigerian writer and feminist Ogundipe-Leslie, it turned out I was using a "locogenetic" approach – that is, a method born out of the field and responding to questions raised by a specific context.[43] Her social criticism questioned who speaks for whom, whose point of view counts, whose experience nourishes the theory. As indicated earlier, the *baraza* implies the idea of council/counselling, which boils down to the exchange of ideas central to the shared authority approach.

It was only when I was back home from Lubumbashi, when I started to carefully watch the filmed *baraza,* that it became obvious that in my role as a researcher I had decidedly influenced it. I chaired the group discussions, suggested topics and requested clarifications. I was a leading voice. However, I was not the only leading voice, and certainly not when discussions became emotional between the ODVs. Group dynamics appeared, and differences in hierarchy revealed themselves among the participants, such as between men and women, or between members of the ODV board and ordinary members of the ODV. I observed the strategies the attendees used to stress their positions; often, the choice of language was far from incidental, and they displayed politics and practices of remembrance of the glorious past to shape the picture of the miserable future awaiting them. The master narrative of *C'était bien à l'époque* was strictly maintained.

---

43 Molara Ogundipe-Leslie, "Literature and Development: Writing and Audience in Africa", in *African Literature and Africa's Development: Mapping Intersections*, eds. Anne V. Adams and Janis A. Mayers (Trenton, NJ: Africa World Press, 1998).

To analyse what happened during the *baraza*, and consequently to be able to interpret my data, I needed to consider the power relations between researcher and researched to be able to classify and interpret the data and conceptualise my findings. I thus needed to explore my first-person practice. Action research theory and practice engages with the process of valuing, leading to decision and action.[44] I needed to be conscious about choices, decisions and actions I took during the interviews and the *baraza* in order to extract my influence on the data. Nevertheless, I also realised that I was not the only one making decisions; rather, in the group dynamic of the *barazaweb*, decisions on topics were made back and forth by all sides, to a greater or lesser degree depending on the hierarchies among the participants.

I was reflecting on the ODVs, my entanglement and our roles during the *baraza* when I read Jiménez's text about the spider web.[45] His metaphor, which I later expanded, proved to be very useful in untangling what I experienced as chaotic intersections of decision-taking. Jiménez uses the metaphor of the spider web to refer to "a world that holds itself in precarious balance, that tenses itself with violence and catastrophe but also grace and beauty, and that calls out and silhouettes promissory worlds of entanglements".[46] Jiménez is interested in the trap that the spider web represents. The trap unites the world of the prey and the predator and he thus uses the image of the trap to describe social theory. He explains that "it is one of my central intuitions that modern knowledge is essentially a trap to itself, such that most forms of explanation are guests unaware they are actually being hosted – predators who do not know their own condition as prey".[47]

Reflecting on the happenings during the *baraza*, I realised that the metaphor of the web that catches the prey was a helpful tool to think about what I had experienced, which until then I had felt was just a vague sense of us all permanently trying to get the upper hand on the issues, interpretation, the word, and so on.

I aimed to produce knowledge, knowledge that became more complex the further the research process went on. For knowledge production, I was looking for the research partners' knowledge. The ODVs wanted to pass on the master narrative to me. While Jiménez talks about the prey's and predator's roles, which are interchangeable, and of prey and predator adjusting to the "trap", I see the benefit of this metaphor in the web itself. Thinking of myself and

44 Coghlan, "What?", 333.
45 Jiménez, "Spiderweb".
46 Jiménez, "Spiderweb", 53.
47 Jiménez, "Spiderweb", 53.

the research partners as being in that very same web helped me to see that I should rather focus on our entanglements than on our position. In that sense, the relations between the researcher and the research partners became one of the research topics.

Jiménez illustrates the changing roles of prey and predator with an example of a research setting in which guerrilla and open-source architectural collectives in Madrid are present:

> We experimented with the format of our meetings: where we met (at cultural centers, in bars, at the Spanish National Research Council), but also with how we conducted a meeting. We took turn taking minutes, which we called *relatorías* (storytelling), and which sometimes read like ethnographic accounts, while at other times they looked like architectural sketches. Sometimes the remit of our activities seemed defined and taken over by the concerns of architects (who were overrepresented at La Mesa, which became a concern in itself), while on some occasions it was the voice of cultural agents or of urban gardening communities that assumed the wisdom of political praxis. Sometimes, even, it was the anthropologists whom everyone turned to for inspiration.[48]

I would like to emphasise again that I do not think of our roles as those of prey and predator, but I find the constant adaptation in the same network helpful. Particularly relevant for this study seems the point of taking the minutes of these meetings. Minutes are – at least in normative settings – the documentation of discussions and serve as the proof of what was taken up and sometimes of what was decided. My archive of the *baraza* is found in filmed *baraza* sessions. The ODVs' archive is found in the minutes noted by the secretary, who chose to attend every *baraza* for this purpose.

Once again, it was only later, when I was back home thinking about my data and research, that I became aware that the secretary's minutes would be necessary to give me an insight into the ODVs – or at least the secretary's – perception of the points that were discussed during the *baraza*. Just like the minutes I had read in the archives of the UMHK, I would have access to a written record. In 2020, travelling to Lubumbashi was impossible because of COVID-19. However, many phone calls and emails to contacts in Lubumbashi, who then contacted the ODVs, were very helpful. I was able to place my request, which was then discussed among the ODVs during their following meeting in their clubhouse.

48 Jiménez, "Spiderweb", 73.

This meeting took place only a few days after a terror attack in Vienna (where I live). They were, via the contact person, asking about my wellbeing, because the news was being broadcast on the channels they watched. As I was later told, they were discussing whether Vienna would be safe enough for me. There was, first of all, their concern for a person they appreciated after three years working together, and second, this person had to tell the world "in the book she is writing" about their situation.

Their concern about the dangerous environment in which I was supposedly living might have speeded up the process. They agreed to prepare a report on the events of July 2019 and some days later I was sent scanned copies. It was a touching moment when I saw these pages; the hand-written testimonies reminded me of the first documents I had read in the UMHK archive in Brussels. This time, however, these were the words of the ex-workers, or at least the secretary's voice. I do understand the secretary's notes as a documentation of our discussions, which is – as much as a careful documentation of the weekly meetings – a complex record-keeping system that maintains the memory and the master narrative. It is very much a site of a corpus that has so far been invisible. It forms part of a new, alternative corpus that consists not only of the archival material in Brussels.

3.5 *An Alternative Archive*

Battley postulates the significance of complex record-keeping systems among communities who traditionally have been "othered" and whose "[r]ecords are embedded and embodied in the community's people, stories, processes and places of belonging".[49] Battley rightly warns us that "[r]emoving community records into an archival institution and arranging and describing them to suit institutional systems strips away the community's own measures of authenticity".[50]

Battley illustrates the point of a record taken from the community to be placed in the archive with the following example, in an interview with a longstanding club member who described going to look at club records that had been transferred to the university's "Special Collections".

> [...] there were also two big photograph albums, which again had been wafting around. They'd come out at Club functions. They used to sit in this wardrobe for a while. When I wanted to look at them, recently, they're now at the Archives in the University, so I had to put white gloves

49 Battley, "Authenticity", 60.

50 Battley, "Authenticity", 61–62.

> on to be able to look at them [laughing], but I appreciate this was policy for Archives, so I guess we've …".

I describe the secretary's report in chapter five in detail to assure the authenticity of his voice. However, it is important to mention his report at this point in relation to his role as chronicler of the history of the ODVs; of course, at the same time he is also an ODV sharing in the same painful experiences.

Seen from this perspective, dependency and capacity for action offer a new methodological turn that opens up the possibility of a new alternative corpus (or "new alternative archive" as Tchokothe suggests).[51] It is one of shared collective memories, while ensuring that the people in the field are not disowned of their archives, knowledge and agency.[52]

The entanglements of participants in the *barazaweb* become visible in the sometimes different representation of the discussions we had. Thus, it was during those moments that I had insight into how knowledge was produced. We find knowledge, as Strathern puts it, only if we relate things to each other. Hence, what counts as knowledge is what counts as relations because "[r]elations are also a means for comprehending a world thought of as connections between persons, however fractious, and however we describe values, collectivities, institutions, alliances, intimacies, and so on".[53] Taking up Strathern's point, Blaser and De la Cadena emphasise

> that the knowledge practices we (modern scholars) have at our disposal are, in turn, conditioned to reinstate themselves. A consequence of this feature is that it may perform epistemic and ontological invalidations – or absences – of the possibility of the multiplicity of worlds.[54]

My aim thus is to present the multiplicity in knowledge production and the entanglements that contributed to this assemblage of knowledge. It is after all, to emphasise Strathern's point, important to know how knowledge is produced. Equally important to me are two more questions: who owns knowledge and whose knowledge counts?

51 Rémi A. Tchokothe, "Archiving Collective Memories and (Dis)Owning. Special Issue, ed. Daniela Merolla on Behalf of the International Society for the Oral Literatures of Africa", *Afrika Focus* 32, no. 1 (2019); Rémi Armand Tchokothe, *'Entré en tant que cousin, sorti en tant que gendarme': Visa Balladur, Kwassa Kwassa, (im)mobilité et géopoét(h)ique relationnelle aux Comores,* Africa Multiple 2 (Leiden: Brill, 2023).

52 Tchokothe, "Archiving".

53 Strathern, "Opening", 28.

54 Blaser and De la Cadena, "Pluriverse", 6.

Knowledge production is based on a process of communicative acts occurring between all those involved. Hence, all data collected is by nature based on the usage of languages and the choice of languages for any given moment. Even if the data has been presented in a text, such as in the annual reports of the mining company or my transcripts of interviews or *baraza*, all these texts are the result of face-to-face and orally mediated exchange that has then been transformed in a textual form. When it comes to the texts produced by the UMHK, for instance in the company magazine *Mwana Shaba*, we have to think of the company's strategies of information management and language strategies. The ODVs equally used strategies to formulate their points of views and stress their perspective.

Let me add a thought on textual practices as discussed by Segall from the perspective of ethnography. He describes ethnography as a meeting place "where a variety of voices are assembled together in a complex intertextual practice"[55] and warns us that:

> [a]s ethnographers, we use, manipulate, alter, edit, discard, reduce and recycle voices from both communities equally. Whether explicitly by signed consent (There) or implicitly through making one's writing (Here) public in journals or books, the voices we recruit – whether from those *in* or *from* the field – equally serve the ethnographer to explain, connect, theorise, concretise, illustrate, and advocate a particular ethnographic account.[56]

I am thus aware that, in the end, I am the one doing the textual representation of the ODVs' voices and there is thus a risk that I might represent their voices inadequately, especially taking into account that "[e]very transcription is a re-telling, a new telling of a previously heard, now newly heard voice".[57]

An appropriate approach to deal with this situation comes from Pillow[58] and Visweswaran[59] and their findings of the benefit of a reflexive approach: "[u]ncomfortable reflexivity, then, is not about better methods, or about whether we can represent people better but", as Visweswaran states, "whether we can be accountable to people's struggles for self-representation and

55 Segall, "Critical Ethnography", 584.
56 Segall, "Critical Ethnography", 584.
57 Segall, "Critical Ethnography", 585.
58 Pillow, "Confession".
59 Kamala Visweswaran, *Fictions of Feminist Ethnography* (Minneapolis, MN: University of Minnesota Press, 1994).

self-determination".[60] I am, as far as the given circumstances allow, able to give an account of the way knowledge was produced because the ODVs were part of it. For them it was important to pass on the master narrative to me, *their* master narrative, which I could not and did not want to destroy. For me the narrative of *C'était bien à l'époque!* represents a sometimes uncomfortable reality.

The analogy of the participants' entanglement in a spiderweb helps one understand how the ODVs' master narrative was negotiated, and the knowledge production in the *barazaweb* helped me avoid the problem of becoming a platform for their goal and of them being instrumental for my goals. Our sharing in the *barazaweb* greatly dissolved the opposition of researcher-researched communities, while at the same time we did not affirm oneness and I did not pretend to avoid "othering".[61] The benefit of the *barazaweb* for the research was thus not "giving voice" to the ODVs in a benevolent way, but accepting that they were taking their voice to frame their master narrative. Hence, their voice is a new voice in the alternative archive.

The following section focuses on the plurilingual situation of the research setting, because an understanding of the different languages and language attitudes in the area of Lubumbashi over the given research time forms the basis for the description of language choices for strategic reasons. These language choices were made apparent not only during the interviews and *baraza* but also in the company magazine *Mwana Shaba*, and to a lesser degree in the annual reports.

4 The Importance of Language Choice

The language(s) used in the documents created by the representatives of the colonial state, the UMHK and later Gécamines, the ex-mineworkers and myself during the interviews and *baraza*, mirror not only what is thought of the most appropriate mean of communication in mostly a plurilingual setting but equally reflect relations of power between those who write or speak and those who listen or read.[62] Those involved in communication likewise chose a language to pursue resistance or offer concession. Thus, the language choice in the texts for this research is meaningful. Swahili and French are relevant in the context of this study, not because other languages were not used in

60 Pillow, "Confession", 193.

61 Segall, "Critical Ethnography".

62 Fairclough, *Language*.

the period in focus (for example, before 1965, immigrant workers brought to Lubumbashi Kilamba, Kiseba, Kilemba, Kisanga, Kiyeke, Wuruwund [Lunda] and other languages, from Zambia, Zimabwe and Malawi)[63] but because Swahili and French were employed for written and oral communication between the UMHK and the workers. Thus, the means of communication demonstrates the constant interaction between the wish to exercise power and the wish to be understood.

Swahili has been spoken in the eastern parts of the Congo, as well as in the region of Katanga and its capital city, what is now Lubumbashi, since at least the arrival of the Arabs. Swahili has been equally useful for European traders, missionaries and "explorers";[64] the coastal form from Zanzibar became the basis for a British controlled "standard" variety. But Lubumbashi Swahili is different. Schicho describes this creolised central variety (or central varieties) as a "broken" version of Lubumbashi Swahili (or up-country Swahili), characterised by lexical borrowings from French and Swahili and other Bantu languages, language switches and transfer of syntactic structures from "Standard Swahili" to Lubumbashi Swahili.[65] These linguistic differences emerged as individual and spontaneous phenomena. Ferrari et al. state that the simplified vernacular (which functioned like a pidgin) transformed into a widespread first language in Katanga: "*Le Swahili tel qu'il est parlé au Katanga est depuis longtemps un symbole du régionalisme katangais*" (Swahili as spoken in Katanga has long been a symbol of Katangese regionalism).[66] In addition, Swahili is part of the linguistic repertoire of immigrants and their descendants.

According to Fabian, Swahili was used in Katanga for two political reasons.[67] First, it was an attempt to create a greater distance between the Congo and southern British colonies. The British colonies constituted a danger because of their interest in Katanga's natural resources. Second, Swahili was considered a convenient means of communication to stabilise the workforce; controlling communication allowed not only the control of work life but equally other domains of life.[68]

63 Tshibanda, «Vocabulaire», 92–93.

64 Fabian, "Missions".

65 Walter Schicho, "Non-acceptance and Negation in the Swahili of Lubumbashi", *African Languages and Cultures* 5, no. 1 (1992): 77.

66 Ferrari, Kalunga and Mulumbwa, *Le Swahili*, 107.

67 Johannes Fabian, *Language and Colonial Power: The Appropriation of Swahili in the Former Belgian Congo 1880–1938*, African studies series 48 (London, New York, Melbourne: Cambridge University Press, 1986); Johannes Fabian, "Simplicity on Command: On Pidginization of Swahili in Shaba (Zaïre)", in *The Fergusonian Impact, in Honor of Charles A. Ferguson on the Occasion of His 65th Birthday. Vol. 1: From Phonology to Society*, eds. Joshua A. Fishman et al. (Berlin: Mouton de Gruyter, 1986).

68 For a discussion, see also Gysels, "French".

Thus, these power relations between colonisers and mineworkers led to Swahili-language textbooks being produced to serve as manuals for use by Europeans in Katanga.[69] The Swahili presented in these guides was an amalgam of different varieties used by Europeans from different backgrounds.[70] It was presented as a deficient medium with a restricted lexicon and rudimentary grammar, inadequate for expressing complex ideas. In fact, this sketched version of Swahili was just the Europeans' improvised manifestation of how they used Swahili to communicate with Africans. The colonisers' wish to control communication is highlighted by Fabian: "in descriptions of Congolese Swahili [...] 'communication and control' – the need to communicate and the intent to control – were inseparable motives".[71]

For the Belgian colonial state and the UMHK, language policies were essential, because those communicating needed to make sure that they would be understood and that their ideas would be followed. At the same time, they tried to propagate Belgian norms through French. French was therefore chosen for colonial publications such as *À chacun sa maison*, publications aimed in particular at the *évolués* ("an upper class of educated Congolese who were granted certain rights following their assumption, to varying degrees, of a lifestyle similar to the European one").[72] French was also the language of choice for company minutes; these documents were meant for internal use and communication with the metropolis.

4.1 *Language in Schools*

In Belgium, the question of the appropriate language(s) in the colony had been discussed from the very beginning. Flemish nationalists in particular protested against the fact, that Congolese children should only be taught French and not it Dutch.[73] However, for primary education in the Congo,[74] the colonial authorities preferred African languages to European languages. Meeuwis states that in the colonial context, in nearly all primary schools the medium of instruction

69 Fabian, *Language*; Gysels, "French".

70 Such as Greek or Flemish employees of mining and railway companies.

71 Fabian, *Language*, 14.

72 Kristien Geenen, "Categorizing Colonial Patients: Segregated Medical Care, Space and Decolonization in a Congolese City, 1931–62", *Africa* 89, no. 1 (2019): 111; Pedro A. G. Monaville, "Decolonizing the University: Postal Politics, the Student Movement, and Global 1968 in the Congo" (PhD dissertation: University of Michigan, 2013); Makombo, *Du Congo Belge*. Geenen ("Categorizing") shows in her paper on the categorising and taxonomy used for colonial patients that further distinctions were in use, such as *indigènes civilisés* and *indigènes évolués* and others, which included divergent professions.

73 Michael Meeuwis, "The Origins of Belgian Colonial Language Policies in the Congo", *Language Matters: Studies in the Languages of Africa* 42, no 2 (2011), 194.

74 Meeuwis, "Bilingual", 1281.

for the first two years was a Congolese language. Secondary education, on the other hand, "was always, and in all locations, organised around French as the sole medium of instruction, except in most technical schools and in teacher training schools".[75] However, the mineworkers were not necessarily very proficient in French, because they usually did not receive formal education before they were recruited by the UMHK. Swahili, the lingua franca, was thus the language connecting the workers and therefore played an important role in the communication between the UMHK and their workers. The schools provided for the workers' children in the camp gave preference to Swahili in the moment of enrolment.

In the annual report of 1950, in a section on courses for workers' general education, the company explains that it would like to offer illiterates and semi-literates an opportunity to increase their knowledge of reading Swahili and spoken French to prepare them for further professional education.[76] Still, the UMHK tried to put the emphasis on what they called "mother tongue", but that referred to Swahili. The workers' ambitions to learn French were criticised:

> Sa grande ambition est de connaître le français, signe extérieur de civilisation. Calcul, mesure, dessin, langue maternelle, lui semblent superflus.[77]

> His great ambition is to know French, an outward sign of civilisation. Calculation, measurement, drawing, mother tongue, seem superfluous to him.

In its 1953 annual report, the UMHK argued that it would be an absolute necessity to start teaching in Swahili, which would become the general language throughout Upper Katanga. However, in the first year, French would be an important curriculum subject. Starting from the third year of primary school, French exercises should include not only oral exercises but also writing and reading. In Grade 5, French should become the first language of instruction. All post-primary education should be taught in French.[78]

Thus, the schools for the workers' children, who were envisaged as the company's future workforce, prioritised Swahili from the moment of enrolment. However, knowledge of at least basic French was also promoted. For the company's future managers and senior workers, French was vital and was therefore taught and regarded as the language of prestige and power.

The UMHK mainly chose French to communicate in written form with the workers, but Swahili played an important role.[79] The UMHK chose a title in

75 Meeuwis, "Bilingual", 1280.

76 AGR 2 – n°655–03046, Rapport Annuel 1950, 32.

77 AGR 2 – n°655–03046, Rapport Annuel 1950, 32.

78 AGR 2 – n°656–03050, Rapport Annuel 1953, 26.

79 No records of oral communication between the UMHK representatives and workers are available.

Swahili for their company magazine, *Mwana Shaba* (copper worker). In the 1956 annual report of the Département MOI, the magazine is described as a bilingual publication in French and Swahili.[80] This decision had two reasons. First, Swahili would ensure that the workers understood the content. Second, French should be used to gradually enhance workers' command of French.

4.2 *Authenticité*

The company's language policy was influenced by political changes, particularly when Congo gained independence in 1960. After his second coup on 24 November 1965, Mobutu Sese Seko intended to change Congo's image. The country underwent a campaign under the motto of *authenticité*[81] (authenticity), which reclaimed the nation's African traditions.[82] The Mobutu government began to change the names of the country's major cities in May 1966; Elisabethville became Lubumbashi, a move that represented a re-baptism, because the Belgian colonisers had already renamed the cities between 1885 and 1935.[83] Mobutu stated: "[b]y the policy of [authenticité], the return to our sources, I hope to mentally decolonize my people, that is to say, to modify the structures left by the colonizer".[84]

This movement implied that he had to find a language for his ideology. Therefore, a conference was organised where intellectuals started debating language issues and made suggestions, but Mobutu was very much in favour of his own language, Lingala. However, *authenticité* did not contain a real language policy in which African languages would gain prominence. French remained the language of the state. The reason for this was the localised use of African languages in Zaire, which did not exceed the limits of the territory occupied by the communities speaking those languages.[85] In 1971, for instance, Mobutu decided to replace the terms *Monsieur* and *Madame*, not with words used in Lingala, or Kikongo, Swahili or any other language from the Congo, but with *Citoyen* and *Citoyenne*, taken from the French Revolution.[86] Mobutu was, however, favouring the French of France over the Belgians: the words *septante* (seventy) and *nonante* (ninety), used in Belgian French, were replaced by *soixante-dix* and *quatre-vingt-dix*, the French words for these numbers.[87] Furthermore, even the

80 AGR 2 – n°657–03053, Rapport Annuel 1956, 44.
81 For a detailed discussion of *authenticité* and its effect on the arts, see for example, Van Beurden, *Authentically African*.
82 Van Beurden, *Authentically African*; Dunn, "Imagining", 235; Ngalasso, "Etat".
83 However, re-baptism does not apply to Lubumbashi, because the Belgians founded the city.
84 Dunn, "Imagining", 240.
85 Ngalasso, "Etat", 11.
86 Dunn, "Imagining", 248.
87 Ngalasso, "Etat", 21.

term of Mobutu's ideology itself, *authenticité*, was used exclusively in French. Intellectuals claimed for an eradication of "foreign" languages and the promotion of national African languages, but Mobutu was not impressed.

In the following section, some extracts from articles published in *Mwana Shaba* illustrate the UMHK's choice of language to communicate to workers. The choice of Swahili for specific topics is of interest – the UMHK wanted to ensure workers' comprehension.

4.3 *Swahili and French*

4.3.1 Announcements

In 1966, *Mwana Shaba* published an order informing workers that they were requested to always carry their identity documents.[88] It published this notification in full length in French and in Swahili. The Swahili version includes terminology that is characteristic of Lubumbashi Swahili, which includes many words borrowed from French. They are marked with quotation marks and end marks in the original:

Kwa maombi ya "service" ya "administration Générale" ya mji wa Elisabethville kwa kutaka kupunguza kazi ya "contrôles" ya wa-"agents" wa kuchunga kanuni wa-"commissaires de police" na kwa faida ya watu wa kazi, tunakumbusha ya kama, kila mkaaji wa nji wa Elisabethville anapashwa kutembea kila siku na :

1. "carte" ya "photo"
2. buku ya mpalata
3. "carte" ya kazi
4. buku ya mkubwa wa jamaa

Vitu hivi ni vya kuonyesha wakate wote pale wakubwa wa kazi ya serikali wanaiomba.[89]

At the request of the services of the general administration of the city of Elisabethville in order to facilitate the controls of the agents of order (police commissioners) and in the interest of the workers we remind any inhabitant of the city of Elisabethville that he must permanently carry his identity documents:

1. plastic card with photo
2. identity card
3. work permit
4. family register booklet

These things have to be presented to the government employees whenever requested.

In the same year, the UMHK announced the creation of shops where employees of the company could buy daily necessities at a reduced price.[90] The text was

88 *Mwana Shaba*, No. 123, 15 April 1966, 15.
89 *Mwana Shaba*, No. 123, 15 April 1966, 15.
90 *Mwana Shaba*, No. 126, 1 June 1966, 2.

given in both languages and included words of thanks by the correspondents addressed to the UMHK to allow the workers to "live better in difficult times".[91]

In the 1 June 1966 issue, *Mwana Shaba* placed an announcement for a section dedicated to letters to the editor, a section that had existed before but had been cancelled for some time.[92] The announcement was published in French and Swahili, and letters from the readers were published in both languages. Each contribution ended with a short comment, such as thanks for the contribution or a reference to further information. The editors of *Mwana Shaba* added these comments in the language in which the letter was composed. The letters to the editors that were published were of course carefully selected and served as a measure to control communicative content by the company. In 1966, *Mwana Shaba* published the following complaint by a reader, which was followed by a reply from the publisher:

M. Lambert Lukuka wa Panda anasikitika ya kuwa Kiswahili inapunguka zaidi na zaidi katika Mwana Shaba. Français ni luga inaonekana kuwa na wasomaji wa kuenea. Habari yetu fupi inayoandikwa katika français na Kiswahili inawezesha kwa wasomaji wengi zaidi kwa kujizoea luga ingine. Lakini français ya vyombo vya ufundi tuseme, ni ngumu sana kwa kuiguza katika Kiswahili. Zaidi ya ile, ukurasa wetu wa "La Boîte aux Lettres" inajibu katika luga ile msomaji alitumia. Tena musisahau ya kuwa kizazi cha sasa kinajua français na kinaituia zaidi na zaidi.[93]

M. Lambert Lukuka of Panda is sad that Swahili is diminishing more and more in Mwana Shaba. French is a language that seems to have a widening readership. Our short contributions written in French and Swahili enable more readers to practise the alternating language. But the technical French, let's say, is very difficult to translate into Swahili. In addition, our "La Boîte aux Lettres" page responds to the message the reader used. And do not forget that the current generation knows French and uses it more and more.

The complaint provided the publisher with the opportunity to expound on the company's view that workers' French language skills should be improved. The response by the editor of *Mwana Shaba* implies the lower prestige that was attributed to Swahili in comparison to French. Swahili was presented as a language useful for communication as long as the topic did not concern any

91 *"Vivre mieux dans des moments difficiles"/"kuishi vema wakati wa magumu".*

92 *Mwana Shaba*, No. 126, 1 June 1966, 14–15.

93 *Mwana Shaba*, No. 127, 15 June 1966, 14.

complex subjects. Furthermore, the company's intention as formulated in the annual report announcing the aim of language choice for *Mwana Shaba* was reproduced: French competence should increase, even though in this comment the argument was formulated openly by mentioning that bilingual texts would help to practise the other language. It was further argued that the language choice was not the choice of *Mwana Shaba* but of the composers of the letters to the editors themselves. The trend went – as they argued – towards French, especially among the youth.

4.3.2 In Memoriam

Obituaries were published in either Swahili or French in most cases: in Swahili for Congolese workers and in French for white staff members. Bilingual texts were published when the Congolese deceased person held a higher position. In 1966, for instance, the obituary for M. Alphonse Hamici was published.[94] He was *chef* of the Cité and is described as the brother of the administrative director of the weekly newspaper *La voix du Katanga*. The hierarchy within the company and society thus had an influence on the language choice.

4.3.3 Swahili

The section *Nouvelles de chez nous* (News from Us) in *Mwana Shaba* was dedicated to news covering leisure and especially sport activities in the different locations in Katanga where the UMHK had its mines and camps. Additionally, letters to the editor were often (but not always) published in this section. Swahili was the choice for all this news, with the exception of the title of this section; sometimes the pictures illustrating a topic were accompanied by a caption in French and Swahili.

De Rooij analysed the section *Habari za Kwetu* (News of/from our Place/Home), as the section *Nouvelles de chez nous* was titled in earlier issues,[95] looking at the letters to the editor in the April 1958 issue. The letters described the problems and concerns of the residents in the late 1950s. De Rooij argues that the letters that made it into the magazine nearly always presented complaints about the loss of traditional values and behaviour in the new urban centres of the Copperbelt. There were warnings against the dangers of alcohol, thievery and the changing attitude of young women who no longer automatically obeyed the old customs. De Rooij points out that during this period of rising political activity and unrest, it did not come as a big surprise that the letters to the editor did not contain any political issues. In addition, "[e]ven if some

94 *Mwana Shaba*, No. 125, 15 May 1966, 15.

95 De Rooij, "Letters".

workers would have had the courage to write about politics, the editors of the journal would have made sure that these letters never got published".[96]

De Rooij argues that the letters in *Habari za Kwetu* are examples of popular literacy because most of the employees of the UMHK were schooled workers. However, the actual proficiency in writing Swahili is difficult to assess. According to De Rooij "[t]he variability in spelling displayed in the letters allows the conclusion that there was no clear written standard variety which the writers could turn to and that to some degree their writing reflects the spoken language of that time".[97] What we gain from De Rooij's analysis of the letters is an idea of the colloquial Swahili in the Copperbelt of the late 1950s.

The UMHK's language policy left its traces in the status that is attributed today to Swahili and French, status that became obvious in the interviews and during the *baraza*. Swahili is the lingua franca among the ODVs. However, in communications between the members and the president of their association, French was more commonly used, even though the president is a Swahili speaker. In many ways the group's language use mirrored the hierarchical structures in which they had been socialised. This resulted, for instance, in very formalised openings of the meetings (three times a week in Cité Gécamines for the board members of the ODV) in French, followed by a prayer in Swahili. The discussions that followed and which I attended were characterised by a typical switching between Swahili and French, in which Lubumbashi Swahili borrows from French and vice versa.[98] Whenever I was invited to talk during these meetings, to present my research project, deposit my interview requests or speak about any other issue, I had to follow the protocol given by the president in French.

I thus addressed them in French, but switched to Swahili after a while because I soon realised that the president or his secretary started to translate French into Swahili for some participants. Ex-mineworkers' knowledge of French depends largely on the category of work they did. Blue-collar workers usually had less formal education and were thus less proficient in French, whereas those whose career paths ended in senior positions were required to have a very good command of French, not least because all the paperwork had to be handled in French. However, since the blue-collar and senior positions were classified into numerous subgroups, there was a broad spectrum of

96 De Rooij, "Letters".

97 De Rooij, "Letters".

98 A description of the code switching and code mixing in Lubumbashi Swahili is not relevant here. In a recent contribution, Mutambwa concludes: "la langue swahilie ne serait aujourd'hui que l'ensemble de ces différentes variétés" (Mutambwa, "Kiswahili", 51).

competence in Swahili and French. I therefore started to adapt to the unwritten rules that French was the appropriate choice because we were in a rather formally organised setting, but that Swahili was equally appropriate when it came to the actual content and transmission of information. The secretary showed me his meticulous minutes of these meetings since 2003. It came as no surprise that all the minutes were in French, the language that has mainly been in use for writing in Lubumbashi, not because French is more widespread but because of the lack of standardisation of Swahili in Lubumbashi. In addition, by using French for the minutes, the language of greater status, the board members emphasised the seriousness of their fight for compensation.

Before I started an interview with the ODVs, I usually asked them what their language preference was. In Cité Gécamines, where ex-blue-collar workers usually lived, they most often were in favour of Swahili, whereas in Makomeno, the neighbourhood of the former cadres, French was usually preferred. In the course of the interviews, however, both languages were spoken. These interviews would certainly serve as a rich database to analyse code switching and code mixing by speakers and listeners with a plurilingual repertoire. However, in the context of this study, the purely morpho-syntactical discussion is irrelevant.

There was one interview that was in French only, although all the communication before and after was solely in Swahili, even without any borrowings from French. This interview took place in Makomeno, in the house of a former manager who had moved with his wife to Lubumbashi from Bukavu, a city at the very east of the DRC on the border of Rwanda. In this region, the Swahili is more similar to the Swahili from the East Coast and thus much closer to the variety I had learned. From the first moment I met him and his family our communication was in Swahili only; they even expressed their delight to speak "their" Swahili. However, for the recorded interview, he insisted on French. As a manager, as he pointed out, he wanted to perform according to what was formally required. Thus, language choice is never only to ensure mutual understanding, but equally an assertion of the status linked to it.

The difference in language choice for a formal and a less formal setting also became apparent in July 2019 within the scope of the trigger event and the *baraza* in Cité Gécamines. The trigger event took place in a hall that belongs to one of the many church organisations in that neighbourhood. The formal setting, with tables for the projector and laptop, the microphone ready for the introduction by the Waza Arts Centre and myself, meant that during the individual welcomes, even the members with whom I usually spoke Swahili chose French, and it was no surprise that unknown people greeted me in French.

It was planned that Patrick Mudekereza would formally open this event and explain the idea of our co-operation. He chose Swahili for this introduction; he is from Lubumbashi and wanted to ensure that everybody would understand. My role during this event was to present my previous research and highlight the importance of the interviews I had conducted with them in 2017 and 2018 and to explain the idea of the group discussions to come. As Patrick and the president of the ODV pointed out to me during the preparatory meeting, I was in the role of the European researcher and the formal setting demanded a presentation in French. The lively debate to clarify issues after the presentation was characterised by a preference for French among those asking questions, and therefore I answered in French, while Patrick Mudekereza of the Waza Arts Centre translated everything into Lubumbashi Swahili.

The *baraza* that followed the week after took place in the meeting room of the ODV board, a room that was familiar to me and to those attending. My introduction and initial statements to initiate the discussions were in French, but often borrowed from Swahili, especially when topics demanded specific descriptions, such as to discuss of the role of the *tshanga tshanga* (the *chef de Cité* in Cité Gécamines). During the discussion, though, I often switched to Swahili, especially when I responded to a participant who had made his or her statement in Swahili. The participants used both languages, some more French than Swahili, others more Swahili than French. What characterised these gatherings most was the discussions among the participants themselves (as I had hoped), who engaged enthusiastically in sometimes highly emotional debates. Everybody spoke according to their choice, it seemed. Nevertheless, I may have influenced the language choice during these discussions simply by my presence as a researcher from Europe.

5 Proceeding from Here

I proceed on the basis of two assumptions: that (industrial) paternalism existed, and that there is an interweaving of people and materiality. Both are relevant in the context of this research.

The ODVs' master narrative of *C'était bien à l'époque!* and their constant recall of what they had been provided with by the UMHK require some remarks on paternalism and the industrial paternalistic approach by the UMHK that is visible in the archival material. Paternalism obviously left traces among the ODVs, in the sense that they felt "taken care of well".

The (ex-)workers' perceptions of paternalistic experiences are not discussed in the literature. The "beneficiaries" of paternalism (which is critically discussed by scholars today) are conveyed as having no power and no voice and there is the sense that anyway there was no need to understand their points of view because no resistance was to be expected. After all, the ODVs benefited and got what they sorely miss today. Nevertheless, within the framework of the *baraza* the ODVs indicated the meaning that paternalism had and has for them. The nostalgic references to it during the *baraza* were evoked by spatiality: that of the *baraza*, or their houses, a location that is a constant reminder of the past. In actor-network theory these spaces are non-human actors.

5.1 *Paternalism*

Young starts his discussion of what he calls the "paternal metaphor" by referring to a comment by the Belgian Minister of the Congo De Schrijver about the rural populations in the colony, made shortly after the DRC's independence in 1960:

> I see these simple populations outside the large urban centers, and I feel myself more than ever the father of a family. And if I have ten children, that has prepared me to better understand these peoples … We know that all the children of a family must work together to achieve the big goals. And these children are like the ten fingers of my two hands. When I am in the Congo, I listen to all the voices … I say to those who only represent two fingers, 'You don't have the right to ask me not to take account of the eight others'.[99]

De Schrijver was, as Young explains, the architect of a radical decolonisation. Considering De Schrijver's position, it was surprising that he used a metaphor that reduced the Congolese to children who needed to be taken care of. Belgium's role of mother and father was the blueprint for the UMHK's approach towards their workforce, as I argue below.

Young further argues that paternalism as a guide to policy can be traced back to the founding of the Congo Free State in 1885, but until World War II the approach was more of an implicit assumption than a political theory.[100] Up to that point, the Congolese had been simply considered immature and with no need of any further "sophistication". But in the postwar era colonialism was on the defensive and needed justifications for its prolongation. This resulted in paternalistic colonial administration policies. "[R]educed to its simplest expression, paternalism required an aggressive expansion in social

99 Crawford Young, *Politics*, 59.
100 Young, *Politics*, 60.

and economic fields, with political advance postponed until some undefined threshold of maturity had been reached."[101]

Colonial "development" gained a foothold on various levels in different domains and in rural as well as urban areas. In the urban areas, for instance, "African housing" was promoted, as well as schools and hospitals. In the rural areas, the Fonds du Bien-Être Indigène promoted welfare activities from sanitary campaigns to the provision of drinking water.[102] At the societal level, for instance, "[t]he sale of liquor to Africans was prohibited until 1955. This restriction dated back to the Brussels Anti-Slavery Conference of 1889–1890; initially, it was no doubt a humanitarian measure to halt the ravages of alcoholism and prevent unscrupulous exploitation".[103]

In relation to companies, in 1946 the legislation adopted the establishment of Conseils d'entreprise, similar to company unions, which were a forum for discussions between labour and management about worker grievances.[104] Half of the worker members were elected. Young argues that these bodies were a determining factor for the slow growth of African labour organisations.

For this study, I use the term "paternalism" to refer to all the measures used by Belgium (and by proxy, the UMHK) to "take care of" or "control" the Congolese or the workers (that were urgently needed). I do so against the background that paternalistic approaches were seen as a strategy to show concern or goodwill at that time. As Young put it:

> Hailey is quite right to add that the "concern of the Administration has not in fact been merely material; there has been a real element of good will toward the African population and its welfare. Good will is implicit in the paternal metaphor."[105]

The goodwill of the mining companies in the region was seen as such by many mineworkers, as Larmer et al. also point out.

> In Katanga, the provision of comprehensive social services by the triumvirate of the mine company UMHK, the Roman Catholic Church and the

101 Young, *Politics*, 60.
102 Young, *Politics*, 62.
103 Young, *Politics*, 66.
104 Young, *Politics*, 62.
105 Young, *Politics*, 63.

> Belgian colonial state created a system of paternalism which many mine-workers and their families genuinely regarded as generous.[106]

I consider the discussions on paternalism mainly as a discourse about a unilateral declaration, because the paternalistic metaphor simply reduces the "beneficiaries" of the measures to recipients lacking agency. For this study, I thus understand paternalism as a setting in which the mining company operated. This paternalistic approach is evident in the ideological orientation of the company's decisions, which can be seen, for example in the reports from the archives.

Since the paternal metaphor is at least implicitly used by the ODVs today as a reference point for a time when they lived in good circumstances, the question arises whether beneficiaries of a paternalistic approach are powerless or whether they find strategies to use the role of supposed powerlessness productively in order to cope with their current situation.

In this context it is worth examining a case study by Mutongi, who describes widows' agency in western Kenya from the 1940s to the 1960s.[107] The widows, the powerless "objects", used strategies to act within the alleged beneficiary roles to use the construction of the feminine, and consequently also masculine, categories for their own benefit. Mutongi describes that the widows

> consciously presented themselves as "poor widows", as idealized stereotypes of suffering females who were believed to become needy and helpless at the death of their husbands. They told their stories in ways calculated to solicit sympathy. And this usually worked to their advantage since it placed men in the difficult situation of having to defend their "ideal" masculinity.[108]

By grieving in public, the widows drew attention to their social and economic needs. They reinforced the importance of the gender categories to prompt men, who had to uphold their own self-image, to guarantee the economic livelihood and social status of the bereaved widows. "Assisting widows in the tasks previously performed by their deceased husbands made men feel 'strong', 'dynamic' and 'paternalistic'."[109] The widows' main aim was to acquire sufficient

---

106 Larmer, Guene and Henriet, *Across the Copperbelt* 15.

107 Kenda Mutongi, "'Worries of the Heart': Widowed Mothers, Daughters and Masculinities in Maragoli, Western Kenya, 1940–60", *The Journal of African History* 40, no. 1 (1999).

108 Mutongi, "Worries", 68.

109 Mutongi, "Worries", 70.

money to educate their daughters, in response to a paradigm shift that had occurred in that time. Young men preferred to marry well-educated young women – women who knew how to manage a modern household – which fit into Christian and European ideas about modernity and civilisation.

Mutongi's case study shows that at approximately the same time that the Lubumbashi mineworkers started their working careers in a paternalistic context, strategies to challenge the passive role existed, though in a different geographical and societal setting. Although I did not find evidence of these strategies in the archive, probably because of the corporate nature of the documents, I think the fact that the roles of beneficiary, passive and agent, can be reversed is important. Taking this line of thought further and applying it to the situation of ODVs, I conclude that they are not paralysed either, but also use strategies to voice their agency. The discourse on the past, the present and the future is thus shaped from different but intertwined roles.

5.2 *Interweaving*

The basic idea of actor-network theory (ANT), first developed by Bruno Latour and Michel Callon, is to bypass the subject-object dichotomy and instead focus on the interweaving of people and non-human "beings". The idea is not, as has often been assumed, to assign non-human things (such as objects, technology, animals, plants) attributes that are usually regarded as special features of the human capacity to act (such as consciousness, intentionality and eccentric positionality). On the contrary, ANT virtually refuses to make any a priori statements about the competencies, qualities and characteristics of the actors involved.[110] Latour suggested that ANT should be understood as the science of associations. The idea is that the concept of the actor should be expanded. Latour argues that we can either follow social theorists and set up at the start which group and level of analyses we will focus on, or "we follow the actors' own ways and begin our travels by the traces left behind by their activity of forming and dismantling groups".[111]

I use this concept of ANT to underline my argument that spatial configurations and objects in a space, as well as materiality, influence society in a dialectical relationship. Law argues that the successful long-distance control by Portuguese colonists was based on an expansion that involved "the

110 Lars Gertenbach, "Die Droge als Aktant: Akteur-Netzwerk-Theorie", in *Handbuch Drogen in sozial- und kulturwissenschaftlicher Perspektive*, eds. Robert Feustel, Henning Schmidt-Semisch and Ulrich Bröckling (Wiesbaden: Springer VS, 2019), 267.

111 Bruno Latour, *Reassembling the Social: An Introduction to Actor-Network-Theory*, Clarendon lectures in management studies (Oxford: Oxford University Press, 2007), 29.

technological, the economic, the political, the social and the natural [...] all seen as being interrelated".[112] He shows that it was the combination of science, drill (a strict set of rules) and physical tools that allowed the Portuguese navy to be successful over a long period of time. Thus, objects are of a structural nature but they are not determinants. Seen from the perspective of ANT, people can be understood as a result of the unfolding web of relationships in which they are involved. And human and non-human actors are interconnected.[113]

In the context of this study, I see spatial objects, especially houses, as non-human actors. I treat them as triggers of nostalgia, as I will explain.

Let me draw your attention to one of the houses that was of great importance for this study: the house in which most meetings with the board members of the ODV and all *baraza* took place. The house was owned by Mama Helene, the "blind widow", as everybody called her. According to her late husband's will, the house was to serve as the meeting place for the ODV board. Her husband had been a member of this board as well as her companion. Mama Helene made the living room of her house available for these meetings. She was therefore usually around during the meetings, sometimes sitting in them and listening to them, sometimes sitting outside in front of the house. She was not a member of the board. Nevertheless, she was a participant in the board meetings, she was the "human infrastructure" who linked the house with the ODVs and facilitated the joint struggle. Thus, in this network Mama Helene linked human agency (the board members of the ODV) and non-human agency (the living room of the house), and the spatial object became the trigger for nostalgia. I follow Bennett, who writes:

> Place can be understood as simultaneously imagined and embodied, an active site for social practices through history, memory, other people, and material things. [...] History is not stuck in the past but moves through the lives of people and places, and is constantly being recreated in the present through memories (Blokland, 2001; Kuhn, 2000) and the presence of material objects (Jones, 2010).[114]

112 John Law, "On the Methods of Long-Distance Control: Vessels, Navigation and the Portuguese Route to India", *The Sociological Review* 32, 1_suppl (1984): 235.

113 John Law and Vicky Singleton, "ANT and Politics: Working in and on the World", *Qualitative Sociology* 36, no. 4 (2013): 491.

114 Bennett, "Gifted Places", 658.

The intertwining of the people involved in the research, with ever-changing roles, the associated material environment and the connection of knowledge from archives with newly created knowledge – the new alternative archive – are at the centre of this study. All these interconnections become visible at the moment they are communicated.

6 Conceptual Background of the Nostalgia-based Master Narrative

Reflecting on nostalgia involves thinking from today's perspective about what has been lost. I approach nostalgia by taking a closer look at the discourse and then suggesting that nostalgia works as a backward projection to solve today's problems.

6.1 *The Object of Loss*

Odhiambo discusses the lyrics of a song by Jumanne Omari, a musician from Samia in western Kenya, whose works often dealt with proletarian labour.[115] The following lines of a song from 1958 illustrate the virtues of humble domestic work:

Kazi ya Kiboi	The work of houseboy
Inapendwa sana	Is very much liked
Na vijana	By young men
Kwa sababu yake	The reason being
Wana pata posho	They get rations
Na nyumba ya bure.	and free accommodation.[116]

The work of a domestic servant is described as being attractive to young men, not because of the work in particular but simply because of the benefits linked to it: food and housing. This example illustrates that work was neither exclusively perceived as exploitative by employees, nor that the topic of this section is unique to Elisabethville/Lubumbashi.

Fabian's *History from Below* is a remarkable work that discusses the booklet *Vocabulaire de ville de Elisabethville*,[117] an account by André Yav, a former domestic servant. Yav's narrative of Elisabethville's history covers roughly

115 E.S.A. Odhiambo, "Kula Raha: Gendered Discourses and the Contours of Leisure in Nairobi, 1946–63", *Azania: Archaeological Research in Africa* 36–37, no. 1 (2001), 262.

116 Translation by Odhiambo.

117 Fabian, *History*.

the years between 1885 and 1958, the years before the song above came to be known.[118]

In Yav's narrative, work conditions are mainly described as difficult and exploitative. "There was not a single worker who was able to open his mouth, even a little bit. […]. Then we boys lived in true misery."[119] The boys' described hardship is also specified in relation to housing conditions. For instance, the lack of sufficient space troubles the father of a family; the absence of sufficient privacy[120] to get dressed before going to work is described as follows:

> Because they thought [it good] to build for the black man just a one-room house. [But] this man had his wife and his children, some of them male, some of them female. Now this poor man with his wife and children suffered when he went to sleep and when he awoke. Who is this man? The poor man, the boy, who sleeps in one small room together with his children, female and male. When he goes to work, the poor boy, when he wakes up, he says to all this grown-up children: Mothers and fathers, you must excuse me. Get up and leave, or go first outside. Me, your old man, I want to put on my clothes first.[121]

Lack of sufficient space is compared to the space available to the employer:

> And should this White man have two rooms, enough to give both to his employee, the boy, he puts a lock on it [to make it] his chicken coop or rabbit hutch. In that respect the White had a very bad spirit indeed. But there were many among them who had a very good spirit and took very good care of their people.[122]

---

118 See Schicho ("Linguistic Notes") in Fabian, *History;* for linguistic and anthropological notes see Pauni and Dibwe dia Mwembu, "Vocabulaire».

119 Fabian, *History*, 75.

120 In her very interesting contribution, Malevez discusses how male architects of colonial architecture contributed to the exclusion of men from domestic work: "Intimacy is one of the notions at the core of this process: by branding the home as an 'intimate refuge from work' for men, domestic manuals and architecture and design magazines implicitly excluded them from participating in domestic work. Intimacy was also a prism through which male architects thought about the layout of houses. Rather than aiming to impress the occasional visitor, they advocated for homes to cater to their inhabitants' needs, discarding at the same time the need for domestic servants. Homes became more rational and practical, but also more 'intimate' as a result." (Malevez, "Les douceurs", 2)

121 Fabian, *History*, 75.

122 Fabian, *History*, 77.

This second excerpt reveals that the relationship between employer and employee was not always considered exploitative, and that in some cases employees were well taken care of. *C'était bien à l'époque!* (It was good at that time!), the most commonly expressed sentence by the interview partners talking about the former times, refers to before 2003. But as in Yav's account, in comparison to the ODVs' narrative, which related to a time long past, the sentiment of being well taken care of was of utmost importance to the ex-mineworkers. The nostalgic narrative of the past is based on the general perception *de ne pas être abandonné* (of not being abandoned). The references to being well taken care of are manifold among the members of the ODV and are discussed further below.

The decline in living conditions is a topic not only among the ex-mineworkers but also in the verbal arts of Lubumbashi today. Sando Marteau is a performing artist who lives in Lubumbashi and is "one of the very few Congolese poets who consistently employ Swahili for their compositions. Full of melancholy tones, Sando Marteau's beautiful, deep songs speak out the pain and malaise of contemporary Congolese society".[123] Rettová provides us with the Swahili lyrics of Marteau's song *Union Minère du Haut-Katanga*:[124]

Alikuwa mama wa Wacongomani wote,	She was the mother of all Congolese,
mama wa watoto wa Katanga,	the mother of the children of Katanga,
mushariki wa ulimwengu muzima,	a companion for the whole world,
na yeye wote walioneyamo.[125]	everyone found his place in it.

The reference to "mother" is used synonymously for the mining company that offered a place for everyone and took care of her "children". Also, the reference to "not being abandoned" is present in this song as it is in ex-workers' narratives.

The second stanza states that "the Congo is in tears" (*leo Congo mu matshozi*), followed by a reference to exploitation, asking the question "for whose benefit?" (*kwa faida ya nani?*) in the third stanza. In the fourth stanza, today's mining companies are criticised: "stranger ate what was on the table" (*Mutoka mbali alikuliya lwe ku meza*) "while the Congolese picked up the crumbs on the

123 Alena Rettová, "Swahili and Swahili Poetry in Lubumbashi: The Language and Lyrics of Sando Marteau", *Archív Orientální* 86, no. 3 (2018): 333.

124 Alena Rettová, *Chanter l'existence: La poésie de Sando Marteau et ses horizons philosophiques* (Středokluky: Zdeněk Susa, 2013), 90. I adapted Rettová's orthographic version (compiling the morphemes belonging to one predicate, noun, etc. in one word) to facilitate understanding for readers of (Standard) Swahili, because Marteau's specific orthographic style is not relevant for this chapter.

125 Rettová, *Chanter*, 90.

ground" (*na Mucongomani alilokota twa tshini*). The fifth stanza describes that the "companies extracted all the riches" (*Wali tshimbula mali fasi zote*) and "left the ponds without fish" (*kwatsha bishima bila samaki*).

The nature of the problem described corresponds to the perceptions of the ex-workers. They explained how today the wealth is taken by foreign companies which leave no benefits for them. In the sixth stanza of the song, Marteau asks where the leaders are, who are missing in these times:

Mabunge tulitshawa muko	Our elected representatives, our parliamentari-
wapi?	ans, where are you?
Viongozi mune tu ongoza	Leaders who lead us, where are you?
muko wapi?	At our place, it's as if we did not have a home;
Kwetu kama aina kwetu,	with us, it's like being perched on top of a tree.
kwetu kama dju ya muti,	Our riches are as if they were not ours,
mali yetu kama aina yetu,	our riches are as if they belonged to someone
mali yetu kama ya benyewe.	else.
Atu oneyemo,	We do not find ourselves in them,
atu oneyemo ma minings,	we do not end up in mining companies,
sisi atu oneyemo.[126]	we do not find ourselves in them.

The same perception of missing leadership manifested in the interviews and during the *baraza*, when statements like "*On a besoin d'un conducteur*" (We need a leading figure [lit. driver]) were made. In Marteau's song and among the members of the Collectif des ex-agents de la Gécamines, the UMHK – the mining company of the old times – is glorified whereas the state enterprise, Gécamines, which succeeded the UMHK, is criticised. Today's politicians and leaders are considered responsible for the economic decline.

Sando Marteau published another version of this song: *Mama wa Wacongomani* (Mother of the Congolese). In this version, "mother" is as a synonym for the UMHK. Many of the verses are similar, but this version includes a second verse that praises the mother for very specific qualities:

Alijenga mabarabara, masomo,	She built roads, schools,
mahospitali, miji mbali mbali,	hospitals, different cities,
wafanya kazi wake wali lipa vizuri,	and the workers were well paid,
mutoka mbali na mwana Congo	foreigners and Congolese
wote walifurahi,	were all happy,
kweli alikuwa mama wa wote.[127]	she really was a mother to all.

126 Rettová, *Chanter*, 91.

127 Rettová, *Chanter*, 88–89.

The building of infrastructure, the payment of good wages and general good conditions for Congolese and foreigners alike correspond to the ODVs' sentiment of *C'était bien à l'époque!* Thus the nostalgia is a sentiment expressed not only by individuals formerly employed in the mining sector, but also by artists of different art forms.[128] The widely heard catchphrase *Union Minière* [*kaji*] *njo baba, njo mama* (the Union Minière [or alternatively, salaried work] is the father and the mother)[129] thus sounds like the abstract of this song, reflecting the perception that the company was like a parental figure.

Sammy Baloji's artworks are prominent in Jewsiewicki's reflections on local collective memory and popular culture. Baloji works with a heritage that does not belong to him "because it was written from the gaze of elsewhere and refers to the generations of their fathers and grandfathers".[130] With these "ruins" that Baloji processes in his works he focuses on replacing old metaphors with new ones, with the purpose of reconstructing what is missing today.[131] This artist's work displays, as in Marteau's songs, the nostalgia that permeates today's society.

In *Native Nostalgia*, Dlamini explains that sentiments of nostalgia confirm that people's lives in the past were different in comparison to the current moment – though not in the way often imagined.[132] The author assumes that nostalgia is "a sentiment of loss and displacement" and "it is about present anxieties refracted through the prism of the past".[133] This sentiment usually erupts in moments when people feel adrift in a world that seems to be out of their control. This is certainly the case for the ex-mineworkers in this study, who regretfully refer to their good life in the past.

Following Boym,[134] Dlamini[135] delineates two types of nostalgia.[136] First, he discusses restorative nostalgia, the emphasis of which lies in "*nóstros*" (return/homecoming). Thus, a person wishes "to rebuild the lost home and patch up

---

128 Schicho (*Le Groupe Mufwankolo*) and Fabian (*Power*), for instance, researched the theatre troupe Mufwankolo, who promoted the local variety of Swahili.

129 Petit and Mutambwa, "LA CRISE", 470.

130 Jewsiewicki, "Leaving", 6.

131 Jewsiewicki, "Leaving", 7.

132 Dlamini, *Native*, 12.

133 Dlamini, *Native*, 16.

134 Boym, *Future*.

135 Dlamini, *Native*, 17.

136 Nadia Atia and Jeremy Davies, "Nostalgia and the Shapes of History", *Memory Studies* 3, no. 3 (2010): 182. "In 1688, the Swiss doctor Johannes Hofer proposed a name for a certain type of wasting disease. The word combined the Greek *Nostos*, 'return to the native land', with *Algos*, [meaning] suffering or grief; so that thus far it is possible from the force of the sound Nostalgia to define the sad mood originating from the desire for the return to one's native land' (Hofer, 1934 [1688]: 381)".

the memory gaps". Reflective nostalgia, on the other hand, "dwells in algia,[137] in longing and loss, the imperfect process of remembrance". People who would be classified as restorative nostalgics would not think of themselves as nostalgic at all; rather, they are convinced that their project is about truth. In contrast, reflecting nostalgics would not take the past for granted, as "there is no monumental past to recreate".[138]

The ODVs did not make a single reference to a wish to convince me of the "truth" of the past. There is no master narrative to correct, as it does not exist. When I referred earlier to the *Vocabulaire de ville de Elisabethville*, it was not an attempt to compare the narratives of the domestic servant of that time with those of the ODVs. The life experiences are not the same (although Yav describes the economic crisis in the 1930s and the ODVs experienced a severe economic decline). It is no surprise that the longing for earlier work and better living conditions was common. In that sense, Worby and Allen's approach to nostalgia seems to add a valuable aspect. They suggest that nostalgia "denotes a specific way of enfolding the past into the present, and indeed the future".[139] Worby and Ally elicit Dlamini's different registers; in the sociological reading, they identify nostalgia as a particular sentiment that represents a symptom, and use that symptom to diagnose and explain an underlying social malaise.[140] The workers' painful longing ("*algia*") does not refer to returning home ("*nostos*") but can rather be seen as an expression of this mood that represents the symptom of the underlying malaise. Furthermore, the "home" may have existed or it may have been purely imaginary; more importantly, it may belong to the past or to the future.[141]

Rosaldo discusses an additional and different aspect of nostalgia. He points to the fact that "agents of colonialism – officials, constabulary officers, missionaries, and other figures from whom anthropologists ritually dissociate themselves – often display nostalgia for the colonized culture as it was 'traditionally' (that is, when they first encountered it)."[142] However, this category of nostalgia is not relevant for this study. The UMHK and the Belgian (colonial) state were far from innocent in altering or destroying "traditional" life. I will

137 In neo-Latin, "*nostalgia*" = homesickness; in Greek, "*nóstos*" = return (to the homeland) and "*álgos*" = pain; today's meaning is probably influenced by the synonymous English nostalgia. Do you need this footnote, having made the point more or less in the footnote above?

138 Dlamini, *Native*, 18.

139 Worby and Ally, "Disappointment", 468.

140 Worby and Ally, "Disappointment", 460.

141 Piot, *Nostalgia*, 20.

142 Rosaldo, "Imperialist" , 107–8.

read the measures they took to control and shape society and workers against the backdrop of actions of control.

Nevertheless, the nostalgia of the Belgians in this sense is an important aspect, which is relevant to Mobutu Sese Seko's undertaking to change Congo's imaginary. For example, he changed the name of Léopoldville to Kinshasa in 1966, and launched a campaign under the motto of *authenticité* (authenticity), which attempted to reclaim the nation's African traditions.[143] In the ideological *manifeste de la N'sele*, published in 1967, he defined *authenticité* and *Mobutism*. From a political point of view, *authenticité* started in 1971 when Mobutu addressed the UN on 14 February.[144] The motto of *authenticité* was created as an all-encompassing African philosophy and "represented a departure from the ferocity of the colonial experience and provided a cohesive and comprehensive value system (cultural, political, legal, and economic) to harmonize the past with the present".[145]

I see the ODVs' narrative of the glorious past as a possibility to elicit their "object of loss" in particular.[146] Their nostalgic narratives are associated less with life as a whole than with different aspects and facets that constitute a worker's life. I thus consider *C'était bien à l'époque!* as a concomitant feature and as a starting point to analyse how the workers interpreted and shaped their world on the basis of different facets expressed in concrete texts that represent the knowledge and thoughts of particular times.

The nostalgic reference to the past serves not only to remember the good times of the past but equally to create a feeling of belonging. Bennett points out that the past "is always viewed from a distance" and therefore it "is often seen as relatively fixed and stable compared to the present (May, 2013)".[147] She argues that it is the belonging that offers a stability that is needed in times of change because

> [i]t is change, rather than continuity, which is more difficult to come to terms with for many people, as it can lead to a loss of ontological security

143 Dunn, "Imagining", 235. For a detailed discussion of *authenticité* and its effect on arts, see, for example, Van Beurden, *Authentically African*.

144 Daviel Lazure Vieria, "Precolonial Imaginaries and Colonial Legacies in Mobutu's 'Authentic' Zaïre", in *Exploitation and Misrule in Colonial and Postcolonial Africa*, eds. Kenneth Kalu and Toyin Falola, 1st ed., African Histories and Modernities (Cham: Springer International Publishing, 2019), 171.

145 Vieria, "Precolonial", 168.

146 Worby and Ally, "Disappointment", 468.

147 Julia Bennett, "Narrating Family Histories: Negotiating Identity and Belonging Through Tropes of Nostalgia and Authenticity", *Current Sociology* 66, no. 3 (2018): 450.

> (Back, 2009; Giddens, 1991; Savage, 2008). A feeling of belonging may mitigate this loss (Bennett, 2012; May, 2013).

I thus see the strategies with which members of the ODV create their belonging to one group as a tool to cope with a life that radically changed in 2003.

Nostalgia is not a unique phenomenon among the ODV, and has been widely discussed under different perspectives in relation to economic decline. Bissell, for instance, examines nostalgia for the colonial past among Zanzibaris whose turning point was also economic change – the moment when the clove industry largely collapsed. "Unable to supply the "goods" of life, the state faced increasing levels of discontent. In the streets, ujamaa socialism was widely seen as the source of economic and social stagnation".[148]

Bissell argues that certain factors are necessary for the emergence of nostalgia. First, there must be a sense of linear historical time, because "[i]f history ends in redemption or if history cycles around in eternal return, then nostalgia becomes redundant".[149] Second, there must be a sense of loss, where

> [t]he present must be compared to other moments and marked as a moment of decline—as in the fall of empires, for example, or national eclipse, or a loss of power and position by a particular social group. Moreover, nostalgia requires an object world to seize on—buildings, fashion, images, and the ephemera of everyday life".[150]

Like Worby, Bissell points out that there is a loss that is connected to objects:

> As a false or fictitious history, the product of fantasy, nostalgia lacks a "proper" distance or objectivity. Moreover, it is typically represented as a reaction to a larger and more encompassing set of forces: modernity or modernization; consumption, spectacle, and the eclipse of history; postmodernism; transnational or late capitalism; and, of course, globalization.[151]

The ODVs' nostalgia is not a "colonial nostalgia" as described by Bissell, because their longing focuses mainly on the company that took care of them, before

148 Bissell, "Engaging", 219.
149 Bissell, "Engaging", 221.
150 Bissell, "Engaging", 221.
151 Bissell, "Engaging", 224–25.

and also after independence. However, the company's economic development is linked to historical events, though that is not represented in an explicit way. Likewise, the ODVs' nostalgia is not linked to an experience of dislocation. Their nostalgia focuses on being employed and being well cared for, which materialised in the access to objects. These objects of loss are discussed in the following chapter.

Nostalgia also gained interest among scholars working on the industrial sector, where it has been described as a strategy to create a feeling of belonging. Strangleman discusses nostalgia in reference to railway companies.[152] He suggests that the past, history and identity are almost malleable and thus used by managements and/or governments to win consent for change, or minimise criticism among workers and the public.

In Strangleman's approach, nostalgia is seen a result of successful strategies used by those in power over others. In his work, managements or governments are responsible for creating a sense of belonging. They create a corporate culture that results in nostalgia among the employees. He refers to Gabriel,[153] who argues that "marginalised workers attach nostalgic meaning to a wide variety of animate and inanimate objects in their work lives, and from such attachments derive ontological security".[154] It is therefore worth examining the discourse of those in power, in the context of this study of a mining company. At the same time, following Strangleman, nostalgia becomes visible in the ex-mineworkers' feelings of being neglected. Equally visible is how this feeling is linked to animate and inanimate objects that are intertwined with the lost employment.

The longing for what is lacking in the present is, following Pickering and Keightley, not only a yearning for what is not attainable anymore, owing to the irreversibility of time; it is also important to take into account that "to condemn nostalgia solely to this position leaves unattended not only more general feelings of regret for what time has brought, but also more general questions for how the past may actively engage with the present and future".[155]

6.2 *Nostalgic Backward Projection as a Solution to Current Problems and the Future*

I have often reflected on the term "surveillance". I encountered it in its French usage in documents of the colonial state and of the UMHK alike in connection

152 Strangleman, "Nostalgia", 729.

153 Yiannis Gabriel, "Organizational Nostalgia: Reflections on 'The Golden Age'", in *Emotion in Organizations*, ed. Stephen Fineman (London: SAGE, 1993).

154 Strangleman, "Nostalgia", 729.

155 Pickering and Keightley, "Modalities", 920.

with measures taken to control the many different domains of a worker's life. In literature, the term is used in the same sense:

A unique feature of the Belgian system was the Commission for the Protection of ~~Natives~~ [DW]. This body was designed to be a sort of moral ombudsman, to maintain *surveillance* [italics DW] on the administration and companies and to expose and denounce any exploitation of the African population."[156]

I therefore read this noun exclusively as a synonym for monitoring, observation, control and as a term that describes a situation of a unilateral performance by a powerful instance, leaving those under surveillance in a position with limited agency. However, the actions of those in the subaltern position also leave traces that influence those in power.

One of the group discussions was dedicated to "surveillance", which we agreed upon at the trigger-event. From my side, I wished to discuss points that I extracted from earlier interviews. However, what I perceived as the control of workers by the company (such as the gong mentioned by almost all interviewees, which marked working hours and free time, or medical examinations to conduct medical experiments, unannounced house inspections or the careful compilation of films screened to workers in the leisure circles) was – to summarise it very generally – described as a feeling of "being taken care of" and "not being neglected". The ODVs linked what I considered as surveillance in all contexts to the company taking care of them.

The nostalgic sentiment of the lack of a general leading figure can be seen in comments by ex-workers during the *baraza*, such as "*Quel papa va nous encore rassembler?"* (Which father will gather us now?), "*Est-ce qu'on peut exister sans papa*?" (Can we exist without father?), "*On a besoin d'un conducteur*" (We need a leader [lit. driver].) or "*On cherche un papa The early paternalist approach, un papa qui va nous conduire au paiement ya franca yetu*" (We are looking for a responsible father, a father that will guide us to our money being paid). All these statements refer to their current situation, where nobody is taking care of them anymore, expressing their feeling of helplessness. The term *papa* has another layer that goes beyond the simple reference to a father figure. It is used to describe a boss, someone from whom they can demand support in exchange for their manpower. However, that working relationship no longer exists. Hence, the call for a *papa* by the ex-workers is also a yearning for employment. Unfortunately, those times are now gone.

It is important to note that there were some voices with critical self-reflection among the ex-workers regarding their nostalgia. One participant in a *baraza*

156 Young, *Politics*, 38.

mentioned that they should be more proactive and take control of their lives, using the metaphor of the father figure in his statement: *"Nous avons dépassé le temps pour un autre papa"* (The time for [searching for] another father has passed). One participant summarised our discussion as follows: *"l'avenir iko sombre"* (the future is dark).

The interviewees and participants of the *baraza* were socialised in a company structure that fostered an approach where workers were to be provided what was needed for life, while workers in return dedicated their life to their employer. Discussions on the dangers of the former paternalistic approach for one's own agency today, however, usually resulted in the interviewees' and participants' reference to the current lack of father figure.

What Strangleman described as a successful strategy used by the ones in power can thus be read as being successful among the members of the ODV. Their longing to be taken care of is a longing for a paternalistic experience. They received objects, animate and inanimate, in return for a life they dedicated to the company. The dangers of paternalistic policy were discussed in 1947 by Malengreau:

> The object of paternalist policy is to make the African a being assisted, insured and pensioned, instead of making him a free man … Each native is provided with his standardized house, mass-produced furniture, pre-determined scale of food, his free time regulated to the last detail without a trace of imagination … Man turned into a sort of vegetable, in an anticipation of the mechanical earthy paradise of Bernanos. But all times, men have found freedom in misery preferable to a comfortable slavery.[157]

The early paternalist approach by the UMHK is illustrated by the following words of a supervisor at the UMHK in 1935, which reflect the slogan *"Bonne santé, bon moral, bon rendement"* ("Good health, good morale, good performance"), launched in 1927:

157 Malengreau cit. in Young, *Politics*, 71.

Le chef d'exploitation surveille l'entraînement de son ouvrier noir (…) Le chef de camp veille à la bonne discipline de son personnel, pendant et après le travail (…) Le missionnaire (…) inculque aux enfants et aux adultes les principes d'une bonne morale et d'une bonne hygiène. Le médecin soigne les malades et prévient les maladies. Tous interviennent dans l'éducation et le relèvement du noir.[158]	The supervisor of the exploitation supervises the training of his black worker (…) The camp leader ensures the proper discipline of his staff, during and after work (…) The missionary (…) inculcates to children and adults the principles of good morale and good hygiene. The doctor treats the sick and prevents diseases. All are involved in the education and raising the black.

Paternalistic actions concerned not only work and leisure, but the most intimate matters, such as marriage. What Cooper postulates for French and British Africa equally applies to the Belgian ideology: "Women as the provided for".[159] Thus, the UMHK supported their workers in getting married as one of the measures of the stabilisation policy, as it is explicitly mentioned for instance in the annual report of 1937.[160]

Les contrats de travail de longue durée (3 ans ou au minimum 2 ans) constituent avec les mariages des travailleurs (surtout des recrues) les bases les plus solides d'une bonne politique de stabilisation M.O.I.	Long-term employment contracts (3 years or at least 2 years) constitute, together with the marriage of workers (especially recruits), the most solid basis for a good stabilisation policy of the MOI.

"Already at the time of their recruitment, labourers were encouraged to take their wife and children with them, if they had any. If they did not yet have a wife, but had already started the 'traditional' negotiations with the family-in-law, the recruiter did everything in his power to make the marriage happen (Annual Report MOI 1947: 24–25)".[161]

The UMHK had a marriage brokerage system that provoked feelings of helplessness among workers as they realised "that they depended on their employer not only for wages, food and housing, but for love and family as well".[162] In

158 Vellut, *Les bassins,* 52.

159 Cooper, *Decolonization*, 468.

160 AGR 2 – n°0654-03037, Rapport Annuel 1937, 12.

161 Cuvelier, "Men", 78.

162 Fetter, *Creation*, 146.

the nostalgic references to the times when a father figure was taking care of workers, the downside of the paternalistic approach were usually faded out.

In the following chapter, I discuss the ex-mineworkers' nostalgia against the backdrop of three concerns that are in the broadest sense linked to the overall topic of surveillance. First, the ODVs' feeling of lacking stability, which I examine on the basis of the concepts of *kazi* (work), leisure, space and the controlling system of *tshanga tshanga* and *malonda*, invented by the UMHK. Second, *heshima* (respect) – all the ODVS reported, although in different ways, their experiences of loss of respect that went hand in hand with the loss of employment. I illustrate this topic with three individual accounts. The third concern refers to matters that I read as relevant for creating identities.

CHAPTER 4

Objects of Loss

"*C'était bien à l'époque!*" requires some explanation. What was it the ex-mineworkers were referring to, what was their point of reference and what were the objects of loss they no longer had? In this chapter I focus on the three domains of stability, *heshima* (respect) and identity, to illustrate the ODVs' sentiment for what they lack today against the backdrop of the situation in which they were socialised and which serves as their point of reference.

1 Stability

I argue that stability is one of the objects of loss constructed by the ex-mineworkers. They are in a daily struggle for survival, and during the interviews and the *baraza* the lack of stability was evident at different levels, emerging repeatedly.

The ex-mineworkers' first memories covered their childhood, their educational path and the start of their working life. Furthermore, narratives by their parents influenced their perception of their (work)life. All the interviewees and participants in the *baraza* were born between the 1930s and the 1950s. Thus, their accounts referred to a time from the early 1940s up to today.

1.1 *Background Events*

At the beginning of the Second World War and in the middle of it, the mineworkers went on strike. During that time, while German forces occupied Belgium, the UMHK's head office was in London. A stable workforce was highly important to the UMHK, to maintain its economic strength and overcome the shortage of workers, which was a major concern. However,

> [P]rotest did not just suddenly happen. It was often the result of motion-time study engineers disturbing the flow of authority between camp managers and the lower echelons of administrators. As a result, workers felt themselves empowered enough to test the validity of the company's wartime demands.[1]

1 Higginson, "Steam", 100.

As Seibert described it:

> [A]round 17,000 workers were not content with the working and living conditions in Union Minière's mines and compounds. The company portrayed itself as a considerate employer and displayed photos and films of smiling workers, clean hospitals, and happy families. Yet this was simply an attempt to build up a model reputation for the entire Belgian colonial project. In reality everyday life for the vast majority of workers was characterised by hard, dangerous, and poorly paid work.[2]

The Second World War had been preceded by a difficult time for the UMHK: the Depression from 1930 to 1933 was accompanied by protests. Higginson argues that the protests were nothing unique for the UMHK, but that:

> [l]ike other industrial firms in southern Africa during the Depression, the company sought to drastically reduce the cost of maintaining and reproducing subsequent generations of African workers. […] Its administration believed that it could do this without undermining the company's legitimacy in the eyes of the workers. The larger context of the mineworkers' experience, therefore, had its roots in this decisive turn in southern Africa's industrial revolution.[3]

On 9 December 1941, the mineworkers in Elisabethville did not go to work but instead went on strike, the culmination of a long period of protest.[4] They argued for higher salaries to compensate for rising living costs (salaries had not increased since the thirties), they generally opposed a situation they experienced as oppressive and they demanded better housing conditions.[5] Kayembe Mwebwe, who was interviewed by Perrings, describes that night:

> We started working [at the smelter] at 3 o'clock in the afternoon and we had to finish by 11 at night. At that time we waited for the others to come relieve us but they didn't come. Then the white men who were working there told us to shut down the furnace and to go back home. As we were

2 Seibert, "Wind", 263.

3 Higginson, "Bringing", 201.

4 Dibwe dia Mwembu, *Histoire*; Seibert, "Wind"; Julia Seibert, *In die Globale Wirtschaft Gezwungen: Arbeit und Kolonialer Kapitalismus im Kongo (1885–1960)* (Frankfurt, New York: Campus Verlag, 2016).

5 For a description of worker protest in Katanga, see for example, Higginson, "Bringing".

> going home we met, at the compound offices, many men. And there were soldiers encircling them … I was scared and I didn't want to stay there any longer so I went home and slept, and in the morning some delegates called for people to go to the football field. Many people went there but a few stayed at home. Then M. Maron [the governor] came and said: "We want to increase your wages but we can't treat like this. You have to point out twelve or twenty from you and we will go to the office to discuss the problem". But the people didn't want to listen. The delegates wanted to make them quiet, to calm them, but the people didn't want to. There was crying and shouting. Then the governor found that he was in danger himself, so he asked the soldiers to fire. Then they shot the people. I myself didn't see anything because I was behind, but those who saw said that Mpoy Léonard, who was a delegate, was the first man to be shot down.[6]

Higginson cites an African clerk telling the director about the workers' desire to live in decent conditions, including being able to receive or visit friends:

> Monsieur le Directeur: Many whites are astonished to hear our demands for better housing and better treatment. They feel that we are asking for too much – in short, that we desire to live as they do […] Permit me to draw attention to the fact that a small dwelling might have served our needs in the past since we spent most of our time in the open air or in the shade of a large tree or lean-to. But now, with new ways of doing things introduced into our country, we can no longer live as we did in the past. We are obliged to live in houses in which we can entertain our relatives, friends and other visitors (1934, 3).[7]

The Second World War was also a battle for the control and exploitation of the world's strategic mineral sources.[8] The workers' protests took place at a time of economic change in the Belgian Congo. The UMHK made a drastic overhaul and expansion of its operations and became the world's main supplier of cobalt and uranium.[9] It multiplied its general output sixfold but with only a twofold increase in its workforce and minimal technical innovations.

---

6 Perrings, *Black Mineworkers*, 226.

7 Higginson, "Bringing", 201–2.

8 Dumett, "Africa", 381.

9 Dumett, "Africa"; Perrings, *Black Mineworkers*.

The UMHK followed the protests closely. The strike on 9 December 1941 was documented dispassionately in the annual report of the Services d'Afrique, Départment M.O.I. Arrests were described; we do not know who performed or commanded them; the incidents were described as "minor" and it was stressed that the situation was under control. The following words explain the main concern of the company:

Il importe de rechercher les causes de ces événements non pas pour établir et doser les responsabilités mais pour en tirer une leçon pour l'avenir : il ne faut plus de 9 Décembre.[10]	It is important to look for the causes of these events, not to establish and balance the responsibilities, but to learn from them for the future: we must not have another 9th of December.

The company looked for a reason for the strike. The annual report pretends that there was no explanation and emphasises the company's surprise. The company judged its workers to be "hardworking, disciplined and happy". The company praised the employees by remarking on their willingness to work overtime as the war demanded greater production.[11] This view of the high level of discipline of the workers indicates that the management did not expect the protest.[12] The report queried how it was possible that such courageous, disciplined and happy workers without any revolutionary germ (*germe révolutionnaire*) were suddenly drawn into such events. The UMHK determined as follows:

10 AGR 2 – n°654-03041, Rapport Annuel 1941, B.

11 *"Les exigences de la production, amplifiées par la guerre, ont imposé une cadence telle que les journées de repos accordées aux travailleur ne représentent que 12,6% du total des journées distribuées au lieu du chiffre normal de 14,2%. Ces mêmes travailleurs ont presté en 1941 environ 500.000 heures supplémentaires"* (B) (The demands of production, exacerbated by the war, imposed such a rhythm that days of rest granted to workers represented only 12.6% of the total number of days distributed, compared with the normal figure of 14.2%. In 1941, these same workers put in about 500,000 additional hours.)

12 *"Que cette population fut disciplinée on ne peut en douter quand on sait que malgré l'intensité de l'effort qui fut demandé aux hommes, il n'y eut que 0,38% de journées d'absences non motivées et 0,43% de journées de prison."* (B) (That this population was disciplined cannot be doubted when we know that despite the very hard work, there were only 0.38% of days of unexcused absence and 0.43% days of prison.)

Il n'y a qu'une réponse possible: il y eut contagion. Le foyer de contamination était *EXTERIEUR* et rien ne s'est opposé à son extension épidémique – Ainsi figure en tout premier lieu, parmi les causes des événements de Décembre chez les noirs, la plus importante de toutes, la cause réellement déterminante : les mouvements de grève chez les blancs.[13]

There is only one possible answer: there was a contagion. The source of contamination was EXTERIOR and nothing opposed its epidemic extension – thus, first among the causes of the events of December among the blacks, the most important of all, the truly determining cause: the strike movements by the whites.

Thus, the strike by Europeans was portrayed as the culprit, but the line of argument did not follow the question of which whites were on strike and why. Rather, it was based on the idea that the Congolese would simply imitate what they saw, like children. This was also stressed by the UMHK in the same annual report, quoting Doctor Mottoulle, medical advisor to various mining companies and one of the driving forces behind the "workforce stabilisation policy" – not without emphasising his long experience in the Congo:

Le colonisateur ne doit jamais perdre de vue que les [sic] ~~nègres~~ [*DW*] ont des âmes d'enfants, âmes qui se moulent aux méthodes de l'éducateur; ils regardent, écoutent, sentent et imitent.[14]

The coloniser must never forget that the N* have the souls of children, souls who mould themselves to the methods of the educator; they watch, listen, sense and imitate.

The argument relates to the supposed sole capacity of the Congolese for imitation, which would then be reproduced. The importance of this point was expressed not only by the choice of words but also by their presentation in capital letters:

ILS VOIENT LES BLANCS – CEUX-LA MEMES QUI SONT LEURS CHEFS AU CHANTIER OU A L'USINE – QUI REFUSENT LE TRAVAIL … Wazungu wanakataa kazi.[15]

THEY SEE THE WHITES, THE SAME PEOPLE WHO ARE THEIR SUPERIORS AT THE WORKSHOP OR THE PLANT, REFUSING TO WORK … The whites refuse to work.

13 AGR 2 – n°654-03041, Rapport Annuel 1941, C.

14 AGR 2 – n°654-03041, Rapport Annuel 1941, C.

15 AGR 2 – n°654-03041, Rapport Annuel 1941, C.

The last sentence was repeated in Swahili, to convey in the language of the Congolese workers the alleged outrageousness of whites refusing to work.

Although the report stated that the strike that broke out among the whites was by far the most important cause of the disruption of order in the camps, the company argued that there were other causes, too, although to a lesser extent.[16] The UMHK acknowledged the rising cost of living for the workers in particular and pointed out that workers would have been helplessly at the mercy of traders:

Le COUT DE LA VIE pour les noirs a effectivement augmenté. A côté du renchérissement des marchandises provoqué [sic] par la situation internationale il y a aussi, de la part de bon nombre de commerçants, une exploitations scandaleuse de la clientèle indigène dont toute l'éducation d'acheteur est à faire. Cette exploitation existe depuis toujours mais la guerre en a décuplé l'ampleur. Quand on lit la chronique judiciaire des journaux relatant les excès commis dans le commerce avec les européens, on peut se figurer jusqu'où vont les abus lorsqu'il s'agit d'indigènes, faciles à leurrer et bien incapables de se défendre.[17]	The COST OF LIVING for black people has indeed risen. Besides the increase of the price of goods caused by the international situation, there is also a scandalous exploitation by many traders of the indigenous clientele, who have to be educated as buyers. This exploitation has always existed, but the war has amplified it tenfold. When one reads the legal column in the newspapers about the excesses committed in trade with Europeans, one can imagine how far the abuses go when it comes to Congolese workers, who are easy to deceive and quite incapable of defending themselves.

Thus, "impudent merchants" were presented as one of the main sources of the exploitation of the workers and the UMHK located the cause for the strikes outside of the company's range of influence. Exactly as in the ex-mineworkers' current assessment of the good old times, when the company took care of their workers, the UMHK presented itself as the protector. The UMHK supported

16 The following additional reasons were mentioned: first, the product was not always good in terms of quality because the production services wanted to achieve a higher return at a lower cost price; second, weak management tended to shirk responsibility and 'cover up' instead. In addition, the judiciary was accused of having an enormous influence on the police services.

17 AGR 2 – n°654-03041, Rapport Annuel 1941, E.

the workers by, among other things, providing canteens to feed the workers.[18] However, the food was not free; its cost was deducted from the workers' wages. The UMHK argued that it had taken steps to improve the remuneration of workers well before the colonial administration cared at all. It was obvious, the company went on to say, that the cost of living would be felt more heavily by households than individuals. Therefore, in November 1940, the UMHK substantially increased not only the food ration entitled to each worker, but also the food ration for every woman and child in the worker's family.

Another report, a summary of the years from 1940 to 1946 by the Département M.O.I. addressed to the general management, mentions that the discipline among the Congolese workers (they used the term *indigènes*) would have suffered during the years of war.[19] The first of several reasons given by the UMHK for this was the "the fall of prestige after our setbacks".[20] The company further explained that, to improve the workers' situation, it increased salaries (with a detailed report on how much in which year), it increased food rations for the workers, their wives and children, and in 1944, opened "canteens" to sell fabrics, household items, and so on.[21] The last measure on the list of improvements to enhance workers' discipline was a newly created award:

Il a, enfin, été décidé de créer un "Brevet de Bons Services" qui sera remis à certains travailleurs anciens, de bonne formation professionnelle qui donnent satisfaction tant au point de vue de leur conduite, qu'au point de vue de leur travail.[22]

Finally, it was decided to create a "Certificate of Good Service",which would be awarded to certain former workers with good professional training who gave satisfactory results both in terms of their conduct and in terms of their work.

After the Second World War, the UMHK's need to stabilise the workforce synchronised with the Belgian colonial state's ideas of development for the colony. In 1949, the colonial government introduced a 10-year plan for the economic and social development of the Congo[23] containing, among other aspects, important infrastructure projects, such as public buildings and housing facilities for

18 AGR 2 – n°654-03041, Rapport Annuel 1941, E.

19 AGR 2 – n°654-03042, Rapport 1940–1946, 2.

20 AGR 2 – n°654-03042, Rapport 1940–1946, 2.

21 AGR 2 – n°654-03042, Rapport 1940–1946, 3–4.

22 AGR 2 – n°654-03042, Rapport 1940–1946, 4.

23 Ministère des Colonies, *Plan décennal pour le développement économique et social du Congo belge* (Brussels: Editions de Visscher, 1949).

the Congolese.[24] One of the propositions was to adopt the so-called Système Grévisse.

Ferdinand Grévisse was a district officer of that time who published a study about so-called "native quarters" in Lubumbashi. He argued that the Africans should be motivated to build houses themselves, although under supervision and with consideration of a long list of constraints.[25] Grévisse's idea was one of collaboration, in the sense that the colonial state would build the foundations of the houses and provide the construction material at a good price, while the future inhabitants would build the houses themselves. In doing so, the colonial state could decide on the exact size and location of the houses on a parcel of land. In addition, this system would minimise costs by avoiding the involvement of construction companies. Furthermore, prefabricated parts, such as windows, doors and roofs, would be used.

Prefabricated parts were also a symbol for houses that corresponded to the idea of a European house, not only in the Belgian Congo. Callaci writes that providing new housing was also a matter of modernisation and, above all, of "civilisation" in the early years of Tanzania's independence.[26] For the first president, Julius Nyerere, building houses was building Tanzania.[27] The modern houses (*nyumba za kisasa*) were covered by a metal sheet roof (*bati*).[28]

For Grévisse, it was not only the material and spatial considerations regarding house building that were important but also the social component.[29] The Système Grévisse would – he argued – lead to the stabilisation of the lives of urban Africans, and the Congolese would thus be easier to govern.

It was precisely at this time, when the UMHK was on the one hand providing the workforce with the most benefits and on the other hand trying to retain workers in order to secure a much-needed efficient and stable workforce, that the ODV organisation was born.

24 Lagae, "Modern".

25 Chapelier, *Elisabethville*, 47–49, 65.

26 Callaci, *Street*.

27 Callaci, *Street*, 18.

28 "After having run for office promising cement houses with metal roofs as a symbol of freedom and decolonisation, he [Julius Nyerere] returned again with a new take on the matter of housing: 'The present widespread addiction to cement and tin roofs is a kind of mental paralysis. A bati roof is nothing compared to one with of clay tiles. But those afflicted with this mental attitude will not agree. Cement is basically 'earth' but it is 'European soil'. Therefore people refuse to build a house of burnt bricks and tiles; they insist on waiting for a tin roof and 'European soil'. If we want to progress more rapidly in the future we must overcome at least some of these mental blocks.'" (Callaci, *Street*, 19.)

29 Ferdinand Grévisse, *Le centre extra-coutumier d'Elisabethville: Quelques aspects de la politique du Haut-Katanga Industriel* (Brussels: Institut Royal Colonial Belge, 1951).

The earliest memories of some members of the ODV referred to the strike, which they had experienced while they were children. In general, however, the generation of the interviewees and participants of the *baraza* had started to work when the colonial state's and the UMHK's measures of stabilisation came to fruition.

The first concept that I link to stability is that of *kazi* (work). It was the prerequisite for the mineworkers to become ODVs and is the basis of what they identify with.

1.2 *Kazi*

The Swahili term for "work", *kazi* links the employee with the employer whereas *kuwa mfanyakazi* describes "being a worker". Workers' nostalgia about *l'époque* is directly connected with these terms. All their painful longing for the old days relates to having been a worker. *Kazi* means more than what we might think of as work, mental or physical activity as a means of earning income. Likewise, "worker" means more than being an employee, especially one who does manual or non-executive work. Work and being a worker meant being taken care of by the employer, and housing was one of the key components of being looked after – or controlled. The workplace defined housing that became the home for thousands of Congolese and newcomers from Rwanda-Urundi. A home was shaped not only by its physical structure but equally by the social activities that went along with work and leisure activities.

Fabian discusses major components of the semantic field of the Swahili term *kazi* in relation to a religious movement known as *Jamaa* (family) during the 1960s. An estimated 130,000 people were involved.[30] The movement was organised on a local level, and membership was restricted to adult and married Christians; it was also "intertribal". The Swahili of Katanga was the language that Placide Tempels, the founder of this movement, chose to formulate his message.[31] Fabian's interest during his research in 1966/67 focused on the everyday world of a typical *Jamaa* member and the relationship between their job and their employer. Fabian describes his bewilderment caused by contradictory statements towards *kazi*. On the one hand, work was presented to him negatively, such as work is hard, wages are low, while on the other hand there were positive connotations, such as being proud to be a worker (*muntu wa*

30 Fabian, "Kazi", 299.

31 For more information about Placide Tempels's thinking, see for example, Emmanuel M. Banywesize, "Placide Tempels et le destin de la pensée africaine contemporaine", in *Lubumbashi, cent ans d'histoire*, ed. Maurice Amuri Mpala-Lutebele (Paris: L'Harmattan, 2013).

kazi). Fabian analysed the *Jamaa* movement against the backdrop of the complexities of employment in the mining sector of that time. These complexities refer to the change of conditions of recruitment. Whereas in the beginning the UMHK forcefully recruited workers, the system of recruitment was later characterised by "a stable self-propagating labor force in which workers and their families were expected to, and did, join the enterprise for extended periods on the basis of freely accepted contracts".[32]

Fabian also discusses the "civilising mission" involved in the employment of African workers, at least from the employee's perspective. The company's efforts to "civilise" its employees went hand in hand with the mission's approaches, and the mission's representatives were paid for their efforts:

> [R]elationships between industrial employers and their African employees cannot be limited to the actions and transactions of remunerative labor. The visible result was the "Camp", the labor settlement as a total society in which all basic needs were satisfied (and controlled) by the company, including religion since missionaries administering parishes and schools in the settlements were on the payroll of the enterprise.[33]

The "civilising" approach also became visible in the official documents of the company, where "the overall *raison d'être* of the industry as well as the essence of labour relationship was, in effect, consistently expressed in the language of moral values, philanthropic aims, and a total theory of history".[34] Fabian describes the *Jamaa* movement as based on the idea of unity and love beyond racial, ethnic and social boundaries. He quotes a member who explains the movement as being "like the Union Minière".[35]

Fabian offers a brief sketch of the semantics of *kazi*.[36] He explains that in Swahili no single lexical term exclusively refers to industrial work, as is the case

32 Fabian, "Kazi", 301.

33 Fabian, "Kazi", 302.

34 Fabian, "Kazi", 302.

35 Fabian, "Kazi", 303.

36 "In Katanga Swahili the noun *kazi* may cover a wide range of activities, moods, attitudes, and attributes. […] In some expressions a specific denotation may be due to idiomatic usage, e.g. in the often heard *kazi yako* 'that's your business, it's up to you, go to hell.' It may also be achieved through a context-specific contrast such as in the opposition between *furaha* and *kazi* […]. But the overwhelming majority of expressions in which *kazi* has a specified meaning is based on complexes formed with the connective particle {a}, especially those which function as characterizations. These may signify a trade or profession: *kazi ya mwalimu* 'being a teacher;' a type of employment: *kazi ya Union Minière* 'being employed by the Union Minière;' a degree of exertion, effort: *kazi ya nguvu* 'hard work.'

for agricultural labour, *kulima*. Therefore he links work to not only an activity itself but also the relationship between an employee and an employer and thus to wage labour. He shows that the *Jamaa* doctrine is permeated in most domains and forms of expression by conceptions of labour and images and metaphors derived from members' experience and lifestyle as an industrial worker.[37]

The term *kazi* also made its way into the Swahili terminology for weekdays.[38] Monday became *siku ya kazi moja* (first day of work), Tuesday became *siku ya kazi mbili* (the second day of work), Wednesday became *siku ya kazi tatu* (the third day of work), Thursday became *siku ya kazi ine* (the fourth day of work) and Friday, *siku ya kazi tano* (the fifth day of work). The UMHK distributed the weekly food ration (*mposho*) on Saturdays to the workers, and so Saturday got the name *siku ya mposho*.[39]

Together with Bogumil Jewsiewicki, Dibwe dia Mwembu conducted research in 2004 on the perception of *kazi* among workers. Dibwe dia Mwembu argues that at the very beginning, *kazi* was put on a level with slavery because living conditions were harsh, accidents numerous and morbidity and mortality rates were high.[40] The first subterranean mine in Kipushi was described as a tomb. Due to the numerous accidents, it was widely believed among Congolese that going into an underground mine meant being buried alive. As a result, worker from Rwanda-Urundi in particular were recruited who were initially unaware of these incidents.were recruited to work there.[41] Dibwe dia Mwembu further argues that during the Second World War, population numbers and workers increased, but so did morbidity due to accidents, probably also because the

Similarly we find that most verbal expressions are complex, combining a verb with the noun *kazi* and often adding further specifications through the connective {a}. Examples are *kufanya kazi ya chauffeur* or *kutumika kazi ya chauffeur* 'to work as a driver.'" (Fabian, "Kazi", 304–5.)

37 Fabian, "Kazi", 319.

38 Dibwe dia Mwembu, "La perception", 162.

39 Dibwe dia Mwembu does not mention a specific name for Sunday in Lubumbashi. The term *mujuma* can also be used for Sunday. See for example the play *Ufundi ya kazi ya mikono*, included in Schicho, *Le Groupe Mufwankolo*, 138.
Personal experience from 2017, 2018 and 2019 showed that either *siku ya dini* (day of the religion) or the French term, *Dimanche,* were used. Standard Swahili from the East African coast was not in use. Its names of weekdays follow the Muslim tradition, where the first day of the week is Saturday.

40 Dibwe dia Mwembu, "La perception", 163.

41 Dibwe Dia Mwembu cites a song among workers that expressed their sentiment before going down into the mine, which meant the fear of dying without being sick (Dibwe dia Mwembu, *L'histoire*, 164.

legal minimum of days off was no longer respected.[42] Furthermore, expensive machinery replaced cheap manual work, and only short-term, semi-skilled workers were employed. A noticeable improvement of working conditions characterised the years after the Second World War and especially the 1950s, mainly as a result of the technological evolution that reduced manual work, as Dibwe dia Mwembu also states:

À cause de la concurrence, les conditions de vie des travailleurs progressent avec l'amélioration du logement, de la ration alimentaire, des infrastructures médicales, etc., et rendent les villes industrielles plus attrayantes.[43]	Thanks to competition, the living conditions of the workers are getting better with the improvement of housing, the food ration, medical infrastructure, etc., which is making the industrial cities more attractive.

Work in the city became a sign of good living (*bien-être*) for the workers and their families, because they had access to utilities that were unknown in the villages, such as electricity or running water. Dibwe dia Mwembu describes photographs that workers sent to their family members in the home villages, which showed well-dressed family members. The pictures portrayed men sitting around a table, chatting, eating and with a beer after hours of hard work, and women in fashionable dresses. The families were shown next to accumulated possessions, such as a bike, a phonograph or sewing machine.[44] At that time, Dibwe dia Mwembu states that the saying "*Kazi ndjo baba, ndjo mama*" (work is my father, work is my mother) started to be used.[45]

The noun *kazi* was often replaced by the name of the company, Union Minière, and the interview partners and participants in the *baraza* referred frequently to this metaphor. During that period of economic prosperity for the company, work valued the workers, they gained respect and were able to satisfy all the needs of a family. *Kazi* thus was a social promotion and offered a certain identity in the late colonial world after independence.[46]

Dibwe dia Mwembu refers to a song by the musician Jean Bosco Mwenda wa Bayeke, who was famous in the 1950s. In the song, the musician expressed his contempt of unemployment that would not allow people to have a good life anymore:

42 Dibwe dia Mwembu, "La perception", 164; Dibwe dia Mwembu, *L'histoire*, 113.
43 Dibwe dia Mwembu, "La perception", 164.
44 Dibwe dia Mwembu, *L'histoire*, 115; Dibwe dia Mwembu, "La perception", 165.
45 Dibwe dia Mwembu, "La perception", 65.
46 Dibwe dia Mwembu, "La perception", 166.

Bulofwa nabo ni bubaya sana sana	Unemployment too, it's a very bad position
Hautakula, hautavala sana sana	You cannot eat nor dress properly
Watu wengine ni wasenji sana sana	Some people are really idiots
Wanaacha kazi, wanakaa paka bure	They give up their work for nothing
Umutazame na bilato habapate[47]	You can see them with no shoes[48]

The musician not only glorified work by characterising the benefits of work (food and clothes), but criticised those who abandoned their jobs and thus did not meet the norms related to work that guaranteed a good life.

In 1967, Gécamines emerged from the nationalisation of UMHR. But economic changes led to a crisis in the Congo and especially for Gécamines. Nevertheless, as Dibwe dia Mwembu points out, Gécamines paid salaries on a regular basis,[49] and they were still higher than at other companies. However, the salaries were insufficient because canteens, for instance, did not offer food at preferential prices anymore. Healthcare services were still provided, though. Until 1975, the company enjoyed a period of prosperity. Then the economy declined and the company was a victim of misappropriations by the Mobutu regime.[50] Gécamines' empire started to collapse in the turmoil of the early 1990s and was not able to meet its financial obligations.[51] Workers were paid irregularly. At this point, the former meaning of *kazi* was fading away.

Workers' nostalgia about *kazi* thus refers to a period when employment stood for prosperity, which was reflected in material things such as housing, food and salary, access to healthcare, education, leisure activities and prestige. There wasn't a single conversation where I wasn't reminded of the benefits that came with *kazi* in the good old days. For instance, *mposho*, the food ration; the ex-workers explained to me in detail the exact amounts of the different foodstuffs they were eligible to get depending on the size of their family. Food was never an issue while they were employed; nowadays, they often starve. It is thus not surprising that *mposho* was a dominant topic.

47 Dibwe dia Mwembu, *L'histoire*, 118.

48 *Umutazame* = lit: you can see him.

49 Dibwe dia Mwembu, *L'histoire*, 120.

50 Dibwe dia Mwembu, *L'histoire*, 121–22; Rubbers, "Women", 214 .

51 With the country heading for bankruptcy, Gécamines was the country's main source of income and was therefore used to cover the regime's cash needs. Poor management strategies led to a general decline of the industry and its collapse. Inflation led to exaggerated price increases for basic necessities and delays in the payment of wages and salaries, which were already inadequate in both the private and public sectors. (Dibwe dia Mwembu, *L'histoire*, 141; Petit and Mutambwa, "LA CRISE", 469.)

1.3 *Leisure*[52]

In 1964, the UMHK's company magazine *Mwana Shaba* published – as in most of its issues –the football results; its sports section reported on the different company teams.[53] A photograph of a football team called "Dragons", which visited the town of Kipushi for a game, appears at the bottom right of the page. The caption relates that the team of *mineurs* (mineworkers), as the players were described, visited the mining facilities in Kipushi before the game took place. The photograph was taken because they arrived as a football team, and the teams that were playing were usually shown on that page in *Mwana Shaba*.

But the team is wearing protective clothes and white helmets. It is possible, of course, that the photo was taken during the football team's tour of the factory, and that protective clothing and helmets were required in this context. However, the photograph showing the team is not that different from the one on the following page, where a photograph illustrates a report on a company delegation during an underground visit at a mining site in Jadotville. The delegation is also wearing protective clothes and white helmets, the same outfit as the members of the football team. *Mwana Shaba* illustrated workers during working hours and workers as members of a football team in their leisure time in the same manner.

Leisure activities did not exist as an activity per se, but as part of the work-life concept. Thus, I use the entanglement of work and leisure as one lens through which I look at company paternalism. As many scholars have stated, leisure cannot be conceptualised without reference to work.[54] The mining company, which took care of all aspects of life, thus also defined leisure activities. The company's approach was in line with the Belgian colonial state's welfare activities.[55]

Leisure activities were provided in an allocated area as a result of the residential segregation in a city that existed solely because of the mining activities.

---

52 See also Daniela Waldburger, "'C'était Bien À L'Époque': Work and Leisure Among Retrenched Mineworkers in the Democratic Republic of the Congo", *African Studies* 82, no. 1 (2023), 8.

53 *Mwana Shaba*, 1964, No. 12, 11.

54 Akyeampong and Ambler, "Leisure"; Odhiambo, "Kula Raha"; Thomas, "Work"; E. P. Thompson, "Time, Work-Discipline, and Industrial Capitalism", *Past & Present* 38 (1967).

55 Vanthemsche, *Belgium*, 47. The welfare policy was gradually introduced between 1890 and 1944. However, it focused very much on rural areas, where Fonds du Bien-Être ~~Indigène~~ [DW] operated a wide range of welfare activities; sanitary campaigns were undertaken, food storage facilities built, livestock provided and vocational schools constructed (Vanthemsche, *Belgium*, 31; Young, *Politics* , 62.)

Dibwe dia Mwembu recounts that the city and work were inseparable.[56] Lubumbashi was not unlike many other colonial cities; you needed a job contract in order to be able to stay there. The unemployed had no place and the formal sector reigned supreme. Callaci, for instance, describes a similar situation in Tanzania. There, in 1976, the government launched a campaign called Operation Kila Mtu Afanye Kazi (Operation Every Person Must Work). Eleven thousand unemployed people in Dar es Salaam were arrested and sent to Ujamaa villages outside the city. "These measures established that the right to the city was based on salaried employment, which would remain a possibility for only a select few."[57]

To ensure a stable workforce, the company kept an eye on workers' efficiency in the workplace, but they also tried to make sure that workers used their time off for healthy leisure activities. As Martin points out, leisure as an abstract issue "is most powerful in the minds of those who seek to impose certain activities or to structure time and space".[58] Thus, the UMHK structured work and leisure temporally and spatially. In terms of the former, the most obvious evidence, frequently recounted by the interviewees, was the sound of the gong that could be heard throughout Cité Gécamines, announcing working hours and the change of shift. As for the latter, the company provided jobs, housing and leisure activities on company-owned land; each activity had its defined area under the company's sphere of control.

In the 1951 annual report, the UMHK stated that to celebrate the company's 50th birthday it had decided to create social centres.[59] As well as providing an area in which to educate women, the centres also served as a space for leisure activities.[60] The report stated that the centres had to include a room for shows, one for meetings, a library, a stadium and a swimming pool.[61] Furthermore, the report mentions the *cercles sportifs*, which had already been created. In his comparative study, Chipande portrays the importance of football on the

56 Dibwe dia Mwembu, "Lubumbashi", 138.

57 Callaci, *Street*, 41.

58 Martin, 7.

59 AGR 2 – n°655-03047, Rapport Annuel 1951, 24.

60 By creating these centres, the UMHK was in line with the Belgian welfare programme. The UMHK and its successor actively promoted the nuclear family and women's roles and responsibilities. For a detailed discussion on the intertwining fields of health, hygiene, home and women's roles in the same period, see Daniela Waldburger, "House, Home, Health and Hygiene – Social Engineering of Workers in Elisabethville / Lubumbashi (1940s to 1960s) Through the Lens of Language Usage", in *The Politics of Housing in (Post) Colonial Africa*, eds. Kirsten Rüther, Martina Barker-Ciganikova and Daniela Waldburger (Berlin: De Gruyter, 2020).

61 The social centres also offered courses for men, such as adult literacy.

Zambian and Katangese Copperbelts from the 1930s to the present, highlighting that the mining companies identified football as a leading leisure activity.[62] He stresses the UMHK's belief in the importance of workers' health, which "was captured by the UMHK motto, 'good health, good spirit and high productivity.'"[63]

Even though the annual reports show that the company promoted football, the UMHK kept a critical eye on it. Football was very popular among workers, but not necessarily the preferred way of controlling their leisure time. The company was not always happy about the lack of educational aspects in certain sporting activities:

Le sport presqu'uniquement pratiqué est le football. Il a incontestablement beaucoup de succès, mais son action éducative est pour le moins douteuse. Il permet à quelques vedettes de se donner en spectacle et a souvent amené des incidents fort significatifs : un chauvinisme exagéré s'y développe, teinté parfois de superstitions et influencé par certains exemples regrettables donnés par les équipes d'Européens.[64]	The sport almost uniquely practised is football. It is undeniably very successful, but its educational action is dubious to say the least. It allows a few stars to put on a show and has often led to some very significant incidents: exaggerated chauvinism develops, sometimes tinged with superstition and influenced by some regrettable examples given by European teams.

The company did not approve of chauvinistic or superstitious behaviour because it needed disciplined workers. The behaviour of some players is also mentioned in the 1957 annual report.[65] Just as Chipande reports for Zambia and Katanga,[66] the educational aspect of sporting activities was important to the company. For example, the UMHK organised athletics competitions, but also championships for team sports such as football or basketball. Chipande points out that "the growing popularity of football among Africans in the Katangese mining towns led the President of UMHK, M. Gillet, to introduce a football competition in 1956 for what came to be known as the Gillet Cup".[67]

62 Chipande, "Football".
63 Chipande, "Football", 104.
64 AGR 2 – n°655-03047, Rapport Annuel 1951, 24.
65 AGR 2 – n°657-03054, Rapport Annuel 1957, 36.
66 Chipande, "Football", 102–4.
67 Chipande, "Football", 107.

The UMHK encouraged sporting activities because a healthy workforce was the foundation of the efficient workforce that the company needed.

In the 1951 annual report, other leisure activities are also listed, such as reading, games, social gatherings at bars, dance, theatre, arts and cinema.[68] The company criticised workers for allegedly showing the greatest interest in the bar, where beer was served, out of all the recreational activities offered:

Il semble qu'actuellement tout au moins, l'intérêt se porte surtout et avant tout sur l'existence du bar où sera débitée de la bière européenne.[69]

It seems that, at least now, interest focuses primarily on the existence of the bar where European beer will be served.

From the beginning, the UMHK kept an eye on beer consumption and gambling activities. For example, two years earlier, the company blamed the workers for their lack of discipline in other areas of life on the fact that they loved beer and gambling too much:

Nous ne pouvons, pour expliquer cet état de choses, que répéter les raisons que nous invoquions dans notre Rapport de 1948, c'est à dire notre refus de vendre à crédit et l'imprévoyance du noir qui ne sait pas s'imposer la discipline de l'économie. Nous sommes cependant tentés d'y ajouter l'influence du jeu et l'abus des boissons qui prennent de plus en plus d'extension.[70]

To explain this situation, we can only repeat the reasons we invoked in our 1948 report, that is, our refusal to sell [the furniture] on credit and the improvidence of the black who is unable to show thrifty discipline in economic questions. We are, however, tempted to add that the influence of gambling and the abuse of drinks is gaining more ground.

In the evenings, most of the workers would drink beer in the *cercle* in the Cité, as this space was called, even though they could have gone to another area in town. However, the prices in the Cité were lower in comparison to the city, and that was how the company attempted to control the radius of movement of its workforce. Dibwe dia Mwembu discusses the bar not only as a place of controlled drinking but also as a space for exchanging news important to the workers (*diffusion de l'histoire orale*).[71]

68 AGR 2 – n°655-03047, Rapport Annuel 1951, 24.

69 AGR 2 – n°655-03047, Rapport Annuel 1951, 26.

70 AGR 2 – n°655-03045, Rapport Annuel 1949, 23.

71 Dibwe dia Mwembu, *L'histoire*, 57–103; Quaretta writes on the importance of beer drinking in Lubumbashi today and discusses three imaginaries that are fairly widespread in

This control of leisure time was also in force at events provided for staff, such as film screenings. Every annual report contains a subsection under leisure activities that reported the number of films shown. In the 1951 annual report, the types of film were discussed as follows:

> Ce métrage se compose en grande partie de films muets éducatifs et documentaires, qui furent commentés en Swahili sur fil sonore, par le personnel du Département M.O.I., et de quelques films sonores commandés récemment à l'Abbé Cornil.[72]

> This footage consists largely of educational and documentary silent films, which were commented on in Swahili on audio wire by the staff of the Department of Congolese and Ruanda-Urundi workforce, and a few sound films recently commissioned by Father Cornil.

The main objective of the UMHK was to educate the workers and families who attended the film screenings. The choice to provide commentary on the films in Swahili reflects the role Swahili played in this environment. The lingua franca among workers, it was also the language that connected the mining company with its workers.[73] The company purchased films produced by the most successful film-maker, Father André Cornil. In 1950, he was asked by the Services de l'Information du Congo Belge to go to the Belgian Congo and produce educational films for the Congolese.[74]

The films had to be commented on not only to provide a translation of the images and subtitles into the appropriate language for the region but also because "[t]he information service leaders soon noticed that simply translating the subtitles was not enough. The images required a more elaborate commentary in order to avoid any misunderstanding of the educative message."[75] Bouchard states that the commentary

> sought to help Congolese spectators appreciate the very modes of cinematographic expression. As one of the most successful of the filmmaker-priests, Father Cornil, later explained to Rolot and Ramirez, "In the

Lubumbashi and Congolese society in general: masculinity, social success and domination – three models of men (Quaretta, "Apprendre").

72 AGR 2 – n°655-03047, Rapport Annuel 1951, 25.

73 See also the subchapter on "The importance of language choice".

74 Vincent Bouchard, "Commentary and Orality in African Film Reception", in *Viewing African Cinema in the 21st Century: Art Films and the Nollywood Video Revolution*, eds. Saul Mahir and Ralph Austen (Athens, OH: Ohio University Press, 2010), 98; Bokonga Ekanga Botombele, *Cultural Policy in the Republic of Zaire* (Paris: The UNESCO Press, 1976), 43.

75 Bouchard, "Commentary", 95.

> bush, where an entire village usually met for a cinema showing, the difficulties in understanding such films proved to be nearly insurmountable. The education of this virgin public had to be complete. The first task was therefore to make rural populations, people who, for the most part, had never attended any screenings, familiar with cinema.[76]

Cornil's film productions reflect the attempt to impose Christian values, such as monogamous relationships, on the audience. Film screenings for educational purpose were widespread in other colonial settings as well. Rice discusses the colonial film projects in the British Empire and points out that "[f]ilm might provide the 'connective social tissue', a means to address, homogenize, and monitor disparate worker groups".[77] However, UMHK acknowledged that moments of pure entertainment were also necessary to keep the Congolese happy. The company noted that therefore the following improvements were being considered:

Il serait souhaitable que la Société fasse l'acquisition d'une douzaine de films de courts métrage, genre Mickey Mouse. Ce genre de film, très prisé par l'indigène, servirait à clôturer chaque séance sur une note de gaieté générale.[78]	It would be desirable for the company to acquire a dozen short films, such as Mickey Mouse. This type of film, highly prized by the Congolese, would serve to end each session on a note of general cheerfulness.

With its colonial and paternalistic approach, the company thus presented itself as a benefactor, providing the worker with entertainment at the times and in the areas it deemed appropriate.

1.4 *Space*

In this subsection, I offer a brief history of the politics of space in the context of UMHK/Gécamines before highlighting how space, as part of the category *stability*, also became an object of loss.

In 1910, the city of Elisabethville[79] was founded in honour of Queen Elisabeth, the wife of King Albert I.[80] By that time, the Belgian government had

76 Bouchard, "Commentary", 98.

77 Tom Rice, *Films for the Colonies: Cinema and the Preservation of the British Empire* (Oakland, CA: University of California Press, 2019).

78 AGR 2 – n°655-03047, Rapport Annuel 1951, 25.

79 In 1966, the city's name was changed from Elisabethville to Lubumbashi.

80 For a comprehensive overview of the history of Elisabethville, see for example Fetter, *Creation*.

taken over the colony from King Leopold II and named it the Belgian Congo. Vice-Governor-General Emile Wangermée in Katanga chose this site on the nearby Lubumbashi River because of its proximity to the copper mine of Etoile du Congo and the copper-ore smelting oven installed by the UMHK. Elisabethville was one of the largest cities in Central Africa during colonial times, and in 2010 Lubumbashi celebrated its 100th birthday. It is not surprising that this city has received the attention of many scholars.[81]

Elisabethville was planned according to a design that would crystallise Belgian colonial apartheid: initially, a "white town" was separated from the African township for the Africans, called *cité indigène* by a neutral zone (*cordon sanitaire*) separating the dwellers of the same city – as was common practice in sub-Saharan colonial cities.[82] The basis of the original plan was a grid pattern of streets dividing the city's 450 hectares in equal blocks of 250 by 120 meters. "The grid testifies to the economic logic underlying the spatial organization of the urban territory. Organizing the city according to lots enabled the Comité Spécial du Katanga to valorise the 900 parcels in an efficient way."[83]

The European district was the political and commercial centre, exclusively reserved for "whites" and their domestic servants.[84] In the "white town", segregation politics continued within the estates: the living areas for the European families were "protected" by the office of the head of the household, which functioned as a buffer zone lying adjacent to the service areas for the "boys". Domestic servants and gardeners were housed in modest accommodation called the *boyerie*, in the garden, next to the garage or storage areas.

In addition to the "white town" and the *cités indigènes*, two big companies had staff camps in Elisabethville: the railway company BCK and the UMHK. The UMHK chose the location of its labour camp close to the workplace and

---

81 Fetter, *Creation*, provides us with an excellent historiography of the city in its earlier years. The city's history has also been discussed against the backdrop of labour and the UMHK (such as by Dibwe dia Mwembu, *Bana Shaba*; Dibwe dia Mwembu, *Histoire*) or significant events in the city and the Katanga region in general, such as the strikes (Higginson, "Bringing"; Higginson, "Steam"). The socioeconomic situation of Lubumbashi within a wider context has also been studied (as in Higginson, *Working Class*; Perrings, *Black Mineworkers*; Seibert, "Wind"; Seibert, *Globale Wirtschaft*; Vellut, *Les bassins*). In addition, architects and urban planners characterised the city from their perspective, as Lubumbashi was planned, like many other colonial cities, according to the ideology of segregation, such as Lagae, "In Search"; Lagae, "Modern Living"; Lagae, "Rewriting"; Lagae and Boonen, "City"; Lagae and Boonen, "Scenes".

82 Lagae, Boonen and Dibwe dia Mwembu, "M(G)R", 180.

83 Lagae and Boonen, "City", 56.

84 Piet Clement, "Une expérience ambiguë d'autogestion le centre extra-coutumier d'Elisabethville, 1932–1957", in Amuri Mpala-Lutebele, *Lubumbashi, cent ans d'histoire*, 117.

far enough away from the "white town" at a spot downwind.[85] The Lubumbashi River served as a natural barrier of the *cordon sanitaire*.

By the late 1920s, the Africans had two choices for urban employment and accommodation. The first option was to work for the UMHK and to live in their camp, which offered good food, housing and medical care but relatively low salaries and little autonomy for miners, who became members of a rigid hierarchy. The other option was to live in the *cité indigène* where there was a chance to be hired by a smaller employer who might offer higher salaries. Similar to the *cité indigène* were independent quarters, which were also reserved for Africans. Living in the *cité indigène* or independent quarters meant much lower living standards than in the UMHK camp but greater freedom. Regardless of these differences, and in contrast to the earlier period, Elisabethville had by then become a desirable place to live for thousands of Africans.[86]

However, as Lagae points out, these ways of life were largely determined by "colonial confrontations" that were typical of any form of colonialism. "The house was such a field where these confrontations took a very tangible form, as it was the meeting place par excellence of two very different cultural groups, the European occupants and the Congolese domestic servants, mainly 'boys'".[87]

Against the backdrop of stabilisation measures, the UMHK began to build infrastructure in their camps. In addition to hospitals, there were theatres, recreational facilities and community centres. "A key role in this new disciplinary device was assigned to community centres (*foyers sociaux*)".[88] The camps for single workers began to disappear and houses for families were constructed. Not only did the family size matter, but also the job classification. Starting in the 1950s, the

> UMHK even gave housing allowances to top-ranked workers (teachers, nurses, and skilled workers) to stay in the *cité*. Formerly based on a simple division between married and single workers, camp space was used to facilitate a more complex hierarchy founded on biopolitical, professional and cultural criteria from the 1930s onwards.[89]

The UMHK also constructed a residential area for the white employees. This district, Makomeno (part of the former *cité indigène*) was located at what the

85 Dibwe dia Mwembu, "History", 22.
86 Coquery-Vidrovitch, "Process", 48; Fetter, *Creation*, 94.
87 Lagae, "In Search", 274.
88 Rubbers, "Mining", 92.
89 Rubbers, "Mining", 92.

UMHK considered a "safe" distance from the camp of the African workers in Cité Gécamines, but was also separated from the "white city" by the intervening neutral zone. Makomeno offered the same infrastructure as the camp. The white employees had their own schools, hospitals, leisure areas, social centres, and so on. After the independence of Congo in 1960, African senior staff begun to access the residential area of Makomeno, once reserved for white workers.

Housing matters were a constant topic of discussion for both the company and the workers, as the annual reports of the UMHK reveal. In 1947, the UMHK introduced the Conseil indigènes d'entreprise (the council of the Congolese workers), whose members were selected by the workers themselves. The company would listen to the council members when they were invited to the meetings. The annual reports address all issues related to the workforce, such as the number of workers, legal aspects, the pension system, infrastructure, the organisation of leisure activities and various issues related to accommodation. Among the topics discussed and recorded in writing are lists of demands by the Conseil indigène d'entreprise. Most related to technical aspects of the house or to requirements related to work and living conditions in general.

The demands by the workers mentioned in the 1957 annual report highlight the very diverse nature of their claims.[90] For example, workers expressed concern that schools were gradually being closed; they asked for a proper road to get to the cemetery; they stressed that mothers should be allowed to stay with a child who was being treated in the hospital; they asked for a bike shed near the workplace; that the canteens in the Cité should be reopened; that the toilets in the Cité should have signs with *femmes* (women) and *hommes* (men). In the annual reports, the demands by the workers are in most cases presented in listed form. In general, no further explanatory details are available about the reasons for the demands by the workers. Sometimes the demands have the remark *refusé* (denied) in brackets, but this addition is not implemented consistently, either over the years or within the same annual report.

Many of the demands repeatedly made by the workers in Lubumbashi or other UMHK sites concerned the housing situation. Firstly, topics related to electricity. Electrification of the Cité was generally a demand (as in 1954,[91] 1955,[92] and 1960[93]). Over the years the workers more specifically asked for electric light in the house (1958)[94] or pointed out that there were still houses

90 AGR 2 – n°657-03054, Rapport Annuel 1957, 46.
91 AGR 2 – n°657-03051, Rapport Annuel 1954, 31.
92 AGR 2 – n°657-03052, Rapport Annuel 1955, 38.
93 AGR 2 – n°636, Rapport Annuel 1960, 87.
94 AGR 2 – n°634, Rapport Annuel 1958, 50.

without illumination (1963).[95] In 1956,[96] they asked for a change in the hours electiricty supply for lighting in the houses in the Cité. The wish to have a power outlet in every room of the house is expressed in 1954,[97] 1959[98] and 1960.[99] The quicker replacement of broken electric bulbs in the houses was mentioned in 1956,[100] 1959[101] and 1964.[102] In 1952,[103] it was decided that theoretically one home should be equipped with one light bulb (referring to Panda comprising 448 living units). Starting in the late 1950s, the complaints centred on the problem of unstable electricity supply. In 1959,[104] workers complained about power cuts during the night; they asked for power 24 hrs/day (1960,[105] 1963[106]). Also, the workers asked explicitly for a provision of 220 volts in every house (1960,[107] 1963[108] and 1964[109]) and for electricity in the kitchen (1964).[110]

Another issue raised was water. One the one hand, workers demanded that water should be distributed (1954,[111] 1959[112]); on the other hand, they explicitly requested running water in all houses (1959,[113]1960,[114] 1963[115]). The shortage of water was raised in 1955[116] and 1964;[117] the bad quality of water was criticised in 1959,[118] while in 1956[119] they found fault with the water pressure. The shortage of water for toilets was criticised in 1963.[120] Workers seem to have been aware

95 AGR 2 – n°639, Rapport Annuel 1963, 93.
96 AGR 2 – n°657-03053, Rapport Annuel 1956, 43.
97 AGR 2 – n°657-03051, Rapport Annuel 1954, 31.
98 AGR 2 – n°635, Rapport Annuel 1959, 47.
99 AGR 2 – n°636, Rapport Annuel 1960, 88.
100 AGR 2 – n°657-03053, Rapport Annuel 1956, 43.
101 AGR 2 – n°635, Rapport Annuel 1959, 48.
102 AGR 2 – n°640, Rapport Annuel 1964, 96.
103 AGR 2 – n° 656-03049, Rapport Annuel 1952, 29.
104 AGR 2 – n°635, Rapport Annuel 1959, 47.
105 AGR 2 – n°636, Rapport Annuel 1960, 88.
106 AGR 2 – n°639, Rapport Annuel 1963, 93.
107 AGR 2 – n°636, Rapport Annuel 1960, 88.
108 AGR 2 – n°639, Rapport Annuel 1963, 93.
109 AGR 2 – n°640, Rapport Annuel 1964, 97.
110 AGR 2 – n°640, Rapport Annuel 1964, 97.
111 AGR 2 – n°657-03051, Rapport Annuel 1954, 31.
112 AGR 2 – n°635, Rapport Annuel 1959, 47.
113 AGR 2 – n°635, Rapport Annuel 1959, 48.
114 AGR 2 – n°636, Rapport Annuel 1960, 88.
115 AGR 2 – n°639, Rapport Annuel 1963, 94.
116 AGR 2 – n°657-03052, Rapport Annuel 1955, 37.
117 AGR 2 – n°640, Rapport Annuel 1964, 96.
118 AGR 2 – n°635, Rapport Annuel 1959, 47.
119 AGR 2 – n°657-03053, Rapport Annuel 1956, 43.
120 AGR 2 – n°639, Rapport Annuel 1963, 93.

of the price of water and asked in 1959[121] that running water should be paid based on consumption.

Toilets were constantly requested. Even in 1960[122] and 1962[123] not all houses were equipped with toilets, and the council demanded the provision of toilets in all homes. Individual toilets, shower and sinks were requested from the 1950s, and that toilets should adjoin the houses (1959).[124] The lack of running water for toilets was criticised by workers, as was the lack of roofs for the toilets (1959).[125]

Other issues linked to the house concerned, for example, the demand for cement floors made by cement in the old houses (1956,[126] 1961[127]), the repair of the roofs of the houses (1958),[128] a wooden balcony and a *cusinière bantoue*, which was an outside charcoal stove (1962),[129] more wood for cooking and heating (1957),[130] and additional sinks outside the house (1963).[131] Generally, bigger and more modern houses were built by the council over several years (1959,[132] 1960[133]), with a special emphasis on larger houses for families with many children (1963).[134] In 1962,[135] houses that were more modern were explicitly described as houses with big windows and interior doors.

Doors were by far the most frequent subject matter among the house-related complaints. Workers requested the installation of interior doors in the houses over several years (1954,[136] 1956,[137] 1959[138] and 1960[139]) or, like in 1957,[140] asked that the process of installing the interior doors should be speeded up. Other laments related to the quality and type of doors. For example, in 1955[141] the

121 AGR 2 – n°635, Rapport Annuel 1959, 48.
122 AGR 2 – n°636, Rapport Annuel 1960, 87.
123 AGR 2 – n°638, Rapport Annuel 1962, 84.
124 AGR 2 – n°635, Rapport Annuel 1959, 47.
125 AGR 2 – n°635, Rapport Annuel 1959, 47.
126 AGR 2 – n°657-03053, Rapport Annuel 1956, 44.
127 AGR 2 – n°637, Rapport Annuel 1961, 78.
128 AGR 2 – n°634, Rapport Annuel 1958, 52.
129 AGR 2 – n°638, Rapport Annuel 1962, 85.
130 AGR 2 – n°657-03054, Rapport Annuel 1957, 46.
131 AGR 2 – n°639, Rapport Annuel 1963, 94.
132 AGR 2 – n°635, Rapport Annuel 1959, 47.
133 AGR 2 – n°636, Rapport Annuel 1960, 88.
134 AGR 2 – n°639, Rapport Annuel 1963, 93.
135 AGR 2 – n°638, Rapport Annuel 1962, 84.
136 AGR 2 – n°657-03051, Rapport Annuel 1954, 31.
137 AGR 2 – n°657-03053, Rapport Annuel 1956, 43.
138 AGR 2 – n°635, Rapport Annuel 1959, 47.
139 AGR 2 – n°636, Rapport Annuel 1960, 88.
140 AGR 2 – n°657-03054, Rapport Annuel 1957, 46.
141 AGR 2 – n°657-03052, Rapport Annuel 1955, 38.

workers asked for better closing doors, in 1956[142] for the repair of the doors, in 1959[143] for the repair of the door hinges and in 1964[144] for interior doors that could be locked. In 1960,[145] workers asked for doors that were more modern; in the same year and in 1963[146] they explicitly asked that the iron doors should be replaced by wooden doors. Requests for specific doors were made, such as doors to separate the dining room from the living room (1962),[147] the shower from the toilet (1962)[148] or a second exterior door (1962).[149]

Windows were a subject of discussion in the 1960s. The workers asked for vertical windows (1960),[150] locks for the windows (1964)[151] and more practical window frames (1964).[152]

Other structure-related requests were noted in the 1960s. In 1962,[153] the workers complained that the paint and chalk used for the interiors was of poor quality; in 1963 they asked that the houses should be repainted before the next worker moved in;[154] they asked for an overhanging roof to store charcoal in 1960[155] and for new or renovated kitchens in 1964.[156]

Furthermore, health, hygiene and disinfection were important to the workers. In 1959[157] they asked for disinfectants to be distributed to them; in 1962[158] they stated that the insecticides they were given were not effective enough and twice they asked for mesh screens to be fitted to the windows and doors to keep out mosquitoes (1962,[159] 1963[160]). Likewise, workers asked for rubbish bins (1954,[161] 1955[162] and 1960[163]).

142 AGR 2 – n°657-03053, Rapport Annuel 1956, 43.
143 AGR 2 – n°635, Rapport Annuel 1959, 47.
144 AGR 2 – n°640, Rapport Annuel 1964, 96.
145 AGR 2 – n°636, Rapport Annuel 1960, 88.
146 AGR 2 – n°639, Rapport Annuel 1963, 94.
147 AGR 2 – n°638, Rapport Annuel 1962, 84.
148 AGR 2 – n°638, Rapport Annuel 1962, 85.
149 AGR 2 – n°638, Rapport Annuel 1962, 84.
150 AGR 2 – n°636, Rapport Annuel 1960, 88.
151 AGR 2 – n°640, Rapport Annuel 1964, 96.
152 AGR 2 – n°640, Rapport Annuel 1964, 97.
153 AGR 2 – n°638, Rapport Annuel 1962, 84.
154 AGR 2 – n°639, Rapport Annuel 1963, 93.
155 AGR 2 – n°636, Rapport Annuel 1960, 88.
156 AGR 2 – n°640, Rapport Annuel 1964, 96.
157 AGR 2 – n°635, Rapport Annuel 1959, 48.
158 AGR 2 – n°638, Rapport Annuel 1962, 83.
159 AGR 2 – n°638, Rapport Annuel 1962, 84.
160 AGR 2 – n°639, Rapport Annuel 1963, 93.
161 AGR 2 – n°657-03051, Rapport Annuel 1954, 31.
162 AGR 2 – n°657-03052, Rapport Annuel 1955, 37.
163 AGR 2 – n°636, Rapport Annuel 1960, 87.

Other demands noted in the minutes of these annual reports relate to work, health (hospitals), social activities, life in general in the Cité and services, such as a better postal service with delivery to the house (1955,[164] 1957[165]), a public phone in each quarter of the Cité (1962)[166] or food distribution during movie nights.

The main concerns remained the same over many years: water, electricity and doors. Doors that could be locked from the inside might allude to the workers' need for privacy. From the 1960s, more comfort-related requests were made, like having more rooms, or updated kitchens, or more public phones nearby. The workers' demands were minuted by the UMHK and thus their voice is accessible to us but only indirectly. Taking that into consideration, the workers' notion of a healthy and hygienic house correspond to a large extent to what the Belgian colonial state and the UMHK tried to promote among them. The house was the workers' own universe in a world largely comprising Cité Gécamines and the workplace. This space was controlled and looked after by the company right into the farthest corners of the workers' homes.

There is another aspect in connection with space and control: the ethnic composition of residents in Cité Gécamines. The UMHK sought to create a detribalised African community[167] and therefore rejected any initiative to have workers of the same origin live or work together. For this very reason, it introduced the position of *tshanga tshanga*. The term *tshanga tshanga*[168] derives from the Swahili verb "*changa*" (to mix) and refers to a crucial solution in the aftermath of previous troubles: workers should be ethnically mixed during work and where they lived. The *tshanga tshanga*'s responsibility was to ensure that workers did not form ethnic alliances, to prevent ethnic rivalry among the workers and to ensure a well-controlled and organised life within Cité Gécamines. The *tshanga tshanga* was responsible in the Cité for mixing populations by allocating worker housing appropriately.[169] However, this endeavour was not crowned with success: "[*L*]*es différentes populations en présence se regroupaient par affinité tribale et ethnique et développaient des stratégies de défense de leurs intérêts respectifs*" (The different populations involved grouped themselves by tribal and ethnic affinity and developed strategies to defend their respective interests).[170]

164 AGR 2 – n°657-03052, Rapport Annuel 1955, 37.

165 AGR 2 – n°657-03054, Rapport Annuel 1957, 46.

166 AGR 2 – n°638, Rapport Annuel 1962, 77.

167 That was, however, not possible in other neighbourhoods where workers were also living. See Grévisse, *Le Centre*, 306–12; Dibwe dia Mwembu, *Faire*, 36.

168 I found different ways of spelling this word and chose the most frequently used form.

169 Dibwe dia Mwembu, *L'histoire*, 36.

170 Dibwe dia Mwembu, *L'histoire*, 37.

Luc Mukendi, who was born during the company's glory years, represented the generation of the children of the interview partners. He describes the spatiality of Cité Gécamines today from his perspective:

> Cité Gécamines has become something else, a melting pot of different people with varied professions. This calm Cité, where life formerly ran its course to the tune of the factory siren, is today filled with makeshift restaurants and drinking outlets. Small-scale trade exists on each plot of land, and the facades of some Gécamines houses have been transformed to add an eating place or an extension for rent; the public taps, the legendary *'malatas'*, no longer work; the schools are in a dilapidated state; and only those with money can afford electricity and water, but even they have to accept the phenomenon of 'load-shedding' (alternate distribution of electricity among several quarters). Cité Gécamines is truly a far cry from its former glory.[171]

Since the economic decline of mining, and especially after wages were no longer paid, workers had to start selling their houses or renting them out. The Cité was therefore no longer inhabited exclusively by employees of the company and lost its primary identity.[172] The economic crises thus changed Cité Gécamines as a whole from an organised, controlled and well-maintained "enclave" inhabited by a homogeneous population to an uncontrolled district of the city of Lubumbashi.[173] Its infrastructure has long been neglected.

The ODVs often emphasised the current lack of regulation and infrastructure in different contexts. "*À l'époque*" a disinfection service regularly destroyed vermin and disease. Today, there are rats running around; there are many more mosquitoes and thus people suffering and dying from malaria. "*À l'époque*" waste was collected and the water supply worked properly. These days, garbage is strewn everywhere and the narrow moats in Cité Gécamines transport waste and germs. "*À l'époque*" the streets were policed and there was neither theft nor violence; today they are no longer safe. "*À l'époque*" one knew the neighbours. Today's heterogeneous society means one cannot trust neighbours anymore; in addition, tribalism has spread. During my stay in August 2018 two murders by poisoning were reported in Cité Gécamines. I was told that this was the consequence of the lack of controlling forces and infrastructure in this

171 Luc Mukendi, "Cité Gécamines and Operation Voluntary Departure", in VANSA/Centre d'Art Waza, *Revolution Room*, 31.

172 Dibwe dia Mwembu, "History", 25.

173 "Homogeneous" here refers to the workers being in the same community because of their employment and thus same living conditions.

district. The expression "*Ba mu Komponyi*" (the people of the company) used in former times had thus lost all its meaning.[174]

In this context, the system of the controlling bodies of the *tshanga tshanga* and *malonda* are noteworthy. The job of a worker defined where he and his family lived. The allocated housing was localised within the Cité, which was divided into different sections. The superior (*tshanga tshanga*) was responsible for the *Cité*, and his associates (*malonda*), were responsible for the sections. The term *malonda* could have its origins in the verb *kulonda* (to follow), from a neighbouring Bantu language.[175] The *malonda* thus describes a person who follows things. In this context, he followed people's actions: he was *les yeux et les oreilles* (the eyes and the ears) of the company.[176] The *malonda* reported to the *tshanga tshanga*, who was chosen by the director of administration of the mining company, while the *tshanga tshanga* chose his *malonda*. Each *malonda* was responsible for one specific area within Cité Gécamines. The ODVs often referred to this system of control to explain the current security problems and perceived lack of moral values.

To better "guide" Africans in the direction desired by the colonial administration, several controlling measures were taken. For instance, in 1944, the administration installed a special information service in Léopoldville. It launched a magazine called *La Voix du Congolais*, compiled by and for Congolese.[177] The administration paid for it, but kept the right to keep a close eye on the content of the articles.[178] Special library-*cercles* were created, in particular for the *évolués*. Lectures, conferences and debates were held to widen their horizons. Likewise, the UMHK created a system of social surveillance. The company established a network of informants who collected information on what was discussed among the African workers during work hours and time off. These informants were known to everyone. They were the *malonda* (police officers of the company) responsible for security in the labour camp.

Dibwe dia Mwembu cites a former *malonda* who started his services for the UMHK in 1940 and who describes his responsibilities:

174 Donatien Dibwe dia Mwembu et al., "Les Communes Et Leurs Habitants", in *Les identités urbaines en Afrique. Le cas de Lubumbashi (R.D. Congo)*, ed. Donatien Dibwe dia Mwembu, coll. Mémoires lieux de savoir (Paris: L'Harmattan, 2009), 107.

175 Dibwe dia Mwembu, email to the author. In Chichewa/Nyanja, a language predominantly spoken on the Zambian side of the Copperbelt, *malonda* refers to traffic and business. I thank one of the anonymous reviewers for pointing out that the verb could also come from neighbouring languages, such as Tshiluba, Kisanga, Kizela, etc.

176 Dibwe dia Mwembu, *Histoire*, 77.

177 The magazine appeared from 1955 to 1959 (Kadima-Tshimanga, "La société").

178 Dibwe dia Mwembu, *Histoire*, 6.

À cause de ma sagesse, il voulait faire de moi son malonda. J'informais le chef de cité [tshanga tshanga, DW] sur tout ce qui se passait dans mon quartier pendant les heures de travail. Ma femme ou ses amies m'aidaient à décortiquer les informations. Après les heures de service, j'enquêtais moi-même avec le concours des amis et des enfants. Je recevais à la maison des gens du quartier avec leurs problèmes et doléances, je tranchais quelques litiges entre les travailleurs et faisais mon rapport au chef de cité. Par ailleurs, j'ai bien dirigé mon quartier. Les informations que je donnais à mes chefs étaient toujours authentiques.[179]

Thanks to my wisdom, he wanted me to be his malonda. I informed the supervisor of the cité [tshanga tshanga, DW] about everything that was going on in my neighbourhood during working hours. My wife, or her friends, helped to dissect the information. After work, I myself investigated with the help of friends and children. I received people from the neighbourhood at home with their problems and grievances; I decided on some disputes between the workers and reported to the supervisor of the city. Besides, I led my neighbourhood quite well. The information I gave to my bosses was always correct.

Being a *malonda* was not only an assignment for the worker who was chosen by the *tshanga tshanga* but equally affected his family and friends. Although the *tshanga tshanga* and *malonda* were known to everybody, Dibwe dia Mwembu also reports on informants who were hired to work secretly.[180] Those informants reported to the *tshanga tshanga* as well and received some money for their work.[181] Dibwe dia Mwembu cites one of these covert informants who explained that the role was not only to denounce workers' bad behaviour but also to impart information on workers' dissatisfaction, for instance with their salary.[182] This informant explained that, during a certain period, several complaints about salaries were reported to him and the company in the end raised the salaries as a result of the *tshanga tshanga*'s clarification of the problem. Another informant stated that he reported bad treatment by the "whites" to the company and that this would have helped to "civilise the Whites".[183] That informant mentioned that he was rewarded for these services by higher food

179 Dibwe dia Mwembu, *Histoire*, 78.

180 Dibwe dia Mwembu, *Histoire*, 78.

181 Here the real meaning of the word *tshanga tshanga* appears, which highlights the problem with its use to refer to people with whom we do research. See also Tchokothe, "Archiving".

182 Dibwe dia Mwembu, *Histoire*, 79.

183 Dibwe dia Mwembu, *Histoire*, 80.

rations and money, and that his life conditions became much better, without anyone knowing about his side job.

In 1966, *Mwana Shaba* published the request of a worker who was not satisfied with the way the *malonda* had solved the question of access to a banana tree in the garden of the house where he previously lived:

Katika mji wa Kipushi, 'Chef de cité' ana zoezi la kuleta nyumba ya vyumba viwili kwa baba wa jamaa ya watoto tatu. Kwa kuwa mie vile vile niko na watoto tatu, nilienda kuomba nyumba ya vyumba viwili na pasipo ubishi, nilipewa ile nyumba. Katika nyumba nilikuwa nakaa mbele, nimepanda-ako ndizi ambayo ilipamba na ilikuwa karibu ya kuiva lakini nikahama ile nyumba.	In the city of Kipushi, the "chef de cité" has the task of bringing a two-room house to a father of three children. Since I have three children, I went to ask for a two-room house, and without any controversy, I was offered the house. In the house I was living before I had planted a banana tree that was growing, but when it was finally grown up, I moved out of the house.
Siku moja nilikwenda katika ile nyumba kwa kutaka kukata ndizi yangu lakini yule aliingia katika ile nyumba sasa, akanikatalia kwa mie kutaka ile ndizi akisema ya kuwa, nilikwisha ondoka katika ile nyumba na sina tena haki ya kukata ile ndizi.	One day I went to that house to try to cut my bananas, but the one who moved into that house didn't allow me to cut the bananas, as I had left the house and therefore no longer had the right to cut the bananas.
Wakati tulikuwa tunabishana, malonda akafika na tukamueleza sababu ya ubishi wetu. Kiisha kumuelezea mambo yote malonda akampa yule aliyeingia sasa nyumbani sheria. Kwanza yule mtu hakujua hata wakati gani nilipanda ile ndizi. Sheria ambayo malonda ameleta kwa yule mtu ni ya kweli sawa vile alikata yale mambo?	While we were arguing, the malonda came and we explained the reason for our dispute. After explaining everything, the malonda said that the new occupant of the house was right. The man didn't even know when I planted the banana. Was the malonda right in his judgement and the way he solved this issue?
Bamba Remy Jospeh.	Bamba Remy Jospeh.
N.D.L.R. Malonda alikata maneno vizuri kabisa. Haukuwa tena sharia hata kidogo ya kukamata matunda katika lipango ya nyumba ulikwisha kuondoka. Ile ndizi inakuwa ya mwenyi kuingia sasa nyumbani.[184]	N.D.L.R. The malonda's words were right. You did not have the right at all to grab fruits around the house you had left. The banana now belongs to the one that moved into the house.

184 *Mwana Shaba*, No. 121, 15 March 1966, 15.

The *tshanga tshanga* was responsible for the allocation of the houses when a new worker arrived or when a worker got married or had (more) children and was thus entitled to more spacious accommodation. The transition from a single man into a married man, and later the father of a certain number of children thus defined the right to a house with a certain number of rooms. The complaint in this example initially related to the duty of the *chef de Cité*, who had to provide him with a larger house owing to the increase in the size of his family. The *tshanga tshanga* also dealt with many other issues related to housing. One had to report marriage, divorce, newborns and any other matters that were significant for allocation of housing to him.

However, the *malonda* of the respective section in the Cité was the one who had to be addressed by the workers for what the interviewees labelled as "social problems"; he was equally responsible for overseeing the distribution of the weekly food rations. In this request in *Mwana Shaba*, the worker's dispute with the tenant of the house where the complainant used to live before was thus solved by the *malonda*. That the editor of *Mwana Shaba* confirmed the decision made by the *malonda* does not come as a big surprise, because the *malonda* had followed instructions by the *tshanga tshanga* who was chosen by the company. This example also illustrates that the company did not recognise legal pluralism at that time.[185]

The role of the *tshanga tshanga* and *malonda* was one of the main themes of a *baraza* dealing with various aspects of surveillance. During the *baraza*, I presented to the group the following four quotations from interviews years before in order to initiate a discussion about these controlling bodies:

1.	Le tshanga tshanga, ah c'était très bien parce qu'il s'occupait des gens.	1.	The *tshanga tshanga*, ah, that was very good because he took care of people.
2.	Il y avait de la discipline.	2.	There was discipline.
3.	C'était bien avec le tshanga tshanga, c'est pas comme maintenant, ici le quartier Gécamines, était urbanisé, c'était propre, c'était vraiment bien.	3.	It was good with the *tshanga tshanga,* it is not like today, here the Cité Gécamines, it was urbanised, it was clean, it was really good.
4.	Le chef de Cité, kitu kizuri, kuiba hapana, kimya, wote salama.	4.	The supervisor of the Cité, a good thing, there was no theft, it was quiet, all was peaceful.

185 Legal pluralism refers to the application of customary, religious and statutory laws in the same social field with or without state recognition. For a discussion, see for example Berihun A. Gebeye, "Decoding Legal Pluralism in Africa", *The Journal of Legal Pluralism and Unofficial Law* 49, no. 2 (2017).

Even as I read these quotations to the participants, a group of six men, they nodded in determined agreement. The first reaction of Papa Gérard was: "*Ah, c'était magnifique avec le tshanga tshanga*" (It was magnificent when there was a *tshanga tshanga*.) Papa Maurice added that everything that happened in the Cité had to be reported to the *tshanga tshanga* and that he had his *équipe* of *malonda* to solve social problems in particular, such as brawls or theft, which had to be reported to the *tshanga tshanga*. He further explained that the *malonda* had meetings with the *tshanga tshanga* every morning before they started to work. The *tshanga tshanga* had to know about births, deaths and sick people.

Another participant added that this system of surveillance was very much appreciated, because – as the quotations from the interview already show – the workers felt that there had been order and discipline. My questions as to whether this instance ever triggered a feeling of being controlled were denied. The system with *malonda* and *tshanga tshanga* is conceived as a form of control that ensured a peaceful life in the Cité, which is not the case anymore. However, one participant added that the system worked so well because everybody was afraid of doing something wrong and people feared sanctions. Nevertheless, the controlling force of the *tshanga tshanga* had its limit. If one went outside of the Cité to another district of the city, nobody could report what one was doing there.

As one participant summarised: "*En dehors, ça c'est une autre chose* "(Outside, that is something different). However, most of the workers took their glass of beer in the evening in the *cercle* in the Cité, even though they were free to go to another district in town; the prices in the Gécamines were cheaper than elsewhere in the city.

Nevertheless, there was one aspect of the system that the participants of the *baraza* criticised: the company did not want to have family members beyond the core family staying with them in the Cité. Thus, visitors had to be preregistered with the *tshanga tshanga* and only then were family members allowed to visit for a few days; they were not allowed to live with the worker and his family for longer than those visiting days. "*Ça nous faisait un peu mal*" (That hurt us a bit), commented participants. Asked about any strategies of undermining the rule, Papa Maurice added that even if it hurt, there was no opposition possible, because one had this job; it was just like that, and one had to accept it. Another participant explained that when the UMHK was nationalised the company became less strict regarding family members staying with them.

The discussion on criteria that made a *malonda* an appreciated one – or not – circled around his ability to solve problems. All participants agreed that a good *malonda* was one who was able to provide them with good advice. A good *malonda* was a person one could address in case of problems, a person one could confide in. Thus, the *malonda* was perceived less as a controlling authority and more as a person who looked after the workers. The criteria for a good *tshanga tshanga* were the same: he had to be a successful mediator.

De Rooij analysed letters to the editors from the section *Habari za Kwetu* (News of/from our Place/Home) in the April 1958 issue of *Mwana Shaba*. In his following example, a man expresses his satisfaction with the work of the *tshanga tshanga* and stresses that it is thanks to the *tshanga tshanga* that they could now live without disagreements:

> In the past, Mr. Changa-Changa used to begin the year by sorting out disagreements that had arisen on New Year's day through drunkenness. This year, I am happy to see that we celebrated [lit.: laughed at] New Year without fighting, that we drank without mad drunkenness, that we rejoiced at this New Year's day in friendship. As a result we know that fighting from drunkenness and shouting from disagreements is worthless, that means we have made great progress.
>
> RAPHAËL SEBUTIMBIRI[186]

The members of the ODV also emphasised the *tshanga tshanga*'s role as a judge. He could impose penalties of one day, three days or five days in prison. If a worker received a penalty of five days twice, he had to leave the company and lost not only his job but also all the benefits that went with it, such as housing.

With the *tshanga tshanga*'s responsability for allocating housing to the workers came the power to demand discipline not only in the spatial sense within the Cité, but also in a moral sense for discipline in life in general. Thus, the ODVs often used the term "*père de travail*" (father of work) to characterise his role. It is noteworthy that in this way the participants discursively linked all aspects of the *tshanga tshanga* with work, even the role also strongly influenced their private lives. I therefore asked myself where the boundaries between private and working life lie when living and leisure activities are considered part of work – boundaries that are of course a result of industrialisation in the 19th century, in Europe and elsewhere.

One participant explained that although the *malonda* was concerned about everything that happened in the Cité, he did not get involved in disputes between couples. Problems of that kind were discussed with the *chef de kabila* (tribal chief). If a couple divorced, the *tshanga tshanga* had to be informed, because a change in marital status and family size affected the housing permit. The participants thus argued that information that was public was transmitted to the *tshanga tshanga*, whereas information that was considered private did

186 De Rooij, "Letters".

not reach him Although the *malonda* was the eyes and ears of the *tshanga tshanga* and thus in charge of non-private matters, he was aware of many problems related to what the participants called "truly private matters". As Mama Marie described: "*Il était là comme un papa*" (He was there like a father).

Many participants spoke of a supervisory authority who controlled them during their "truly private time" – at night. This supervisory authority was called *batumbula,* a kind of spirit that wandered at night and frightened people so that they would stay home then.[187] Rubbers explains that the *batumbula* were recruited by *simba ya Bulaya* (the lion of Europe), a white man who ate Congolese people:

> [Batumbula are] recognisable in popular paintings by their coat, their hat, their torch and their dark glasses – to kidnap men and women in remote places and to confine them in some prison (pit, cellar, attic, etc.). There, victims are fattened with salt until they see hairs growing on their body and they turn into pigs. Unless they put them into cans, White people, along with their guests, will consume them at Easter, Christmas or New Year.[188]

Rubbers further argues that the accounts of *batumbula*

> seem to offer an allegorical comment on various aspects of urban life such as work hierarchy, camp discipline, the symbolic power of dress and the politics of marriage. Today, the old still pass on memories of the White ogre to younger generations, saying that they themselves only just escaped seizure by his subordinates.[189]

---

187 Luise White, *Speaking with Vampires* (University of California Press, 2000), 18–9. White discusses the meaning of the term pointing out the many ways to read it: "[t]he term for those who captured Africans for the Europeans who ate their flesh in colonial Belgian Congo was *batumbula* (singular, *mutumbula*), from the Luba *-tumbula,* translated in Shaba Swahili as to "butcher." […] *Batumbula,* a term that took hold among the migrant labour population of the mines of colonial Katanga, may have been interpreted by Swahili speakers with one set of meanings and by Luba speakers with another. The power and viability of the term lay in its many meanings, which allowed the word to encompass all the things *batumbula* were said to do, from digging pits, to giving their victims injections, to eating their flesh. And in Belgian Colonial Congo, *batumbula* was also glossed by the Shaba Swahili term "*simba bulaya*", the lion from Europe, another animal term to describe the predatory cannibals who left their victims' clothes behind."

188 Rubbers, "Story", 278.

189 Rubbers, "Story", 279.

However, Dibwe dia Mwembu cites one of his interviewees who refused to think of the Whites as being involved in anthropophagy.[190]

Dibwe dia Mwembu describes the *batumbula* in reference to the UMHK's attempt to keep workers in the camps:

> Comme le camp de l'UMHK était séparé de la cite Kamalondo par une brousse où, croyait-on, se cachaient les batumbula, la peur d'être capturé la nuit par ces derniers a eu un effet bénéfique dans la mesure où nombreux étaient les travailleurs qui préféraient se contenter de ce que leur offrait le cercle récréatif, pouvant ainsi regagner leur logis le plus tôt possible, vers vingt et une heure.[191]
>
> As the UMHK camp was separated from Kamalondo by a bush where the *batumbula* were believed to be hiding, the fear of being captured by the *batumbula* at night had a beneficial effect in so far as many workers preferred to make do with what was offered to them in the recreational circle, thus being able to return to their homes as soon as possible, around 9 p.m.

Dibwe dia Mwembu further describes that the *batumbula* significantly contributed to the rhythm of the night of workers and families. Not only were the streets deserted, but after 9 p.m. they used pots instead of toilets outside the houses for fear of the *batumbula*. Children were no longer allowed to play outside and the residents sang: *Wasipo kwako, ende mu pori, bakamutumbule kiko batumbula*! (Whoever does not have a family home should go into the bush to be captured by the *batumbula*).[192]

The ODVs confirmed that the *batumbula* were still active. However, their power was diminished because, as the participants pointed out, thefts and violence at night were constantly increasing in Cité Gécamines. The ODVs miss the rigid, controlling system that offers security.

The nostalgia for a strict system of control in Cité Gécamines is also evident in the context of the ex-workers' explanation for the increase in violence as a result of ethnic conflicts. In this context, the importance of the *tshanga tshanga* was emphasised. The *tshanga tshanga* had the explicit duty to mix workers of different origin in order to build "a deracinated African community"

190 Dibwe dia Mwembu, *L'histoire*, 68–69.

191 Dibwe dia Mwembu, *L'histoire*, 68.

192 Dibwe dia Mwembu, *L'histoire*, 68.

and "to annihilate customary diversity and to form an unnamed, anonymous society".[193] The *tshanga tshanga* thus formed a population that was united on two levels: first, by their shared employer, and second, by neighbours they knew and trusted. Neither would be the case today, the ODVs pointed out.

Dibwe dia Mwembu reports on one of his interview partners who also describes peaceful coexistence nostalgically:

Nous vivions [...] en harmonie comme les enfants d'une même famille. Nous étions comme une même tribu. D'ailleurs, le problème de tribu ne se posait pas.[194]	We lived [...] in harmony like children of the same family. We were like one tribe. Moreover, the problem of tribe did not emerge.

The fact that workers and workers' families lived together left its mark on the terminology used to describe the housing situation. For instance, those sharing a house (*les maisons jumeleés*) talked about their neighbours as *ndugu ya musalani*, referring to the one with whom they shared the wall of the toilet, or about their *ndugu ya nyumba* (sister/brother of the house), referring to the one with whom they shared a duplex house.[195]

Another term used was *kambolokoni*, which referred to a single room for single men; the term also describes bowls with a specific smell that were put into the urinal.[196]

Hönke and Fetter argue that two authorities maintained the "totalitarian subculture" in workers' settlements.[197] First, the "compound head", responsible for discipline maintenance – the *tshanga tshanga* – and second, the "[Catholic] teacher preacher responsible for morals and learning".[198] In spatial terms, the labour settlements were isolated from other African districts with the idea "to isolate the bubble of social order made by industrial production and a particular regulatory regime of discipline and control from a social environment represented by Europeans as 'hostile' and 'disorderly'".[199]

Vellut describes the interlocking tasks of the *tshanga tshanga* and the religious representatives as follows:

---

193 Dibwe dia Mwembu, *L'histoire*, 36.
194 Dibwe dia Mwembu, "La perception", 165–66.
195 Dibwe dia Mwembu, "La perception", 165.
196 Dibwe dia Mwembu, personal communication with the author.
197 Bruce Fetter, *L'union*; Jana Hönke, "New Political Topographies. Mining Companies and Indirect Discharge in Southern Katanga (DRC)", *Politique Africaine* 120, no. 4 (2010): 113.
198 Hönke, "New", 114; Vellut, "Mining".
199 Hönke, "New", 114.

[L']Union Minière conçut ses camps sur la base du mélange ethnique. La société voulait créer dans ses camps une nouvelle tribu, celle des Tshanga Tshanga ("tout mélanger") unis par le même esprit de la maison. Mgr de Hemptinne, dirigeant l'Eglise catholique à Elisabethville, précisait toutefois qu'il fallait avant tout créer "la paroisse des Tshanga-Tshanga".[200]	[The] Union Minière conceived its camps on the basis of ethnic mixture. The company wanted to create a new tribe in its camps, that of tshanga tshanga ("to mix everything"), united by the same spirit. Bishop de Hemptinne, head of the Catholic Church in Elisabethville, said however that it was above all necessary to create "the parish of tshanga-tshanga".

The *tshanga tshanga*, who chose the place of residence and controlled the area, served as a kind of caretaker who provided security and thus stability in daily life. Papa Bruno pointed out: "*Depuis 2003, on a le sentiment d'être abandonné, on est des esclaves même quand on n'a plus de travail*" (Since 2003 we have the feeling of being neglected, we are slaves, even though we don't have work anymore). From the perception of the workers, slavery was thus no longer linked to work but to the lack of it.

Cité Gécamines was a unity in every respect: the inhabitants were known, everything was controlled and everything could be named. It offered stability in spatial terms. Stability was also a key aspect of the ODVs' work. Although it is surprising to hear Papa Bruno speaking of joblessness as slavery, one has to pay close attention to the context to understand his point of view. In becoming jobless, workers/men lost what they regarded as their freedom, financial security, family, communities and social status, social ties, prestige, gendered roles, masculinity and especially the sense of respect/honour, *heshima*.

2 Heshima

Among the ODVs, *heshima* (respect) meant many things: firstly, recognition by the company for the work done in the form of wages and social benefits such as health care and food rations; secondly, the appreciation of their families, because through the work their needs – and perhaps more – were met; thirdly, social appreciation in the form of prestige because they were a member of the "UMHK family" and did work that was important. ODVs who used to hold a senior staff position in particular raised the last point, while both blue-collar workers and senior staff members expressed a sense of appreciation in

200 Vellut, *Les bassins*, 69.

terms of salary and benefits. Regardless of the job classification, another issue connected to *heshima* in this cultural context was the highly valued ability to be a good host. I will discuss and illustrate these points using the work biographies of two men and two women.

2.1 *Papa Paul*

Papa Paul managed various hospitals in the course of his professional life and had been in a managerial position since the beginning. He first worked for the government and was in charge of a hospital. Then he was hired by Gécamines in Bukeya and was responsible for a hospital with 300 patients. Although the beginning of his career dates back more than 40 years, Papa Paul remembers every detail and date.

He explained that when he was first employed by UMHK as a hospital manager, the doctor in charge there was a German who lived with the "religious" (the nuns or brothers). Papa Paul was married at the time he got this job and he explained that the company immediately declared it would build a house for him and his family. Because the builders worked from 6 a.m. to 6 p.m. every day, his house was ready after only one and a half months. He told me that he felt respected because, although Gécamines decided what kind of house he would get, he was able to express his wishes.

For example, he was asked where he wanted the doors. Papa Paul described in detail his considerations at the time, such as not wanting to go through the kitchen to take a shower, and asking for bigger windows, a veranda and an additional kitchen outside. Recalling the construction of this house, he sighed and pointed out that at that time all tasks were done immediately and that the company's service was fantastic. However, he was aware of the fact that he was privileged compared to the workers, as he had the opportunity to decide on the appearance and structure of his house.

Papa Paul then showed me maps from 1977 with the houses to be built for workers in the Cité. Among other things, he was responsible for the hygienic standards of the accommodation. Using these maps, he explained to me the different types of houses for different types of workers and illustrated this by explaining that with each promotion in the job came a move to a new house.

Later, Papa Paul got a new job in Likasi, where he was given a seven-bedroom house. He worked there for three years and was responsible for occupational medicine, a new field at that time for both him and the company. He was then sent to Kakanda to manage the UMHK health sector. There were problems with a "Congolese doctor" who was the successor of a "white man". What started as a three-month work assignment in an urgent crisis turned into a long-term position of 14 years.

Papa Paul told me that he loved this work, but that his house there had only three bedrooms. The small number of bedrooms was a problem, because, as he pointed out: "*C'était un peu difficile pour les visiteurs*" (It was a bit difficult when I had visitors). Three bedrooms were needed for the family members: one for the parents, one for the girls and one for the boys. At that time, he was a father of six children. Therefore, he could not offer visitors a guest room as he was used to and as was expected of a person in a higher position (which shows the social aspect of *heshima*). However, he went on to explain that he was otherwise given what was due to him in his position, including a gardener and two domestic servants who lived in an outbuilding on the compound, the *boyerie*.

He then worked in Kipushi for a few months, staying in a guesthouse on weekdays and going home on weekends. The company paid for the transport. In 1992, he finally moved to Lubumbashi to take up a new position as head of a hospital. In Lubumbashi, the company gave him the choice between two already existing houses. He explained that he had chosen this house because it was not a *maison à étage*.[201] He argued that he was afraid that in old age he would no longer be able to climb the stairs, even though, as he said, the houses of the upper class would be *maisons à étage* (two-storey houses), because this

201 William Cunningham Bissell, *Urban Design, Chaos, and Colonial Power in Zanzibar* (Bloomington, IN: Indiana University Press, 2011), 61. Multi-storeyed houses have gained interest among scholars particular in relation to the Western idea of these houses as being a symbol of civilisation and modernity. Bissell, for instance, discusses the *nyumba ya ghorofa* in Zanzibar's Stone Town. There "[i]t also mirrors an older tradition in Swahili cultural analysis that seized on the multistoried stone house – *nyumba ya ghorofa* – as the defining feature of Swahili urbanism. Swahili towns, then, were depicted as 'stone towns' even in the majority of instances when mud and wattle dwellings surrounded a few stone structures. Similarly, concentrations of stone houses were typically singled out as 'Arab' quarters, in distinction to 'native' huts because of Western beliefs that African urbanity was a contradiction in terms." However, in Lubumbashi, the people did not appreciate these houses. Lagae and Boonen discuss this topic on the basis of the neighbourhood Ruashi in Lubumbashi, where in the 1950s, the Office des Cités Africaines (OCA) constructed different kinds of houses. The two-storey houses were so unpopular that the OCA started a campaign: "The local government also undertook several initiatives to 'educate' the African population in new dwelling practices, such as the publication of an informative brochure on the *maison modèle*, creating a fully furnished *maison témoin* that could be visited, and organising a series of competitions honouring the most beautiful house/garden/interior of the cité. Deeply rooted in the paternalistic rationale underlying postwar colonial policies in the Belgian Congo, such initiatives were also in tune with then current practices in the mother country that sought to educate the Belgian housewife in 'modern living' via a variety of popularising media targeting a broad audience (exhibitions of model houses and interiors, lectures, publications in newspapers and women's magazines etc.)" (Lagae and Boonen, "Ruashi", 82–83).

kind of house represented what a man in his position would normally prefer. He explained that there were also *maisons à étage* in Cité Gécamines. Workers could usually move in as soon as they reached a higher position in the system. Papa Paul added that workers usually appreciated living in a *maison à étage*, not because they particularly liked this architectural form but because it was a prestigious type of house that was seen as a reason to be respected (*-heshimiwa*, passive form) by others.

Papa Paul also explained to me in detail the system of the property bonus that workers received from the mining company. Initially, workers would have received this bonus after eight years of service, but the union managed to get the bonus paid after only four years. Therefore, as Papa Paul stated, there was money every four years to upgrade something in the house. When I asked him what the most important thing in the house was to keep it up to date, he mentioned the armchairs in the living room; after all, he stressed, it was important to receive visitors properly.

Papa Paul lost his employment on 9 January 2004. At that time, four people were still living in his household. And he explained that he had some time to prepare for these changes in life, because it did not come as a surprise. He was now the owner of this house and decided to commission an architect to remodel and extend the *boyerie*, which was empty at the time, as the domestic staff and gardener had left. He expanded the *boyerie* with a living room, one bedroom, an additional toilet and a kitchen. Every month he and the architect had sat together and calculated the costs to determine what could be done with the remaining money from his savings.

Papa Paul's actual house was rented out and served as the new source of income. His first tenant was a Congolese who was building his house and needed accommodation during the construction period. After that, a Polish citizen rented Papa Paul's house for a period of eight years until his job assignment was finished. The following tenant was an American woman, and nowadays the house is rented by a non-governmental organisation.

Papa Paul explained that since he started to rent out his house, he and his family lived in the extended *boyerie*, with enough space, although it was far less comfortable and luxurious than before. He remembered the moment of moving out of the house into the *boyerie* as a very difficult moment. The two children still living at home were especially unhappy. It was, as Papa Paul pointed out, difficult because the house was the symbol of the prestige he enjoyed with the company, even though he had bought the house from the company over the years. The house was the symbol of the position he used to hold. With the move to the *boyerie*, the symbol of his professional career was immediately lost, which also implied the loss of his social *heshima*. He finds comfort in knowing that the job he did was an important one and he is proud to have improved the health and hygiene conditions of workers and families. Occasionally, he is still consulted by those in charge of the hospital.

Blue-collar workers were less likely to cite their job duties as a source of pride, but emphasised that they were proud of the income and benefits they received from their work. Often, they also pointed out the *mposho* (the food rations) and the possibility of being a parent who could educate their children. However, senior staff members also saw their workplace as a place where they could contribute to the development of the company or improve conditions for other workers, such as Papa Paul, who managed hospitals and improved the health services in many ways. Therefore, the loss of the job had an even greater impact on Papa Paul's self-esteem.

2.2 *Papa Laurent*

Papa Laurent was born in 1948 in the province of Kivu, where he went to school before moving to Kinshasa to study economics and finance at university. He explained that he got a job at Gécamines immediately after finishing his studies, on 6 November 1974, which he remembers exactly, as well as all the other dates related to his working life. He explained that he had not looked for this job but that the company had reached out to him and that was why he accepted. On 6 August 1976 he was transferred to Lubumbashi. In the beginning, he was accommodated in a guest house for a short time until the company could provide him with a house that was appropriate for his position in the finance department of the company. The house was located in Makomeno, the neighbourhood for senior staff. In September 1976, he moved into the house where he still lives today.

When he moved into this house as a bachelor, it was a bachelor's house divided into four smaller flats. Papa Laurent married in 1978 and in 1984 the company converted the house into a *maison jumélée,* with two flats. After the couple had two children, he applied for a bigger house, but at that time there was no suitable house available in Makomeno. Therefore, the company decided to convert the house into a four-bedroom detached house. Today he is the owner of the house (purchased through monthly deductions from the salary) and the only interviewee who had not built an annex to rent out for extra income. He explained that he was lucky that he had found another job (and was therefore still working despite his age), as was his wife, so they were still doing well financially, although much worse than before 2003. His account of the past therefore also reveals a sense of nostalgia, especially in terms of finances and security, but also in terms of the company's general attitude towards looking after its employees.

Papa Laurent's eyes lit up most when he told me how much he loved his job. He stressed that there had never been a complaint against him during his 40 years of service. He emphasised his very good working relationship with his supervisor and explained that once he was the boss, he tried to follow suit and give top priority to good relationships with his staff. This, he stressed, was also important because of his Christian values. Therefore, he appreciated it when his employees turned to him when they had problems, when he could help them, because then he felt respected (*-heshimiwa*).

At the end of each year, if an employee's performance had been satisfactory, the company gave out a *cotation*, a positive grade; accumulating several positive grades led to a higher classification and thus a higher salary. Papa Laurent explained that times became difficult from the 1990s onwards because wages were paid irregularly. However, as he mentioned, he continued to work normally, because he wanted to be there and do his job, even without pay. He felt responsible for others; his position meant everything to him.

When we talked about Makomeno, Papa Laurent said that this neighbourhood was very well organised and maintained until the late 1980s. For instance, there was a waste collection service and the *service d'hygiène*, which came on a regular basis to disinfect houses to combat mosquitoes, and there was electricity. Not only from a health perspective, but also in terms of the demographic structure, he was nostalgic for the earlier times: "*C'était un quartier très calme, que des agents et les domestiques*" (It was a very quiet neighbourhood, there were only workers and domestic servants). He explained that in the well-organised times, every visitor had to register: "*C'était bien organisé le quartier ici. On était dans la sécurité. La garde faisait la patrouille*" (The neighbourhood here was well organised. We were safe. Guards used to go on patrol). But things began to decline in the 1980s, when everything was gradually neglected. Papa Laurent explained that selling the houses to the workers was one of the many reasons why the situation in Makomeno started to change. The company sold the houses to the workers because the maintenance was a very expensive undertaking and the houses had to be renovated regularly. However, Papa Laurent indicated, selling the houses as private property was the turning point in terms of security.

The company was no longer able to control who visited the houses and who sold them,. "*Le quartier est devenu le quartier de tout le monde*" (The neighbourhood has become everyone's neighbourhood). By "everyone", Papa Laurent meant those who were not workers or domestic servants and therefore did not feel bound by the norms and rules that prevailed when Makomeno was a residential area for only Gécamines' employees. Since this change, lamented Papa Laurent, nothing could be done if a neighbour did not keep their house and property clean. And one could not prevent them from building annexes on their plots.

In the past, Papa Laurent concluded: "*La surveillance ilikuwa nzuri kabisa*" (The surveillance was very good). He explained that the security provided did not disturb individuals but protected them from attacks and aggression. He drew attention to the system of whistles that he appreciated very much. The company provided each household with a whistle. If you heard something unusual or disturbing during the night, you used the whistle to alert your neighbours and the guards. With this system intruders were deterred simply and effectively.

Non-material benefits, such as leisure activities, were also among the things Papa Laurent missed. He explained how well the *cercles* were maintained, how much he appreciated the possibility to go out for food or drinks, his enjoyment of sports activities and going to the cinema with his wife. He specified that he especially liked the cinema nights because the movies were for senior staff members only ("*pas des mineures, pas d'enfants*" – no minors, no children) and thus allowed an evening among equals and a feeling of luxury that one deserved.

Papa Laurent was also very pleased with the schools and hospitals, which he considered to be of very high quality. This laid the foundation for the successful lives of his children. Eight of them later entered university and became successful in their lives. One son still lives with his parents, as he was born with Down's syndrome. Papa Laurent emphasised that the company's hospital also offered very good specialists for children with special needs. Those times, when human beings were respected, were now gone.

2.3 *Mama Marie*

Mama Marie, a former senior staff member, was born in 1949 in Kipushi as one of six children of parents who were both working for the UMHK. She had a childhood typical of a worker's child and attended the school that was provided by the mining company. Her mother left while she was a child, so she grew up with her father and siblings. She would have liked to study but it was difficult because of financial and family issues. She therefore started her professional career in 1967 after her compulsory schooling:

J'ai commencé d'abord par être formée. Par être formée ici aux usines pendant disons trois mois, en dactylographie. J'ai mon attestation comme une dactylographe, j'avais terminé avec trente-six mots à la minute.	I started by being trained first. By being trained here in the factories for let us say three months, in typing. I have my certificate as a typist; I finished with thirty-six words per minute.

She remembers her performance at the beginning of her career exactly. The speed of typing was the prerequisite for what turned out to be a successful career. After her training as a typist she started working for the mining company as an office employee of class seven in Lubumbashi. Her supervisor at the time was then transferred to the HR department in Kipushi and wanted her to come along as well. There, she says, she was the first Congolese woman to hold such a position:

M : C'était alors que je suis rentrée. Je suis rentrée maintenant au service du personnel de Kipushi.	M: It was then that I came back. I then returned to the staff in Kipushi.
DW : Ah vous étiez//	DW: Ah you were //
M : //du groupe. J'ai été affectée comme secrétaire. Toute en étant première femme noire. Et cela m'a donné un peu de choix. J'ai accepté de travailler là-bas. J'ai travaillé, les gens venaient me regarder à la fenêtre "Eh mwanamke mweusi ananapiga machine!". J'avais (.) j'étais très fière.	M: // of the group. I was assigned as secretary. While being the first black woman. And that gave me a little choice. I agreed to work there. I worked, people came to watch me at the window "Eh, the black woman is typing the machine!". I had (.) I was very proud.

With the sentence "And that gave me some choice" she refers to the financial scope she had thanks to her employment. She did not want to marry at that time, she explained, and thus wished to earn her own money. In fact, she had no wish to marry at all, even though she later married and became a mother of five children. She said that her husband had kept an eye on her since school and since then had tried her to convince to marry him. With the decision not to study, but to start working, Mama Marie was also supporting the higher education of two of her brothers. She expressed her pride that by working for the UMHK she was able to provide for her brothers' education. Talking about one of them, she said:

Mais comme il n'y avait pas moyens que je rentre aux études, j'avais un petit frère qui venait après moi, j'ai préféré supporter les études de mon petit frère qui malheureusement est mort. Il fût ingénieur. Il était en Europe, en Suisse là-bas, il est sorti avec cinq diplômes.	But as there was no way I could go back to study, I had a little brother who came after me, so I preferred to support the studies of my little brother who unfortunately died. He was an engineer. He was in Europe, in Switzerland over there; he accumulated five degrees.

Mama Marie was very much appreciated by her superior. She worked for and with him for many years. He wanted her services in Kipushi and in Lubumbashi, therefore she moved whenever he was appointed to a new position. Mama Marie's future husband also took a position in the UMHK in Kipushi while she was based there. After marriage she gave birth to five children in Kipushi, but she continued to work. Mama Marie, who worked in human resources, describes becoming a member of the senior staff and then being entitled to a house bigger than her husband's:

[À Kipushi] J'avais eu aussi une grande maison, à travers mon mari on avait une petite maison. Comme j'ai travaillé au service du personnel, le service qui a distribué les maisons, avec mon influence, nous avons eu une grande maison.

[In Kipushi] I also had a big house, through my husband we had a small house. As I worked in the human resources department, the department that distributed the houses, with my influence, we had a big house.

In 1978, the family moved to Lubumbashi because Mama Marie's supervisor took a new position and wanted her to join and continue to work for the HR department; her husband got a position in the electrical department that serviced the plants. Since then she had been living in the house where she welcomed me several times. Despite the fact that her house is located in Cité Gécamines, it is one of the luxurious larger houses for Congolese executives who were not allocated flats in Makomeno at the time. The house has three bedrooms and a living room.

Mama Marie loved her job because she liked her position as secretary in management, which was full of responsibilities and not only offered her many contacts but also opened her eyes to the outside world:

J'aimais le travail parce que ça m'a beaucoup donné disons l'ouverture vers le monde extérieur, d'abord le monde de l'entourage, j'avais des relations, et puis dans la famille avec cet argent j'ai formé les neveux, les cousins, etc.

I loved the work because it has given me a lot, let's say, the opening to the outside world, first the world around me; I had connections, and then in the family, with this money I earned, I paid for the professional training of nephews, cousins, etc.

She also expressed that her earnings enabled the education of those family members outside the nuclear family who could not benefit from the schooling offered by the mining company because they were not children of UMHK/

Gécamines employees. Mama Marie expressed her pride that many family members were well educated and could now take care of her and others in a difficult economic situation. Her own children attended the schools provided by the company and were later sent to study, because education was one of Mama Marie's main concerns.

Since there is no work in this region today, her firstborn moved to Malawi, where he found work. Her second-born son is an engineer based in Kinshasa. Her first daughter became a dressmaker, another one a nurse. Her youngest son became a carpenter and was working for a Chinese company in Mbuji Maji. Mama Marie's children, cousins and nephews got a good education that, as she expressed: "*C'est ce qui m'as fait la fierté d'être femme travailleuse*" (That is what made me proud to be a woman who had a job). Mama Marie often referred to herself as *femme travailleuse* to express in a rather moderate, but no less serious way, that she was the one who was the main breadwinner of the household. However, she also talked about her leisure activities. Like Papa Paul, Mama Marie not only held a senior position but was equally a proud sports person during leisure time. She was a member of the female soccer team of the company and expressed her joy in playing, as well as her joy in having a drink afterwards:

Nous avons joué au football, nous avions une équipe de la Gécamines Lubumbashi et de la Gécamines Kipushi. Dans les concours que nous avons préparés nous-mêmes, nous les avons joués à Kipushi, si nous gagnions, nous avions encore une chance. Ensuite, nous sommes allés prendre un verre au Cercle.

We played football, we had a team from Gécamines Lubumbashi and Gécamines Kipushi. In the competitions, which we organised ourselves, we played in Kipushi; if we won, we still had a chance. Afterwards we went to the Circle for a drink.

Talking about her children, she explained that all her children were born in the maternity clinic in Kipushi. This topic initiated an extensive discussion by Mama Marie of the excellent healthcare services in the former days. She explained that the healthcare facilities closely monitored child development during the first five years with regular health checks and a vaccination programme. If the mothers missed these consultations they were punished. Mama Marie was very happy with this procedure. "*On doit avoir tous les vaccins. Là, en tout cas, la Gécamines nous a bien soigné*" (We were expected to have all the vaccinations. Gécamines treated us well). Given her current health status – she is suffering from cancer and lacks adequate treatment – it comes as no surprise that her nostalgia emphasises the former provision of healthcare.

2.4 *Mama Aimée*

Mama Aimée's narrative showed how she adapted impressively to the new circumstances that came with the economic decline. She was in her fifties, and I went to meet her for the second time in August 2018. I had interviewed her for the first time the year before. Mama Aimée grew up in the Gécamines and had spent almost all her life here. As she said, she experienced the rise and fall of the living and housing conditions of the workers of Gécamines. As a child, she benefited from the infrastructure provided by the company. She summarised her childhood memories as well as the memories of her early adult life with the same words everybody else used: "*C'était bien à l'époque*!"

It was on one of those dry days in August 2018, with a pitiless heat around noon and a wind that blew the red dust through the unpaved alleys of Cité Gécamines, that Mama Aimée warmly welcomed me. We sat down in her office to get some shade and find a quiet place to talk. Continuously, assistants, friends, family members or acquaintances stopped by, curious about the visitor. I never walked through those alleys without being noticed.

A few years earlier, Mama Aimée had founded an NGO to take care of the most vulnerable children: those whose fathers were mineworkers but whose mothers were not official wives, women who often were *les petites femmes* (here understood as prostitutes). These children (and of course their mothers) have suffered most from the decline of the mining sector and the resulting financial difficulties. They often lack a stable social environment and the financial means to attend school. For Mama Aimée, these children are *une bombe à retardement* (a ticking time bomb) for society if they are not well taken care of. She fights against future vandals, thieves and rapists, as she describes the scenario, by providing what she calls "home", a place to sleep, meals, education and, most importantly, affection and attention.

She was also successful in raising funds to employ herself and others to run the NGO. That Mama Aimée runs this NGO at all, that she possesses management and accounting knowledge, that she was able to open a bank account, is far from self-evident. Only when she was already a mother of four did she insist (despite the social pressure of her husband's family) on getting her degree. She dreamed of having a good job with responsibilities. The moment of her graduation was the beginning of the economic crisis of Gécamines. Her husband, a Gécamines worker, was affected, like thousands of others, by irregular payments in the 1990s. Their situation became financially precarious. Mama Aimée described how they started to sell everything at least partly valuable so that the family would have something to eat. They first sold the wall clock and the television, then furnishings, then even the beds and mattresses; only some few cooking utensils remained. All of them, children included, slept on the floor, on cardboard.

To have a bit more privacy for our discussion and to avoid the constant flow of visitors, Mama Aimée guided me out of her office into her house to show me every room. Her office is an annex towards the street in front of her house which was expanded on all sides and now stands in the middle of the property. A huge room for a sewing school she opened is located between the office and her husband's private rooms. Their bedroom is small and dark, every corner filled with personal belongings and clothes, and the couple share this room with five cats. There is another bedroom, the bigger one, where the children of the NGO sleep. We continued to the living room, carefully decorated and well-furnished with a sofa. Mama Aimée told me that normally she would have invited me to sit here for our conversation, but as there was a power cut on that day, it was a bit too dark. She therefore suggested that we go back to her office, which she felt was almost as suitable for receiving her guest as the living room.

In 2003, within the context of the Opération Départ Volontaire, Mama Aimée's husband received compensation totalling USD 2,500. This sum was a drop in a bucket in comparison to what her husband would have earned if he had continued working. Mama Aimée described the moment when they finally had some money again. While her description of their situation at that time, all sleeping on cardboard, was on my mind, I asked her if she could remember what things they first bought with this money. Mama Aimée answered: "a sofa and two armchairs". The money was spent as follows: USD 2,000 on the most important things, such as furnishings; USD 500 as an investment to start her project.

Although she felt ashamed that they were sleeping on cardboard, and she knew that many others were sharing the same experience, she explained that it was most important to have a living room to finally be able to welcome guests again, to be guardians of *heshima*. Being a welcoming family was not only a matter of societal norms but also important to her to demonstrate her ability as homemaker, as she stressed, regardless of the fact that she was the one largely financing the family with her activities. This takes me to gender roles and the third object of loss, identity.

3 Gender Roles and Identity

Être gécaminois (to be a [worker at] Gécamines) is, as I have outlined, the essence of everything that unites the ODVs, the working life they had, the life they lost and the experiences and memories they share. This applied across genders. In both the archive material and in the interviews and discussions, gender-related concepts repeatedly came up. I refer to concepts of masculinity and femininity and the expectations attributed to them in the archives, on the one hand, and in the interviews and the *baraza*, on the other.

3.1 *Masculinity*

One of the workers' main concerns was often mentioned only implicitly: their current inability to fulfil what was socially regarded as male norms and behavioural patterns. Their perceptions of work were strongly linked to their understanding of masculinity. The benefits and privileges granted to the workers and their wives were shaped by assumptions regarding their respective gender roles.

> Several generations of Katangese boys grew up with the idea that, in order to be recognised and treated as real men, it was absolutely essential for them to get access to paid work, or *kazi*. They were taught that men's dignity and respectability depended to a very large extent on their ability to secure the livelihoods of their household members.[202]

When I refer to the term masculinity, I do not intend to open up a discussion on gender in general but am referring to a "cluster(s) of norms, values and behavioural patterns expressing explicit and implicit expectations of how men should act and represent themselves to others".[203] Here, I limit this aspect to the participants' subjectivities and thus to the discourse on norms, values and behavioural patterns as expressed by them.

During a *baraza* on surveillance and control, the participants told me that their leisure time on workdays was usually between 6 p.m. and 10:30 p.m. They described this not by using the term "leisure", but as *le temps pour s'amuser* (time to enjoy yourself), stating that they spent most of this time in Cité Gécamines and less than 20% of this time in other parts of the city. Considering that leisure activities were provided in the social centres and the *cercle*, I wondered what kind of activities they enjoyed outside. I did not get an answer until finally a woman in another group discussion started to complain that "in the good old times" many men had relationships with other women outside. In that rather emotional discussion, it turned out that men did agree on that point and one participant stated: "*Avoir deux femmes c'était presque la mode.*

202 Jeroen Cuvelier, "Work", 8.

203 Lisa Lindsay and Stephen Miescher, *Men and Masculinities in Modern Africa* (Portsmouth: Heinemann, 2003), 4.

Car la vie était si facile" (To have two women was almost fashionable, because life was so easy).

"Easy" in that context meant that they had the economic power to sustain relationships outside the boundaries of the life provided by the company. During the company's prosperous years, it tried to prevent relationships with women other than wives through their measures against *parasitism,*[204] and by promoting the duties of wives, such as providing their husbands with a pleasant home that would prevent them from having extramarital sexual relations elsewhere. However, workers did have the financial means for extramarital relationships prior to 2003 and therefore many workers, as was repeatedly emphasised during the *baraza*, did take advantage of the possibility of a *deuxième bureau* (literally a "second office", or second woman). As a female participant commented, the "other woman" was the other side of the coin that the wives accepted, because the husbands provided them with a good life and a house. The men's object of loss today is therefore not only the option of being able to afford a *deuxième bureau* but also the threat to their notion of masculinity, because, as the male participants explained, relationships with other women were also a matter of prestige.

Cuvelier analysed work and masculinity among young artisanal mineworkers in contemporary Katanga. Within the group of men from the same social class, he observed two trends of masculinity practices. Firstly, the attempts to become a distinct social group in order to distinguish themselves from other men in Katanga, and secondly, the workers' awareness of differences among themselves, which led to the development of their "own styles of masculinity" and their "own ways of dealing with the masculinity ideals".[205] In this way, both blue-collar workers and senior officials came together, as *départs volontaires*, in their nostalgia.

Moreover, unlike Cuvelier's description – namely, becoming a distinct social group – the ODVs did not exhibit what Cuvelier calls masculinity practices, such as rude language, a preference for expensive clothes and generally visible signs of what they would consider masculine. However, the ODVs stressed that they suffered from the loss of what they associated with masculinity: not being able to provide for their families, no longer competing in sports, not being able to have a beer with their male friends after work and the financial freedom to enjoy the pleasures of life, one of them being extramarital affairs.

The loss of income affected other areas that the ODVs linked to their role as men. As many of them said they now depended financially on the income of

---

204 See the next section on women's roles and agency.

205 Cuvelier, "Work", 5.

their children. They presented themselves as powerless and stressed that they would be unable to fulfil what they considered to be their duties as fathers and as breadwinners, following a colonial role model established in the years of economic success.[206]

Workers associated the concept of masculinity with that of pride. Above all, the job had offered them an identity as a member of the company, regardless of whether they were blue-collar workers or senior members of staff. Whereas blue-collar workers usually highlighted the benefits of being a worker, such as the income, the ability to educate their children and access to food rations, senior members of staff referred to work as a place where they were able to participate in the development of the company. This conception of work, security, pride and masculinity is contradictory to the roles that were assigned to most women in this context. The last section of this chapter throws light on the well-calculated expectations of domesticity placed on women by the company and the mineworkers.

3.2 *Women's Roles and Agency*

The role of women, especially in relation to domesticity, was shaped by the colonial authorities and the UMHK/Gécamines, and controlled as a strategy to maintain the productivity of workers. Even so, domesticity gave agency to women. Women's roles were presented and discussed by the ODVs, and are the basis for the reference point for men and women today when they look back to the "good old days".

Women were of crucial importance to the productivity of the workers. While they were a danger to that productivity, on the other hand they ensured it. The colonial authorities were generally concerned about the role of women and thus their influence on husbands and men, and on the hygienic conditions of their home, as the following quotation, referring to France's governmental concerns in Senegal, shows:

Je crois que le facteur qui freine l'évolution du fonctionnaire africain est la femme. Il y a en général un décalage trop important entre l'instruction et l'éducation de l'homme et de la femme. Cela se traduit dans la vie matérielle de	I believe that the factor that hinders the evolution of the African civil servant is the woman. In general, there is too great a gap between the education and training of men and women. This is blatant in material

206 Rubbers, "Claiming", 336.

façon flagrante : on verra simultanément par exemple un mari sortant d'une grande école fédérale, à l'esprit ouvert, excellant en son métier, et une épouse aspergeant de jets de salive à la cola les murs de son logement.	life: for example, we will see simultaneously a husband who graduated from a prestigious federal school, with an open mind, excelling in his job, and a wife sprinkling the walls of her home with sprays of cola-flavoured saliva.
L'éducation ménagère de la plupart de femmes de nos fonctionnaires reste à faire.	The housekeeping education of most of the wives of our civil servants is still needed.
Un logement de fonctionnaire célibataire est presque toujours parfaitement propre ; dès qu'il se marie le désordre et surtout la saleté risquent d'entrer chez lui.[207]	A single civil servant's home is almost always perfectly clean; as soon as he gets married, disorder and above all dirt is likely to enter his home.

As this French commander stated, with regard to Senegal in 1952, women had to be educated because otherwise a house would not be clean and safe for an official to live in. Thus, she was a danger to workers' wellbeing.

Secondly, the Belgian colonial state and the UMHK considered women important because they played a central role in maintaining a healthy and thus productive workforce. It was therefore essential not only to control the actual workforce, the workers, during work and leisure time, but equally to educate and constant surveille the women. In this way, they were assigned different roles, spatially and socially, on three intertwined levels – the Belgians' idea(l) of the nuclear family and middle-class life, moral standards, and health, all of which were important pillars of workers' productivity.

3.2.1 Nuclear Family/Middle-Class Life

The nuclear family as the second anchor in a worker's life (besides the work) became relevant after the UMHK concluded that male workers would be more reliable if they got married and became parents. From the 1930s, the company and the colonial administration actively engaged in supporting the marriage of single workers[208] and consulted rural kinfolk to find a spouse.[209] After the

207 Territoire du Sénégal, Cercle Linguère Rapport politique, Commandant du Cercle Gienger, Sénégal 1952, 22–231, FR ANOM 14 MIOM 2738, AOF 2G52/214. I thank Walter Schicho for sharing this file with me.

208 Dibwe dia Mwembu, *Histoire*, 55–61; Rubbers, "Women", 216.

209 AGR 2 – n°2424, Réunions du conseil d'administration, 24.11.1955, 288. The UMHK aimed at stabilising the labour force for a predetermined period between 3 and 18 years; the rural

Second World War, this system was abandoned, and instead the workers were granted leave to find a wife and get married.[210]

The choice of wife was controlled, in that marriages between partners of the same origin were preferred, as Perrings shows: "Where for example men attempted to contract marriages with women of another tribe, the compound managers would refuse to register or recognize the unions, and would not therefore provide either housing or supplementary rations".[211]

In addition, workers were advised to have a civil and church wedding. The company's policy was to promote life-long monogamous marriages, not only to be in line with Christian norms but also to deter men from taking another wife. Polygyny was to be avoided and controlling mechanisms were established. This policy was supported by the colonial administration "which taxed the economic activities of single women in cities and took measures to eradicate the practice of polygamy (Hunt 1991)."[212]

At the end of the colonial period, more and more children born to workers married among themselves. Therefore, there was no more need to search for partners from the villages. Rubbers notes that girls who grew up in Cité Gécamines had a good reputation because they were well educated, and "[i] n contrast with village women, they could speak some words of French, iron clothes, or cook some European food. They were *'évoluées'* ('civilized' women) who could share the 'modern' lifestyle to which these educated men aspired."[213] The women equally appreciated marrying a worker because his wage work promised a comfortable life. By that time, in economic prosperity, workers and their families benefited from the employer who took care of all aspects of life.

In order to place the concept of the nuclear family at the centre of the organisation of a life that corresponded to Belgian ideology, all the traditions brought by the workers from the villages had to be, if not completely eradicated, then at least controlled. In the annual reports of the Département M.O.I.

---

areas would continue to guarantee social security in the event of discharge or retirement. Thus, the UMHK even supported the rural communities financially, for example with 30 million francs in 1955.

210 Rubbers, "Women", 216.

211 Perrings, *Black Mineworkers*, 128–29.

212 Rubbers, "Women", 217.

213 Rubbers, "Women", 219. Rubbers also points out: "Although marriages between spouses of different "tribal" origins became more and more common among the members of the urban elite, they were generally discouraged by both families for practical and moral reasons. Following the Katangese secession (1960–1963), it was also feared that marriages between people from Katanga and Kasaï, or from North and South Katanga, would lead couples to separate if new political tensions re-emerged."

a section on *parasitism* appeared. In 1948, the UMHK stated that it would continue to fight against bigamy and that the second woman should be ignored under any circumstances. The company described the efforts as difficult:

Ce n'est que petit à petit, par une inlassable propagande éducative que nous pourrons définitivement éliminer ces situations anormales. Il faut aussi espérer que le Gouvernement donnera suite au vœu [sic] exprimé par le Conseil de Gouvernement – Session 1948 – de voir interdire progressivement la polygamie dans les centres extra-coutumiers.[214]	It is only little by little, by tireless educational propaganda, that we can definitively eliminate these abnormal situations. It is also hoped that the Government will respond to the wish expressed by the Governing Council – Session 1948 – to progressively ban polygamy in extra-customary centres.

The "abnormal" existence of several wives was not in line with the company's idea(l) of the nuclear family. In addition, bigamy – and extramarital relationships in general – constituted a financial problem. Because workers acknowledged the – according to Europeans' perspective – illegitimate children, they demanded the same rights with respect to housing, education and food rations for these children and their mothers as were granted for the official wife and children. In the annual report of 1947, the UMHK's financial concerns were explicitly verbalised and they emphasised the important status of the nuclear family.[215]

The UMHK and its successor actively promoted the nuclear family and women's intended roles and responsibilities, most of all by the education offered to women in the *foyers sociaux* (social centres). They were, as Hunt describes, "a colonial project to revise and refashion gender roles, family life, and domestic space enacted by European nuns and social workers and African women within classrooms, households, and an African urban community".[216]

The *foyers sociaux* were not specific to the UMHK but had already been introduced by the colonial state in the 1920s.[217] Courses offered to workers' wives focused on domesticity in all its facets. This ensured a clean house, a

214 AGR 2 – n°654-03043, Rapport Annuel 1948, 18.

215 AGR 2 – n°654-03042, Rapport Annuel 1947, 21.

216 Hunt, "Domesticity", 449.

217 "The Union des Femmes Coloniales established the first lay-operated housekeeping and social welfare centers for young girls in two Congolese cities in 1926. Directors of Catholic missions and private social service agencies, with the agreement of the Belgian administration, sent the first social workers to Leopoldville in 1933, Elisabethville in 1934, and Coquilhatville in 1938. Foyers sociaux were opened to

home for the husband and a healthy environment for the family. The UMHK tried to fulfil its efforts to educate women by providing courses, such as sewing classes in 1937:

Dans les sièges de Panda et de M.P.I : les ouvroirs sont dirigés par les Révérendes Soeurs de la Charité. Les fillettes de nos travailleurs y reçoivent un enseignement ménager et des leçons de couture. Au camp de Lubumbashi, l'ouvroir est surveillé par une dame. Cette œuvre est très populaire et les fillettes s'y rendent volontiers.[218]	In the Panda and M.P.I. sites: the workshops are directed by the Reverend Sisters of Charity. The daughters of our workers receive housekeeping and sewing lessons. At the Lubumbashi camp, the workshop is supervised by a lady. This workshop is very popular and the girls attend voluntarily.

On the following page of this report is a detailed overview of the types of clothing the girls had sewn in the course of this workshop. For instance, in Jadotville in 1938: 326 workshop overalls, 3,109 trousers for mineworkers, 3,350 capitulas (shorts) for workers, 2,630 coats for mineworkers, 222 blouses for hospital staff, 1,180 hospital shirts, 225 pillowcases, 504 mattress toppers, 250 uniform dresses and 212 skirts.[219] The girls who attended these sewing classes thus worked for the company, sewing the different types of clothing that the mining company needed and making an economic contribution to it while being trained.

The report further reveals that the UMHK considered only the older girls, who already knew how to sew, as the efficient ones. They were "paid" by being given the food ration entitled to an adult woman:

Ce sont les grandes jeunes filles qui interviennent évidemment le plus dans cette fabrication importante. Elles sont d'ailleurs rémunérées pour le travail qu'elles fournissent et touchent une ration de femme adulte.[220]	It is the older girls who are obviously most involved in this important production. They are also paid for their work and receive an adult woman's ration.

teach home economics and maternal hygiene, in response to what was considered an urgent problem: women living in urban centers". (Hunt, "Domesticity", 450.)

218 AGR 2 – n°654-03038, Rapport Annuel 1938, 12.

219 AGR 2 – n°654-03038, Rapport Annuel 1938, 13.

220 AGR 2 – n°654-03038, Rapport Annuel 1938, 13.

The company and colonial administration argued that women needed to have "useful employment" in order to avoid extramarital activities.[221] Being good homemakers was the focus of this policy. Control of the wives' performance ensured that they would follow these norms.

> Social workers made regular surprise visits to each household, checking that the house was well-ventilated, that beds were made, or that children were clean: if their report was positive, the hostess got a reward; if not, the company summoned her husband to take sanction against him. According to some informants, this control was particularly strict with the members of the Main-d'oeuvre indigène/civilisée (the category of "civilized" employees) and, immediately after independence in 1960, future Congolese managers. Destined to leave the mining camp for managerial villas, the latter had to develop a lifestyle matching up with their future professional status, beginning with the house.[222]

Not only regular surprise visits of homes, but also contests for the most beautiful house, funded by the colonial urban authorities in the 1950s, were meant to "encourage residents of the African urban quarters to decorate their homes according to European tastes".[223] That "not women but married couples entered these contests" (ibid.) demonstrates that the European idea(l) of a marital relationship was also enforced through housing.

The provision of housing was a prominent topic in a propaganda film produced by the UMHK in 1956 to celebrate its 50th anniversary.[224] The film described in detail the benefits of working for the company. These ranged from flying in recruited workers, to the educational system, evening courses, health services and leisure activities. Key topics advertised, besides housing included the company's educational programmes: from kindergarten to primary school, to vocational training for the men, driving lessons and evening courses. to courses especially designed for the workers' wives covering all aspects of a woman's life – according to the colonial perception – childcare, shoe shining, sewing and ironing ties.

In this way, workers and their families were conditioned according to the Belgian ideal of middle-class life. This can be seen, for example, in the description of a typical Sunday. Very similar to Sundays in Europe, it was stated that

221 Rubbers, "Women", 217.

222 Rubbers, "Women", 217.

223 Hunt, "Domesticity", 468.

224 *En Cinquante Ans*, https://www.youtube.com/watch?v=9z4GtyCvlCg&sns=em.

the workers and their families went for a walk or met friends. This particular scene on Sundays ended with the depiction of several people sitting outside at a table covered with a tablecloth with perfectly set glasses. The UMHK used the medium of film to propagandise not only the workplace but also the private life they offered to workers. The company's perception of family life was crucial, with the house, home and domesticity at its centre.

The film comments that (in 1956) 80 per cent of the workers were married. Their civil status, and the wives and their contribution to the workers' wellbeing, was important to the UMHK. The company preferred married men because they were less tempted to go back to their traditional lives and thus its investment in their education was more rewarding.[225] Furthermore, the Belgian authorities and missionaries were concerned about the demographic imbalance in their colony, with men outnumbering women.[226] The reference in the film to the almost balanced ratio between men and women shows the company's awareness of a balanced gender ratio and its pride in the demographic pattern achieved.[227] Still, by presenting an alleged balanced ratio between men and women in the camps, the film depicted a situation that differed from that outside the workers' camps. Compared to unmarried women in the city, married women in the camps were in a stronger position. Hunt states that

> [c]olonial commentators thought women in the cities were floundering, disoriented, vulnerable, and corruptible due to idleness, excessive leisure, and a void of custom. The notion that the moral authority of customary culture did not extend to urban centers was ubiquitous in Belgian Colonial discourse.[228]

Two years before the colonial states' 10-year plan for the development of the colony was published,[229] the layout of an ideal family home started to be discussed by the UMHK, as in colonial publications, interweaving technical aspects with moral values. In the annual report of 1947, for instance, the UMHK briefly mentions the ideal family home under the section "housing", where more technical issues were usually presented. In this annual report, the company explained the advantages of the newly adapted family houses, improved

225 Perrings, *Black Mineworkers*, 82–83.

226 Hunt, "Domesticity", 451.

227 Dibwe dia Mwembu, "La structure", 172, reports that the UMHK indeed managed to balance the ratio. Whereas in 1925 there were 18 women to 100 men, the number rose to 85 women per 100 men by 1960.

228 Hunt, "Domesticity", 451.

229 See also the early section of this chapter on "Stability".

from two to four rooms, designed for larger families. They included, among other rooms, a spacious living room and a cooking area inside and outside. However, the spatial structure was established together with indications of who should use the kitchen and living room:

Si on obtient, grâce à ce living où se réunira la famille, que la femme y prépare les repas, y vive avec son mari et ses enfants et, dernière mais difficile étape, que les repas y soient pris en commun, un pas énorme sera réalisé vers l'évolution de la femme indigène et la constitution de familles suivant la conception européenne.[230]	If we achieve, thanks to this living room where the family gets together, the woman preparing the meals there, living there with her husband and their children, and – the last and most difficult step – the meals being taken together, then a huge step in the evolution of the Congolese/Ruanda-Urundi woman, and the constitution of the family according to the European concept, will have been realised.

The kitchen and the living room served as the anchor point of a woman's existence. She was responsible for cooking and family meals, two aspects that were considered important by the UMHK in the women's evolution towards a "European concept" of their roles.

Domestic work responsibilities of women thus corresponded to a "modern" lifestyle. Rubbers points to the opposing "villagers" who were regarded as "illiterate 'bumpkins'" who maintained village customs. "In such households [...] father, mother, and children were still eating separately, not during a family meal."[231] The scene on sharing the meal in the UMHK's propaganda movie as well as the dining room mentioned in the brochure *À chacun sa maison* thus projected what was successfully implemented among the population's perception.

The "modern lifestyle" not only tied women to domestic work but also meant that they did not have the possibility to engage in any economic activities elsewhere, as participants of the *baraza* stressed. However, Rubbers states that after 1960 it was only the cadres that could fulfil the ideal of "modern" domesticity. It is this group in particular that indulged most in nostalgia.[232]

230 AGR 2 – n°654-03042, Rapport Annuel 1947, 29.
231 Rubbers, "Women", 224.
232 Rubbers, "Women", 224.

3.2.2 Moral Standards

Malevez cites a Belgian domestic manual from 1901 which clearly outlines the woman's duty as a loving wife:

Après une journée de rude labeur, le mari n'est-il pas plus content lorsque, près d'une table bien servie, il trouve une épouse qui l'accueille le sourire sur les lèvres ? Il se sent si heureux qu'il oublie ses fatigues, et, savourant les douceurs de l'intimité, il n'a nulle envie d'aller au dehors chercher des distractions. (Detienne and Voituron-Liénard 1901, 6)[233]	After a day of hard work, is the husband not happier when, at a well-set table, he finds a wife who welcomes him with a smile on her lips? He feels so happy that he forgets his labours and, savouring the sweetness of intimacy, he has no desire to go outside in search of distractions. (Detienne and Voituron-Liénard 1901, 6)

Such domestic manuals established the moral standards for women, whose role was to serve the family and to maintain society. Malevez argues that

> Women's care and involvement in their home meant that, for men, it was the perfect place to forget about the tiredness resulting from their working life and to indulge in « *les douceurs de l'intimité* », which was encouraged, instead of going to the café, for example. The home was deemed an appropriate space for men and it was promoted across social classes as a barrier against moral depravation.[234]

Women's duty as loving wives was also visible in the letters to the editors in *Mwana Shaba*. De Rooij gives us an example from the April 1958 issue, written by a female reader:

> The women who write to Mwana Shaba are few in number, and yet, I know that they like the paper very much and that they would all have things to say. Today I am writing you to ask you if it is silly for women to embrace their husbands when they go to work or when they return. Is that something that makes one laugh or, rather, is it an act of love and reverence that will bring joy to our husbands?
>
> CÉCILE KIBAMBE[235]

233 Malevez, "Les douceurs", 44.
234 Malevez, "Les douceurs", 4.
235 De Rooij, "Letters".

The editor responded with the following note:

> My dear reader [lit.: woman reader], this is not a foolish thing. Rather it would be very good if all women would do like this. To embrace your husband before he goes to work, is just like saying: "It is because of you that we get our soundness, go in peace, I will stay to watch over the house and the children". And if you embrace your husband when he returns it is [like] showing him openly your joy caused by seeing him with you. We transmit to our readers that Mr. Kisimba François from Shinkolobwe calls this a token of love of the Congolese woman.

The main role created for women was thus that of a loving wife and mother who could rely on the husband as the breadwinner. Of course, there is the question whether these letters were actually written by readers or composed by the editors to communicate the desired ideal of the woman.

Not only men, but also women, were to be protected from moral depravity. Although most attempts to clarify women's roles were made by foregrounding their domesticity, in later times there were also some explicit references to *femmes légères* who were seen as the opposite of the ideal woman because they would not contribute to the development of the newly independent Congo. In addition, they were seen as shameful in the context of the emancipation of women and of women who could work and study, as the following excerpt from *Mwana Shaba* in 1966 illustrates:

ETUDIANTE … ET BELLE DE NUIT! Nous rencontrons dans les cités de nos grands centres des jeunes filles qui mènent une double vie: étudiantes pendant la journée … et garces pendant la nuit!

[…] Elles vous diront avec un petit air gêné, qu'il faut se méfier des garçons : "Elles ajouteront même : Il ne faut surtout pas répondre à leur bonjour de peur qu'ils ne poussent plus loin leur politesses. Car du "bonjour" … on passera au "comment va la santé?" ; de là au "où habitez-vous?" et patati et patata … !

STUDENT … AND LADY OF THE NIGHT [prostitutes]! In the housing estates of our major centres we meet young girls who lead a double life: student during the day … and slut at night!

[…] They will tell you, with a little embarrassment, that you should beware of boys: They will even add: "You should not answer their hello for fear that they will push their politeness further. Because from 'hello' … they will move on to 'how's your health?; from there to 'where do you live?' and blah, blah, blah!

[...] Je le répète, vous avez la chance inouïe de pouvoir faire des études et de devenir les premières intellectuelles du pays, de notre Congo qui en a tant besoin. Ne vous laissez pas impressionner par la faux brillant, par le luxe des femmes légères.[236]	[...] I repeat, you have the incredible opportunity to study and to become the first intellectuals of the country, our Congo, which needs it so much. Don't let yourselves be impressed by the false brilliance, by the luxury of "light women" [prostitutes and promiscuous women].

In this text extract, it becomes clear that female students who are out at night are "sluts". The text is addressed directly to such potential readers and formulated in the direct form of address. The middle part even describes how they warn each other about boys who are far too polite and would not bring the luxury they are looking for. In the last part, they are directly called upon not to squander their opportunities. This excerpt emphasises that the role of women was not always depicted as to take care of the home, but always in connection with a call to the tasks they have to perform for society: in this example, in the period after independence, when intellectuals were much needed.

Mama Aimée's earlier account shows not only her outstanding engagement with children of mothers who were *les petites femmes*, but also that unofficial women were always the victims of the moral standards. During colonial times, and before 2003, the UMHK tried to prevent relationships between their male workforce and prostitutes and second wives in the countryside by promoting marriage and by preventing access to the benefits eligible to official wives and children. Equally, the provision of leisure activities in Cité Gécamines was one measure to stop workers from going to the city centre. The hierarchical situation and spatial separation between the official wives and *les petites femmes* was also expressed by a participant during a *baraza*:

La Cité pour les femmes légitimes, les autres ailleurs pour les jours de repos.	The City for the legitimate women, the others elsewhere for the days off.

The "others" thus did not belong to Cité Gécamines. The moral norms were preserved within Cité Gécamines (and also Makomeno). The interviewees were aware that the children of the other women suffered from their unofficial status, as shown in the following statement by a participant who emphasised that there was a time when one was at least able to recognise own's offspring:

236 *Mwana Shaba*, No. 127, June 1966, 11.

On n'a pas reconnu la femme mais avec Mobutu on reconnaît les enfants.	The woman was not recognised but under Mobutu's regime the children were recognised.

3.3 *Health*

UMHK's concern for hygiene and health reflected the Belgian Colonial's endeavour to keep their workforce healthy and productive. In 1953, the *Bureau de l'Information pour Indigènes* (INFIND) *Service des* A.I.M.O. *du Gouvernement Général* published a brochure called *À chacun sa maison*. The main objective, as described in the introductory part of the brochure, was to encourage the Congolese to build houses according to the Grévisse philosophy. This brochure was dedicated to the technical aspects of house building, but interspersed with statements reflecting Belgian ideals about housing in general. The preface started by referring to the house not in a technical sense but as *le vrai foyer* (a real home), not the material object but rather an abstract idea. "Home" was the place where a devoted and loving wife (*l'épouse dévouée, la femme aimante*) and healthy children (*de beaux enfants pleins de santé*) were waiting for the husband. Home and house were thus discursively linked:

Qui n'a rêvé d'être propriétaire d'une jolie maison, d'avoir à soi un vrai foyer où se retrouvent chaque jour l'épouse dévouée, la femme aimante et de beaux enfants pleins de santé?[237]	Who has not dreamed of being the owner of a nice house, of having a real home where every day a devoted wife, the loving woman and handsome healthy children are waiting?

The brochure promoted a certain type of house – European style; it acknowledged that a "traditional" house (referring to Congolese architecture) would be sufficient to meet basic needs but that it could become *plus saine et plus agréable* (healthier and more pleasant) – without investing much more money – if a few improvements were made according to the Belgian ideal. A slogan in bold, capital letters concluded this section, referring to health:

CIVILISATION implique MAISONS SAINES ET CONFORTABLES[238]	CIVILISATION implies HEALTHY AND COMFORTABLE HOUSES

237 Editions du Bureau de l'Information pour Indigènes (INFIND) Service des A.I.M.O. du Gouvernement Général, 3.

238 Editions du Bureau de l'Information pour Indigènes (INFIND) Service des A.I.M.O. du Gouvernement Général, *A chacun sa maison*, 10.

The discourse on housing was dominated by a concern with cleanliness. The UMHK attempted to ensure hygiene by controlling those who were responsible for the house – the workers' wives. Women were not only trained for domestic work in the *foyers sociaux* but later the company also tried to reach women through *Mwana Shaba*, in particular with the section *Votre page madame* (Your page madam). In this section, some articles very explicitly discuss hygiene.

For instance, in the first issue of 1965, *Mwana Shaba* published the article *le grand nettoyage* (the big cleaning).[239] In great detail, every step of cleaning a house was described. Readers learned, for instance, that the woman was expected to use a wet cleaning rag, how to scrub clothes and much more. As a term, however, "the big cleaning" also referred to general domestic hygiene. It stated that it was inappropriate if children slept in dirty clothes. They were supposed to be clean and sleep in a clean bed (*Il faut que l'enfant soit propre pour s'endormir dans un lit propre*).

Moreover, the text emphasised that even insects would not enter a house that was kept clean. The article ended with the notification that the UMHK's *service d'hygiène* would regularly enter a house to disinfect the rooms. Insects, more particularly mosquitoes that passed on malaria, not only threatened an individual's health but constituted a major threat to the productivity of a UMHK worker. As a result, measures to ensure hygiene were articulated in instructions on cleaning the house itself, avoiding health risks from outside, and keeping its inhabitants clean.

In addition, the text was written in the first person imperative, mainly addressed to the reader in direct speech, thus simulating advice from woman to woman. For example, "You should leave all the furniture inside the house" (*Vous devez laisser tout votre mobilier à l'intérieur de la maison*). Direct speech creates proximity between the voice of the narrator and the reader, and thus facilitated the transmission of the UMHK's instructions.

In the same year, in the October issue, the strategy to create proximity to the reader was used in another article that highlighted the woman's role in terms of cleaning.[240] The text described a sewing pattern for a cleaning dress. The reader was again directly addressed, for instance in the concluding sentence "And you will be, Madame, the most elegant housewife" (*Et vous serez, Madame, la plus élégante des ménagères*). The brief preface of this article was written in Swahili and French. Its main message declared that a woman did not have to look sloppy while doing the cleaning. Instead, wearing the proposed cleaning gown would give her a lovely appearance (*ravissante allure*).

239 *Mwana Shaba*, No. 1, January 1965, 13.

240 *Mwana Shaba*, No. 10, October 1965, 19.

This suggestion was followed by the list of the material needed and a manual on how to sew the dress.

Two roles were ascribed to women in this article. Firstly, and as in the first example, a woman was the one responsible for the cleaning (and again, hygiene). Otherwise, the cleaning dress would not have been a topic at all. Secondly, she was expected to fulfil this duty in a style that matched the desired appearance. Her look also mattered, at least in the view of the UMHK. Again, it was the worker's wife who was responsible for a clean house and thus a hygienic environment. Hygiene was essential to the health of a worker and the maintenance of his productivity.

The title of this article, "The joyfulness of housekeeping" (*Le ménage en gaieté*), thus "sold" the UMHK's concern for hygiene under the umbrella of an attractive activity. First of all, the sewing was an activity that was usually carried out in the *foyers sociaux*, where women got together. Second, doing the housework itself was presented as a chance to be "the most elegant housewife", at least if she wore the suggested dress. Her personal appearance mattered, as demonstrated by the numerous articles on women's beauty. Articles were published on the questions of appropriate hair length,[241] a good manicure (complete with a picture of a European woman),[242] good-looking skin[243] and perfect make-up,[244] just to name a few. Women's style received equal attention, from the perfect handbag[245] to how to wear sunglasses.[246]

Many articles referred to a woman's responsibility as a wife and as the one in charge of the household, with recipes, advice on specific problems, such as the right way to clean a scarf,[247] and how to arrange flowers.[248] The art of flower arrangement is interesting because, as Lambertz hints, this was a new concept for the Congolese. Flowers were associated with plants and plants were traditionally used for medicine and not as a decorative object.[249] This article on arranging flowers was written in direct speech and the initial sentences advise the woman to:

---

241 *Mwana Shaba*, No. 10, September 1964, 18.

242 *Mwana Shaba*, No. 10, September 1964, 19.

243 *Mwana Shaba*, No. 12, November 1964, 10.

244 *Mwana Shaba*, No. 9, September 1965, 19.

245 *Mwana Shaba*, No. 10, September 1964, 19.

246 *Mwana Shaba*, No. 11, October 1964, 17.

247 *Mwana Shaba*, No. 11, October 1964, 17.

248 *Mwana Shaba*, No. 13, December 1964, 10.

249 Peter Lambertz, *Seekers and Things: Spiritual Movements and Aesthetic Difference in Kinshasa* (New York, Oxford: Berghahn, 2018).

Fleurissez-le, et votre mari, le soir sera heureux après sa journée de travail de retrouver son beau foyer, et d'y rester …	Fill it [the interior] with flowers, and your husband, in the evening will be happy after his day at work to find his beautiful home, and stay there …

Thus, flowers were presented not only as home decor but first and foremost as a tool for emphasising after-work domesticity to please the husband. The imperative form chosen to address the housewife further attributed to her the power and responsibility for creating the conditions for a worker to be and to remain productive. The wife, who provided him with a comfortable home, should also prevent moral depravity in her husband.

In summary, it can be said that the colonial state and the UMHK promoted women as the ones responsible for domesticity and family, and they tried to save women from moral depravity. Key issues linked to that were health, hygiene, and the preservation of the husband's productivity. The roles ascribed to men (productive worker, breadwinner) were closely interwoven with the roles ascribed to women. Women's agency was essentially reduced to the domestic space. Therefore, the year 2003 and the economic decline that began earlier changed the roles and agency of women enormously.

Mama Aimée's account exemplifies what I was told by all participants and interviewees: the house was the only thing the family had left at the lowest point of the economic crisis. Monthly instalments deducted from the husband's salary resulted in the ownership of private property at a certain point. The house continued to be the place of women's domesticity (because the woman continued to have these duties, as everybody explained to me) but equally was the starting point of their economic activities. Rubbers recalls the local metaphor used since 2003: women are the "locomotive" or "engine" of the family.[250] At the beginning of the economic crisis, many of the interviewees and participants started to build an annex to rent out to tenants and generate an income.

Building additional structures to rent out had its downsides. Many complained that tenants' payment discipline would be poor, that they would not be able to rely on it and would themselves get into trouble with covering their expenses. Sharing a parcel of land implied less space for the property owner, which could lead to less privacy and the potential for conflict. Most of these economic difficulties forced women to search for additional income.

The UMHK's annual reports do not include any comments by women. To talk to women affected by the loss of their husband's income was therefore most insightful. Papa Guillaume, who used to work as a teacher in Cité Gécamines, signed up for a *baraza* on the topic of the roles of women. On the day of this discussion he arrived a bit earlier and handed a very

250 Rubbers, "Women", 224.

neatly hand written document to me, which, as he stated, noted the responsibilities of women "*à l'époque*". He made direct reference to the propaganda movie by the UMHK that I had screened to the members of the ODV some days earlier to share my research material. He said that all he saw in the movie was correct, but that he would like to be very honest with me and add some clarifications.

He listed six points and he interpreted the topic of women's roles as domestic responsibilities that wives had to fulfil towards their husbands. His document was written in French, reflecting first his position as a teacher and therefore his knowledge of French; second, it shows that Swahili was rarely used for written purposes. Over the course of the group discussion, I asked Papa Guillaume to read his points to our group, who consisted of one other man, six women who were wives to workers, and myself.

Two kinds of hierarchy characterised the discussion. First, the respect that Papa Guillaume had among the other attendees because he was a teacher, and second, his command of French. His was the leading voice in the discussion. When he was reading out the points to the group, I invited the others and especially the women to comment. Papa Guillaume translated the points into Swahili because he assumed that the women would understand them better. After each point was read, I asked the women if they agreed and if they would like to add anything. They nodded in agreement and commented *njo vile* (That's the way it is). Papa Guillaume listed the following points:

1.	Être soumise à son mari et le satisfaire dans le besoin sexuel afin d'accomplir la procréation que prône genèse.	1.	To be submissive to her husband and satisfy his sexual needs in order to accomplish procreation as Genesis advocates.
2.	Être toujours prête pour son manger avant d'aller au travail et le réveiller en cas où il a pris un verre de trop la veille.	2.	To always have his meal ready before he heads to work and wake him up in case he drank too much the day before.
3.	S'occuper de la vaisselle, de la lessive et autres travaux ménagers.	3.	Take care of dishes, laundry and other housework.
4.	Préparer chaque jour de l'eau pour son bain après les heures de travail et son repas du soir.	4.	Every day prepare water for his bath after work and his evening meal.
5.	Préparer les enfants chaque jour avant d'aller à l'école et s'il y a lieu amener le bébé à la pesée au centre de santé.	5.	Prepare the children every day before sending them to school and if necessary take the baby to the weigh-in at the health centre.
6.	Faire les achats pour le menu du jour au marché de la place ou dans les magasins.	6.	Make purchases for the day's menu at the market place or in the shops.

The first point Papa Guillaume listed most surprised me. During the interviews in the previous two years, nobody had ever mentioned sex explicitly. His wording refers to the biblical commands to "grow and multiply", from the book of Genesis. In the Swahili translation for the women though, he erased this reference and simply translated it into "make children". Therefore, I assumed that the French version was mainly addressed to me; the reference to a biblical quotation legitimised raising the sensitive topic of women being responsible for the fulfilment of men's sexual needs by arguing that this corresponded to the assignment in the book of Genesis. The production of offspring, though, was also in the interest of the mining company. Children who grew up as children of workers were the basis of the future workforce.

A woman's responsibility for preparing meals is addressed in the second and fourth point. In connection with breakfast, her duty to wake up her husband is mentioned. He needed to be woken up, especially in case he had a glass too many the night before. Implicitly we learn that, for men, the consumption of alcohol during their leisure time was considered reasonable; this was not expected from women. The company controlled where workers drank because of the lower beer prices in the *cercle*, while it was a wife's duty to ensure that he would still be on time and productive the next day. As point three shows, the wife was responsible for converting him from a working man to a man at leisure by preparing the bath water. However, I read the perception of women's duties by Papa Guillaume not primarily as an assessment by him in his role as a husband, but rather as a representation of the education system for women that was characterised by its essentially practical and utilitarian orientation.[251] The utilitarian approach of the Belgian colonial system marginalised women, preventing them from entering the areas of administration and industry, and aimed to keep them in their roles of wives and mothers.[252]

The wife was presented as responsible for childcare, as point four illustrates. Point six refers again to a wife's responsibility for meals and grocery shopping. Papa Guillaume added a line to the last point, the importance of *mposho*, the weekly food ration that was given to a single man, couples without children and families, but which differed in quantity. He explicitly mentioned flour, meat, fish, beans, rice, palm oil and potatoes. Thus, the women were buying additional ingredients on their daily shopping trip.

There was obviously no legal basis to Papa Guillaume's presentation of women's responsibilities, but it reflected the norms that women were expected to uphold within that community. He added that to access finances women

251 Masandi, "L'Éducation", 498.
252 Masandi, "L'Éducation", 498.

were dependent on their husbands sharing their income. Taking care of the house, domestic work, the children, the husband and their health was thus the key to her financial resources.

Papa Guillaume stressed that Christian marriage, as the UMHK promoted it starting from the colonial period, was still the ideal. Marital relationships, however, faced important changes. Rubbers states that his interview partners claimed that "they were now living according to the ideal of the Christian couple" and that

> [T]his celebration of fidelity and cooperation between husband and wife at least partly comprised an attempt by workers to rationalize more recent developments that were not entirely desired or expected. Their discourse about proper marital life was passing over a complex history in silence – a history rooted in Gécamines social policy since the 1920s.[253]

Rubbers argues that the husband-wife relationship has changed since the 1960s. As mentioned earlier, the UMHK considered women as a key factor for the stabilisation of workforce and ensurement of productivity.

The participants during the *baraza* emphasised that men were expected to take care of the family financially. The loss of income thus radically changed the relationship between men and women. Men could no longer fulfil their role as the breadwinner. One interviewee stated, in a resigned way, that many of them, himself included, had been left by their wives, and that they would have no chance of finding another wife because they were no longer able to provide a good life, as they had been able to at the beginning of their working careers.

In the mid-1990s, the economic situation of workers became difficult for two reasons. First, due to hyperinflation, and second, the irregular wages paid by the Gécamines. This situation had two implications for women. Firstly, women, who had been housewives since their marriage, were forced to contribute to the household income due to the miserable economic situation of the family, e.g. by expanding their activities to starting farm land outside the Cité Gécamines or by starting to run small businesses. Secondly, families had to sell everything they had in their house.[254]

I have outlined objects of loss about which the ODVs' were particularly nostalgic: stability, *kazi*, leisure, space, *heshima*, masculinity, and women and domesticity. With regard to women and domesticity, it was revealing to see

253 Rubbers, "Women", 214.
254 Rubbers, "Women", 224.

that what male workers mostly considered a privilege of masculinity was in fact a calculated means by the company to monitor other aspects of domestic life for the sake of better productivity and cost reduction. These are guises of workers' nostalgia, the main subject of the book framed in the first words of the book's title: "*C'était bien à l'époque mais l'avenir iko sombre*". In the following chapter, I review an attempt to mediate their nostalgia by putting forward the discussions that are the basis of our joint knowledge production, which is indicated in the book's subtitle: *Negotiating Nostalgia with and among Ex-Mineworkers in Lubumbashi* (DRC).

CHAPTER 5

Negotiating Nostalgia

It was a sunny Sunday afternoon in Vienna and I was going for a walk during another COVID-19 lockdown, when a dozen WhatsApp messages reached me from Lubumbashi. Marc thought he was in trouble. And I knew that he usually spent Sundays with his wife at church. Something really must have been bothering him. He texted that he could not yet send me the ODVs' scanned minutes of the *baraza* because the secretary of the ODV had asked him for the exact name of "my cameraman", by which he meant my colleague Carl-Philipp Bodenstein, who was documenting the *baraza* together with the Lubumbashi-based video artist Gulda.

Marc added that the secretary had presented a draft of the minutes to him but felt that it was not yet ready to give to me, and that the secretary wanted to find someone (provided that I pay for this service) to type up his handwritten minutes. Marc (himself born to a UMHK worker) commented in a slightly cynical way: "*Ils sont trop administratifs, ce sont des vrais gécaminois*" (They are too bureaucratic, they are real Gécaminois). I thought this was an extremely interesting comment. It reflected what Marc and I both had noticed during our meetings with the ODVs: that they are organised in a most formal way. Their approach would have been – as Marc assessed it so often during my stays in Lubumbashi – "a little out of time".

The ODVs were very strict about meeting procedures, which seemed – as Marc and I noted earlier in Lubumbashi – like an imitation of the organisational procedures of the UMHK/Gécamines they had worked for in the good old days. We interpreted this as their appreciation for an approach that was used when they were still being cared for. Marc's remark also revealed how the next generation views their parents. I had often heard similar words: they are Gécaminois. Therefore, they would have their own interpretation of things and focus too much on the past.

It took a few messages back and forth to clarify that I would be happy to have the opportunity just to read the minutes. I told Marc that I was used to reading handwritten texts and therefore did not need a typed version; I would have to type the extracts I would present in this publication myself anyway. And above all, the verbatim minutes of that time would be more valuable to me than a revised version. Hours later, I thought about what I had written to Marc and realised that I had once again violated my own claim to let the ODVs decide for themselves what they wanted to tell me, and how. I wanted to see the minutes

 | DOI:10.1163/9789004724907_006

at that very moment to have an "authentic" snapshot of them and was ignoring their wish to provide me with a proper and well-prepared document.

That was part of the content of the messages I received that afternoon. The rest of the news was about money. Marc reported that at the last meeting the other ODV board members had expressed that they also were in a precarious economic situation. The "also" was triggered by me sending money to the secretary through Marc to fund his efforts to compile the minutes of the *baraza* for me and scan them in a shop in town. Marc had advised me to compensate the secretary for his effort and of course expenses. From the beginning of my research trips to Lubumbashi, Marc had always advised me well and knew how to navigate me through the very difficult issue of money. He was well aware that my research budget included what research budgets usually include (flight, accommodation, sometimes a daily allowance). He knew at which moments it was appropriate for me to offer at least food and drinks, copies of pictures taken, allowances for transport, etc.

I will not go into detail about the finances, because this is a very complicated question. I mention it here because the "also" in the sentence made me angry that afternoon. Maybe I was just having a bad day, but I was so tired of the money issue and I felt, I realised later, like prey in a spider's web. The ODVs and I had discussed this again and again at every meeting I had attended, and I had made it clear that I would not be able to solve their problem and get them the compensation they were asking for. They were fully understanding each time; they expressed their satisfaction and hope that I would write about them. They gave me gifts, like the copper rooster and malachite jewellery. And at the same time, we kept discussing money.

I comment on that Sunday afternoon's WhatsApp messages for two reasons. First, they illustrate, in brief, the challenges and opportunities, the beautiful and the displeasing sides of research with a group whose economic situation is dire. Second, thoughts in this context are important to me because of our roles, which were constantly adapted while being entangled.

To think of our entanglement helped me to better understand the negotiation processes during the research. In this chapter, I explain the communication between the participants and the reading and interpretation of themes and roles. After all, it was a challenge for everyone involved to discuss and negotiate a master narrative that I, but also the children of Gécamines ex-workers, felt was ever-present.

To begin with, I describe the report provided by the ODVs on the research visit in July 2019, to illustrate what they presented as the key message of our *baraza*. I classify their report as a strategy of performative nostalgia; they reconstruct our joint discussions in such a way that their core message remains in the foreground.

1 Report by ODVs on Research Stay in July 2019

The four-page report on the events during my research stay on the occasion of the *baraza* was written in November 2020 and is based on the notes taken by the secretary of the ODVs at all meetings and events related to the *baraza* (see Appendix 1). The formalistic text fits the genre of a "protocol", as they called it.

The first thing one notices is the full details of the participants' names and locations. I am referred to as "Mlle Daniela Waldburger" and later in the report as "Mlle Daniela".[1] During our conversations, I addressed my interlocutors as "*mama*" or "*papa*" and their first names, thus exactly as they were introduced to me or had introduced themselves.

However, the board members had to be addressed by the title of their function, as this was how they were introduced to me. I addressed the president as "*Monsieur le president*", the secretary as "*Monsieur le secrétaire*", and so on. The ODVs also addressed the board members in this way, even though they had been friends and colleagues for decades. As Marc noted, the ODVs were acting out the hierarchical structure of the company in which they had been socialised, even in the period after their employment and their collective struggle for compensation. For example, the president is mentioned several times in the report, with his title and full name. The director of the Waza Arts Centre is also mentioned by title and name; however, his wife and business partner is titled only as "*Madame*" and her first name. The secretary signed the report as "*secrétaire rapporteur*" and his full name. The two video artists were referred to as "*cameramen*" followed by their full names.

The correct names of the videographers were of importance to the secretary. As Marc's message conveyed, the secretary felt that the report would not have been correct without the name of my colleague from Vienna. Although the president and secretary are highlighted by mentioning their functions, they were nevertheless constructed as part of the ODVs, as "*nos camarades*" (our comrades). The term unifies all those suffering and fighting together; the secretary uses the possessive pronoun "our" and thus describes himself and the president as equal to the other ODVs. The in-group of the workers is described at the very beginning of the report: *ex-agents de la Gécamines* (*surnom départs volontaires*).

The report starts with the section *points de vue* (points of view), where two short points serve as the abstract. The first point states that the meetings, interviews and *baraza* (in July 2019 – the date is not mentioned in the sentence)

1 The ODVs called me "*Mama Daniela*" during my visits, using "*Mama*" as a term of courtesy. "*Mademoiselle*" is traditionally applied to unmarried women but is also often used to stress the youthfulness of a female counterpart.

were about understanding the social life of ODVs; the second point states that the purpose was to understand the time before, during and after employment (the secretary chose the term "*service*"). Seven lines are then dedicated to explaining that the president was informed by the director of the Waza Arts Centre about my arrival and my wish to talk with the ODVs. Thus, the secretary frames the events that were planned for "Mitaani #mapping Moments" by the Arts Centre and myself as my wish, even though the Centre and the members of the ODV board had already held a preparatory meeting before my arrival to discuss the idea of the *baraza* and shared authority.

The next point describes the first meeting with the ODVs after my arrival. It took place at the Waza Arts Centre, and all participants from Waza, the video artists and I are mentioned by full name, whereas the ODV board members who attended are not named. The secretary adds that the members came after their weekly meeting on Friday, a meeting that was supervised by the president. Although this point seems irrelevant to me in terms of what happened at our meeting on this Friday, it was important to the secretary to mention it. He then explains that the delegation, referring to the Waza Arts Centre, my colleague and myself, got in contact with the local ODV branch who "*répresentent tous les ex-travailleurs de la Gécamines*" (represent all ex-workers of Gécamines). Thus the ODV delegation is presented as the voice of all ex-workers and therefore their individual names do not matter.

The report goes on to say that to plan the interviews in Cité Gécamines we met in one of the churches. The secretary uses the term "interviews" in reference to the *baraza*. Choosing the church as the right place to discuss the *baraza* was done after the representatives of the Waza Arts Centre and I had gone on a tour to search for a place that would offer enough space; we suggested the church to the ODV board, who agreed. In the following sentences the secretary reports on the event that we (members of Waza and myself) called the "trigger event". This event was held to share my research idea and archival material with the ODVs, and to discuss the forthcoming *baraza*'s possible topics, not only with the ODV board (who had already agreed to the idea) but also with the other ODVs, who approved them.

In reference to the archival material I presented, the secretary mentions only the screening of the propaganda film, produced in 1956 on the occasion of the 50th anniversary of the UMHK. He records that the film portrays the situation during the colonial period and emphasises his view of it, namely, that indeed "*la vie des travailleurs était très bonne*" (the life of the workers was very good). The report then summarises the discussions among the participants that followed the screening during the trigger event, taking up the ODVs' narrative:[2]

2 The extracts from the report are quoted faithfully, without correction of typos.

La vie sociale des travailleurs était bonne, les salaires étaient payés chaque quinzaine du mois et les ravitaillements étaient réguliers, les écoles foncionner normalement et les soins medicaux étaient au rendez-vous.

The social life of the workers was good, wages were paid every fortnight of the month and supplies were regularly replenished, schools functioned normally and medical care was available.

The next section describes what happened after 2003, which the secretary describes as a turning point, but which was not part of the event's discussion. I think he included it because it was important for him to once again emphasise the precarious situation of the ODVs today. It is therefore a statement that is dedicated to me, as it contains details that are known to all the former workers concerned, to remind me again, as the researcher, of the ODVs' struggles:

Les ex-travailleurs de la Gécamines vivent actuellement dans la precarité qui n'a pas de nom; la vie sociale ne se justifie pas tout a été jeter dans l'eau. Avant de mettre fin à la carrière, l'ex travailleurs de la Gécamines ont fait trente-six mois d'arrières des salaires, ensuites les miettes payes à compte goutte ont durée six mois, on payer cent personnes par jour. Debute au mois d'août 2003 pour cloturer en janvier 2004.

The former Gécamines workers are currently living in a precarious situation that has no name; social life is not justified, everything has been thrown into the water. Before ending their career, the former Gécamines workers were thirty-six months in arrears on their wages, then the crumbs paid in dribs and drabs for six months, paying one hundred people a day. It started in August 2003 and ended in January 2004.

The section that follows is titled *Évaluation*. Under this point the secretary sums up that after the screening of the film the participants were served drinks and baked goods. The other archive material I presented remains unnamed, but the exact name of the venue is repeated in full length, as well as the fact that I had asked the *camarades* to register for interviews and photos. Once again, here, "interview" refers to the planned *baraza*. By using the term "*camarades*" I am represented as a fellow campaigner of the ODVs.

The secretary does not mention that during this event the topics discussed for the *baraza* were based on suggestions that I had extracted from interviews during my previous two stays in Lubumbashi. The secretary mentions the photo sessions that would go along with the *baraza*; these had not been suggested before nor been a topic in the earlier discussions. However, he lays out a wish, knowing from previous years that I had a camera and that I took pictures whenever the ODVs asked me to do so, and provided them with printed copies.

There was always a very high demand for printed copies. The secretary continues to describe that around 50 *camarades* signed up for the *baraza*.

In the next point the topics of the *baraza* are listed. However, the secretary framed the topics in the way he thought to be correct. What I, for instance, described as "*surveillance*", he described as "*sécurité*". What I intended to describe as the roles of men and women is described as *marriage and divorce*.

The following part of the report records that during the *baraza* the video artists had taken pictures. During the trigger event, it was discussed whether the ODVs would agree to be filmed, and there were no objections. The representatives of the Waza Arts Centre argued that the videos would not only serve as the raw material for the video artists to produce a movie about them but would also preserve the voices of the ODVs and ensure that their statements would not be forgotten.

The report continues by stating that all participants of the *baraza* (again the term "interview" is used) received an invitation for what we called the *grand baraza* at the Waza Arts Centre. The secretary then noted that during that event the participants were welcomed by the director of the Arts Centre and shown the drawn and labelled boards, referring to the cartoons created by the artist Colby (see Appendix 2), which illustrated the interviews between the ODVs and Mlle Daniela. To finish our sharing, as described in the report, beer and soft drinks were offered by Mlle Daniela and Monsieur Carl-Philipp. The last part of the report mentions that each participant received an envelope with money to pay the bus transfer costs to the Waza Arts Centre and back home to Cité Gécamines. The following sentence concludes the report:

En gros-modo, voilà l'arrivée et le retour de Mlle Daniela Waldburger et Monsieur Carl Philipp Bodenstein parmi les ex-travailleurs de la Gécamines (surnomé ODV) licencie abusivement.	In short, this is how we can describe the arrival and return of Miss Daniela Waldburger and Mr Carl-Philipp Bodenstein among the former workers of Gécamines (nicknamed ODV), the unfairly dismissed.

With the last two words, the secretary stresses that the ODVs were treated unjustly, and refers to Opération Départ Volontaire, when they were made redundant in 2003. He thus sustains the ODV narrative in his conclusion to the report on the *baraza*. In summary, the report encapsulates what the secretary considered to be the most important points, but does not represent the different points of view that shaped our discussions and negotiations during the *baraza* on concepts and terms.

2 In the *barazaweb*

Following Deppermann et al. on communicative practices, specific body-object-space constellations are indispensable as co-players in a situation where communication takes place.[3] Thus, bodies and spatial constellations become constitutive participants in many action situations.

As described earlier, the *baraza* were held in the house where the ODVs had their regular meetings. We (members of the Waza Arts Centre and myself) were thus guests, "intruders", although very much welcomed. In the following, I focus on the negotiation processes during the *baraza*.

The ODVs' aim – to frame it provocatively – was to maintain their narrative and convince me repeatedly of their precarious economic situation. They therefore first had to create their group, their community. Bennett explains that the "idea of an original community means that the sense of place, for these people, is 'driven by time'".[4] I consider the ODVs to be driven by time, in that the turning point in 2003 radically changed their life.[5] The association of the ODV was created in that moment. The members share a history as employees of the UMHK/Gécamines and the experience of a shaken present with an uncertain future.

Writing about her research on the importance of historical, social and material connections in belonging to place, Bennett indicates:

> The respondents were all keen to create an identity for themselves as authentic members of this community in the past, as did Back's (2009) market traders. Back (2009), Green (2013), Savage et al. (2005), Robertson et al. (2008), Fortier (1999) and Blokland (2001, 2003) all show how individuals place themselves in an explicit moral relationship to a past community through eliciting memories which are distant enough to create

3 Arnulf Deppermann, Helmuth Feilke and Angelika Linke, "Sprachliche und kommunikative Praktiken: Eine Annäherung aus linguistischer Sicht", in *Sprachliche und kommunikative Praktiken*, eds. Arnulf Deppermann, Angelika Linke and Helmuth Feilke, Jahrbuch des Instituts für Deutsche Sprache (Berlin, Boston: De Gruyter Mouton, 2016).

4 Julia Bennett, "Narrating Family Histories: Negotiating Identity and Belonging Through Tropes of Nostalgia and Authenticity", *Current Sociology* 66, no. 3 (2018): 452.

5 Makori, who also writes about the ODVs and their nostalgia, raises the question of what configures the local experiences of time: "[g]iven the tumultuous history of the emergence of pensioners and creuseurs in Congo, what particular event can be designated as the rupture that fundamentally altered economic life in Katanga?" Makori's interest focuses on his interviewees'experiences in ways that often confound strict periodicity, such as "colonial" and "post-colonial" era, "industrial past" and "liberalised present", or the end of the Cold War (Makori, "Artisanal Mines", 111–16.)

> a distinct sense of "otherness" with the present. "We" then become the group who can "remember", and "they" are those who cannot (Blokland, 2001). Being an authentic member of the community is, as Back (2009) says, "a moral project". Only the authentic "we" can draw on the nostalgic tropes of memories of "our" past.[6]

Bennett concludes that authenticity is connected to nostalgia because people create a sense of continuity by linking back to shared origins. Thus, I consider the construction of the "we" among the ODVs to be one of the underlying aspects of their nostalgia. Nostalgia can be seen to happen only in the present and only in opposition to the past. The creation of an authentic "we" brings past and present together.

Bruner discusses narratives that he evaluates as "a version of reality whose acceptability is governed by convention and 'narrative necessity' rather than by empirical verification and logical requiredness".[7] He identifies ten features of narratives, of which the second in his list, "particularity", is useful for my undertaking to pin down the ODVs' master narrative. "Narratives take as their ostensive reference particular happenings. But this is, as it were, their vehicle rather than their destination."[8]

> Particularity achieves its emblematic status by its embeddedness in a story that is in some sense generic. And, indeed, it is by virtue of this embeddedness in genre, to look ahead, that narrative particulars can be "filled in" when they are missing from an account. The "suggestiveness" of a story lies, then, in the emblematic nature of its particulars, its relevance to a more inclusive narrative type. But for all that, a narrative cannot be realised save through particular embodiment.[9]

The individuals' perspective on the past that existed before that moment may vary, but among the ODVs they are all connected as *camarades,* as they stressed frequently. They share being *départs volontaires* and are thus united as an in-group. The creation of that "we" first required that former staff of different categories – senior staff and blue-collar workers – agreed to join together in one group. Thus, the social relationships distinguished by class while they were employed, and could be categorised as one-dimensional, changed to a

6 Bennett, "Narrating", 453.

7 Jerome Bruner, "The Narrative Construction of Reality", *Critical Inquiry* 18, no. 1 (1991): 4.

8 Bruner, "Narrative", 6.

9 Bruner, "Narrative", 7.

creation of "we" beyond the former labels of being a blue-collar worker or a senior staff member. Consequently, the ODVs, formerly separated not only by the classification of work and its hierarchical affiliation but also by the neighbourhoods in which they were living (blue-collar workers in Cité Gécamines and senior staff members in Makomeno), created a network beyond geographically confined boundaries.[10] Unsurprisingly, though, the members who had been working in blue-collar positions outnumbered the members in senior staff positions.

During the *baraza* the participants thus presented themselves as an in-group, as *camarades* beyond the formerly existing class differences, and as one group that adhered to their master narrative. The following is a description of the six *baraza* with some excerpts that illustrate how the ODVs maintained the narrative.

2.1 *Baraza One*

Planned to talk about the role(s) of women.

Setting: Two men (the secretary of the ODVs and a former teacher), six women (one of them the widow who was the owner of the house that served as the meeting place of the ODVs; she had no teeth, which made communication difficult, but she usually expressed her joy by dancing and singing at the end of a baraza), myself, Carl-Philipp, Gulda, Patrick Mudekereza and Sari Middernacht of the Waza Arts Centre, the last two both taking notes.

We (the ODV board members, members of the Waza Arts Centre and myself) agreed that my role should be to officially welcome everybody and start the *baraza*. However, it was one of the two men, the secretary of the ODV, who took a leading role at the beginning by suggesting that everybody should introduce themselves. To state our names was important to him and most likely to the other participants, so that the attendees from the Waza Arts Centre, who were there to take notes, would be able to carefully report on those attending. And the secretary, who was present as participant and/or observer during most of the *baraza,* equally noted down all the names as part of his careful documentation of the process. He wrote these notes in the very same book where all the weekly meetings of the ODVs were written down.

10 Urban neighbourhoods in Europe from the 19th century to the 1950s were also relatively class homogeneous. Blokland describes the small-scale areas with clear borders and cohesive communities in Rotterdam and argues that class is also tied to space, and that people can use the production of places to form social identity (Blokland, "Bricks", 268).

I started the discussion by stating that we agreed during the trigger event that during this *baraza* we would talk about the roles of women. The former teacher announced that he had prepared a list of the duties of women and started to present them, but I interrupted him by asking if he was referring to wives of workers, working women or women in general. I insisted that we should clarify the terms "*femme travailleuse*" (working woman) and "*femme*". So, I learned, "*femme*" usually referred to a woman married to a worker and preferably a mother of several children, because as the former teacher stressed: "*la femme, zamani uko pale kusoutenir bwana*" (the woman, in the former times, was there to support the husband). On my request that he continue after my interruption, he stated that ideally, at that time, the woman stayed home, and then continued with the list of duties. He concluded that "*anasurveiller nyumba, anasurveiller batoto*" (she takes care of the house, she takes care of the children).

However, he stressed, a "*femme travailleuse*" was not able to fulfil these responsibilities; her house was dirty. This was also the reason, as the two male participants added, why it was the husband who decided if the wife was permitted to take up employment. Women who worked for the company were, as the teacher explained, treated very badly at the workplace. Therefore, men usually preferred that their wives take care of the house and the children, a role for which they got *heshima* (respect). In addition, they were in a place where they were treated well.

The attending women kept quiet, listened and did not add anything to these points, but nodded in agreement. The manner of the men's discussion did not invite the women to contribute; it was a presentation by the teacher to me of how things had been during those glorious times. The teacher, the educated one, took on the role of the historian to explain how things had been. The women were silent, the form of language expected from them.

During the individual interviews I had conducted in the two previous years, however, I was very often told by women that for them it was extremely important to have employment too, because it was there at the workplace where they would have experienced *heshima*, and not at home. During the *baraza* this point was not raised, and therefore I queried whether working women would have experienced *heshima* at work too. The attending women stressed that it was very important "*kuheshimia baba ya nyumba*" (to respect the head of the household). However, they did not explicitly say that they experienced *heshima* at home. Thus, it seemed that they did not want to contradict the teacher's statement directly; they confirmed that it was important to respect the husband without referring to the actual question.

We agreed during the trigger event that the ODVs should choose and attend whichever *baraza* they were interested in. There was no *baraza* exclusively for women. However, there was no guarantee that a women's discussion group would have revealed more insights into their perspective than the mixed group did. What is more, to hold one could have raised unnecessary suspicions about my project.

There was not only the question of gender but – and maybe equally important – that of the hierarchies among the participants. The secretary and the former teacher both had a leading voice in the ODVs' battle for compensation and were the leading voices when we discussed this point. One of the reasons might have been the language choice. Whereas I was using French and Swahili, the two men spoke French only. The teacher took on the role of interpreter, as indeed some of the women seemed to be more competent in Swahili than in French. Linguistically, the women were thus handicapped. With the teacher translating most of the French quotations, it was with "his help" that the women agreed to the men's conclusion that it was a matter of "*mentalité et education*" (mindset and education) that women preferred to stay home instead of taking up employment. Most women worked before they married, but, the teacher emphasised, the woman's *heshima* grew with the change of marital status.

We then discussed the status of unmarried women and married women without children. The teacher stated, and all the women nodded in agreement, that if a couple did not conceive children there was pressure applied on the husband by his family to search for another woman: "*Il était obligé de solliciter d'une autre femme d'essayer un peu d'avoir la chance*" (He was forced to ask another woman to try a bit of luck).

I drew attention to "unofficial women", by citing a woman I had interviewed a year earlier who stated that "in the Cité men behaved liked saints but those who had children in the city were numerous". I intended to discuss the perceptions of different hierarchies among women in the society based on whether they were married to a worker or were in an unofficial relationship with him. The first reaction of one of the two men was to point out that this was the system of polygamy. The other took the floor and agreed that there were indeed "those women" but that we were now in this *baraza* to talk about the roles of women – in their understanding, the duties of women. The discussion thus reached a point where the master narrative of the male ODVs as victims of circumstance was challenged by a topic that was not mentioned in the interviews before: the existence of "other women".

At this moment one of the women spoke up. Whereas earlier she was silenced, or preferred to be silent, she became the leading voice. She confirmed that other women existed, but underlined that it was the *femme de ménage* (housewife) who was the respected one. "*Les deuxièmes femmes ne puissent pas déranger les femmes Gécamines, la femme était bien respectée par la Gécamines*" (The second women could not bother Gécamines women, the official woman was well respected by the Gécamines), someone commented. When I then asked if the women who worked for the company were respected in the same way, she explained that the problem of the working woman was that the husband was neglected and it was no surprise then that he went to see another woman. The participant who uttered this statement was a wife of an ODV who had stayed at home to take care of the children and the household, as I knew from the interviews in the years before. I thus understood her statement mainly as making clear to me that she was respected, in contrast to the (possible) "other woman". I read her statement as a self-empowered expression of the respect she had had, and lost, like everyone else.

The discussion moved on to the *femme célibataire* (single woman), who the participants considered to be in a kind of waiting room until she got married. Thus, as the attending men and women concluded, to have children within a marriage was the most important matter for women as well as men: "*On était respecté*" (one was respected) – again the notion of *heshima*.

I asked the attendees how respected a woman was who was a senior staff member and married to a blue-collar worker. I was told that this was rarely the case. However, in such a case, she would not have been as respected for her senior position as a man, because – and this would have been true for all aspects of life – "*le pouvoir était toujours avec le mari*" (the power was always with the husband).

The question of power and the right of the man over the woman took an interesting turn when we discussed access to wages. The former teacher asserted that in the case of the woman and husband both being employed, the two wages would have been combined. However, the women present objected immediately. One of them said that if the woman was employed it would have been her money, while the two men shook their heads to demonstrate that this had not been the case à *l'époque*. It is worth noting that none of the women attending this *baraza* had been employed in earlier times; they were married to former workers and took care of the house and the children. They were thus sharing their opinion on this topic during the *baraza* without first-hand experience.

The secretary and the teacher then linked the point of access to money to the many cases they knew where a man had been left by his wife around 2003 because he was not able to offer her a good life anymore (the secretary emphasised that he personally had been affected by this). On the one hand, the two men criticised such women for indirectly expressing their greed with regard to the man's salary. On the other hand, they stated that the Opération Départ Volontaire in 2003 was the pivotal moment that left them powerless to take care of their wives. Thus, losing their employment was when many lost their wives. They saw 2003 as the turning point when good marital relationships were destroyed, which boiled down to the loss of an aspect that remained crucial to them: respect – *heshima*.

The women in the group then took the lead and recounted their own experiences of pay day, which was on the 15th of every month. The woman who started this discussion said that on the 15th, he (the husband) was the boss; then he disappeared, and on the 25th he came back and then she suffered. The other women nodded in agreement while the men disagreed; an emotional, very fast discussion ensued for several minutes. I was able to follow only partially. When they calmed down, the teacher summarised for me in a very short sentence that the women had sometimes suffered but that this would have been the exception. That a husband would have used the money for his own enjoyment certainly would have been an exceptional case. In this way, the teacher attenuated the women's complaint; I understood his move as a strategy to provide me with an image of decent and upright fellows, which reinforced his performance of masculinity as understood in this cultural context.

Since the teacher had presented the duties of women *à l'époque*, I asked about the duties of the men. The secretary said that this was not something to discuss; the man was the one working and thus had no obligations. Nobody commented on that statement. So I switched topic and asked the women what they considered to be the most important issues in their life before 2003. They mentioned harmony between husband and wife, to be respected and what they described as "*éducation dans la famille*" (education in the family). The teacher did not nod to the woman who mentioned these three points but at me, and he commented: "*Elle a bien répondu*" (she responded well). Thus the teacher was in a position that he thought required him to assess the woman's statements and he did so by using the third person singular and addressing his judgement of the woman's performance to me.

It is obvious that the teacher and the secretary wanted to ensure (consciously or unconsciously) that the group's performance this day was in line with the narrative of *c'était bien à l'époque*. The criticisms by women of some men who used the salary that was for the family for outside pleasures were not translated by the teacher at all, or only in an abbreviated version. Thus, he again deleted the women's voices, although they were present. It was mainly the teacher and the secretary who set up the rules of this *baraza*: first, by their choice of language for the *baraza*, insisting that the official language of the discussion would be French, the language the women were less familiar with; second, by deciding whether a topic was worth being discussed or not. I regard this as masculinity at play, or nostalgic attempts to keep some lost privileges.

2.2 *Baraza Two*

Planned to talk about surveillance and control.

Setting: Six men (one of them the teacher), myself, Carl-Philipp, Gulda, Patrick Mudekereza and Sari Middernacht of the Waza Arts Centre, the last two taking notes.

During the trigger event we had agreed on this topic for a *baraza* after I had suggested it, based on my archival material and the interviews. I had proceeded from the assumption that the ex-mineworkers must have suffered from the measures taken by the UMHK/Gécamines to control their work life and private life. However, during the *baraza* it became clear that the ODVs missed the surveillance and control of that time and that they understood these concepts differently from me. For them, surveillance and control were proof of being taken care of well.

We started this session with an introductory round of statements, everybody sharing why they chose to attend this discussion. The first participant stated that this topic was important because his former employer had indeed offered surveillance, in taking care of workers who were ill; in addition, their health was surveyed because there used to be a health check every three years. The second participant agreed that these were exactly the reasons that motivated him to join this discussion. The third participant stated that his former job was to control machines and so he felt that he wanted to contribute to this discussion. The fourth participant also held a position that was, as he explained, linked to surveillance. He used to work for the mining company's department of industrial safety. Another participant added that he had joined this *baraza* to talk about two types of control: in a material sense, and in relation to people. He stressed that he was interested in both forms. The sixth participant told us he had a position where he was responsible for control, without further elaboration.

I began my contribution by describing my previous research in the archives, where I had come across the institution of the *tshanga tshanga,* and added that during the interviews many had talked about these controlling bodies. I explained that, from my perspective, I would classify the *tshanga tshanga* as one of the most influential bodies used by the company to control the life of the workers far beyond working time. One participant immediately claimed: "*C'était magnifique!*" (It was wonderful!)

He continued, arguing that this system represented true management and that thanks to it there were no social problems or fights in Cité Gécamines. It took me several minutes and several attempts to frame my reading of this system to the participants, as one that did not protect the workers and the families but controlled them beyond what I considered ethical. However, it was clear that our understandings differed. One participant vehemently declared that they were not controlled in the way I understood control, because they were not controlled everywhere. He argued that the *tshanga tshanga*'s influence was limited to the area of Cité Gécamines and there was still the possibility to go elsewhere (*ailleurs*); he was referring to other parts of the city, where they were free to move around.

However, one difficult side of this controlling body was brought up by another participant. He added that the company did not allow family members to visit them in Cité Gécamines, and he concluded: "*Ça nous a fait un peu mal*" (That hurt us a little). One participant countered that because of these regulations of visitors there were fewer problems in the Cité Gécamines. He concluded that this was difficult, but in the end was a good way to live in a safe environment. Another participant explained to me, "*Nous les Africains, nous les Congolais, nous avons vécu en famille* élargie" (We Africans, we Congolese, have lived in an extended family), thus indicating the importance of family visits. I was framed as the outsider, because I was not part of *nous* (we) and not familiar with the Congolese way of living. From the beginning, the UMHK and Gécamines tried to prevent their workers from living in extended families by promoting the nuclear family preferred by Belgian (European) ideology. The participant's comment thus referred to a difficult situation for "them" since the start of the Belgian colonial approach to family. And his comment was one of the very few explicit criticisms of life as an employee of the mining company.

The workers' leisure time outside Cité Gécamines was the next point we discussed. One of the male participants mentioned that only about 20% of the workers went outside for pleasure activities. Most stayed in Cité Gécamines after working hours because the *cercle* offered everything. Recalling what the *cercle* offered triggered the next statement by another participant, who added that the company offered everything, not only in the *cercle,* except one thing – a decent salary. That was the second criticism during this *baraza.* However, another participant countered this statement in the following way:

Les gens étaient contents sans le savoir. Nous étions comme des domestiques. On te donne tout mais tu ne penses pas à l'avenir, il n'y avait pas de développements.

People were happy without knowing it. We were like servants. You are given everything but you do not think about the future, there were no developments.

This participant defended the company without mentioning it explicitly: "*On te donne tout*" (you are given everything). Another participant took up this statement to criticise the mining company: "*La société nous a pris comme des esclaves. On était sans avenir*" (The company took us as slaves. We were without a future). He not only explicitly mentioned the company, but also described the workers as slaves and not "only" as servants. Like the previous speaker, he emphasised the lack of a future. The next speaker explained that the slogan "*Gécamines njo mama njo baba*" (Gécamines is the father and the mother), which I had heard very often before and after this *baraza*, meant that your parents would give you everything because you were a child; you received housing, food, health care, simply everything. However, by reference to the mantra in this context, the benefits offered called for the beneficiary to accept the role of a child. Children receive what they need, but not more. The participant explained that with the very low salary they received, there was no opportunity to save money.

Today there is *libertinage* (liberation), but, as the same speaker further explained, there is no more discipline; everybody does what they want. This seemed to be an explanation for the fact that life in the Cité Gécamines had become dangerous. The discussion went back to the role of the *tshanga tshanga*, who, during the "good times", had authority because there were only UMHK/Gécamines workers living in this neighbourhood and not "all sorts of people", as is the case today.

I wanted to share another point that I linked to surveillance after going through the archival material: medical surveillance. In the archives, I had read about the medical examinations the UMHK carried out among workers in the early years – not only to make sure that they were healthy, but equally for medical experiments. The participants, however, insisted that all the examinations they experienced were solely intended for their wellbeing. One speaker explained that before someone was employed they had to go for a health check, including radiology and laboratory work. At this point a medical record of that person was kept. Every three years the health check was repeated except if there were urgent medical issues.

When I tried to dig deeper to understand if they ever felt discomfort or the sense of being treated as an experimental object during these check-ups, one person explained that this had not been the case because "they [those examining them] were Congolese". This means that the sense of trust was built on the fact that the medical staff were Congolese, blinding them to the possibility that Congolese medical staff could have been the perfect actors to gain cultural and relational trust while carrying out hidden experiments.

The speakers then explained that silicosis was quite widespread, caused by the work they did. However, it was presented as a disease one simply had to accept, and that the risk could be taken because the company cared for them if they were affected, and they received very good treatment. Furthermore, other work that could be carried out with this chronic disease was then offered to the worker.

The next statement then repeated what I had heard many times before: today, there was no more medical care, they were neglected. Even the NGO Caritas had neglected them. One participant said that this NGO had left because those responsible did not "see the truth", as he put it. He was referring to the overall precarious situation. The discussion around silicosis was thus turned into a complaint about the overall bad healthcare today and that nobody would see the truth that they were neglected, even by the NGO.

As it was rather late and I knew that some participants had a long way to travel back home, I suggested that we summarise this *baraza* and come to a common conclusion of our understanding of surveillance and control. Everybody agreed. One participant immediately declared: "*Il faut nous payer!*" (We must be paid!). At first, this surprised me, because it did not refer to any point we had discussed during this *baraza*. But it summed up the ODVs' general fight for compensation. It also underscored the need to be attentive to the differences between the researcher's interests and the interests of the communities we work with. Then he added: "*Nous sommes comme des combattants. Il faut nous donner ce qui nous est dû, les salaires*" (We are like fighters. We have to be given what we deserve, the wages).

Wage is a term that usually refers to the money one earns when one is employed. In the ODVs' terms, the compensation they were fighting for did not correspond to a salary. The speaker's wording can probably be interpreted as an expression of the wish to still be employed by the company or the wish to be in a situation as existed before 2003. The concluding remarks repeated this request for compensation and payment several times. It was a repetition of the master narrative's goal – to get compensation – without making explicit reference to what we had actually discussed during this *baraza*, which was surveillance and control. At a distance from the moments of our exchange, I now perceive this emphasis as legitimate.

2.3 *Baraza Three*

Planned to talk about health and hygiene – the president's baraza.

Setting: Three men (one of them the president of the ODV), one ODV woman, myself, Carl-Philipp, Gulda, Patrick Mudekereza and Sari Middernacht of Waza Arts Centre, the last two taking notes.

We started this discussion as with the other *baraza*: each participant was invited to explain why they had chosen to join this *baraza*. The president of the ODV opened the *baraza* and explained that he had been employed in the health sector. The next speaker, the woman, added that she had joined this group because the health situation was very bad these days. The following speaker stated that he, his wife and his son had needed medical care for 16 years but had not received it. The two other members nodded in agreement. Furthermore, one person added: "*Nous mourrons chaque jour ici*" (We are dying every day here). Accordingly, we started the *baraza* with this statement on our minds.

The president led the conversation. He started by explaining to us – or most likely to me – in a long monologue, the chronology of health-related issues there and how they had changed, while the other participants nodded in agreement. In those days – referring to the times of UMHK – two diseases predominated: malaria and typhus. Therefore, the *service de l'hygiène de UMHK* disinfected the houses regularly, and every evening the streets were fumigated to prevent people from contracting disease. Every three years, workers and their families were vaccinated against typhus. It was mandatory. But nowadays, he added, something like this did not exist anymore. Even worse, he continued, today a member of the ODV even lacks the chance to buy simple aspirin. And he added: "*Un ODV malade est une invitation de la mort*" (A sick ODV is an invitation to death). In the good times, the company even provided the workers and families with prevention tablets against malaria if they went on holiday. Nowadays, nobody cared for the ODVs anymore, and the president asked the rhetorical question: "*Comment va-t-il vivre?*" (How will he [a member of the ODV] live?) Then he used the slogan: "*Gécamines njo baba njo mama parce que on avait tout*" (Gécamines is the father and the mother because we had everything).

As the president paused, I raised the question of whether there was a difference in health care for blue-collar workers and for senior staff members who lived in Makomeno. The president explained that everybody got the same medical care; the only difference was that senior staff members were immediately examined by a doctor whereas blue-collar workers were examined first by a medical assistant and only then by a doctor, in case that was needed. I asked the group if this made them feel like second-class workers. The president spoke up and denied this. He stressed that the medical assistants were "*formés par les Européens*" (trained by Europeans) and thus were, in his judgement, very competent.

I alluded to the fact that in another *baraza* we had talked about the unofficial women. I did so because I wanted to bring up the question of health issues related to them. The president immediately reacted and explained that at that time life was so easy and that therefore, yes, that would have been the case (that were unofficial women). Another participant then added that men went to see other women because: "*Ici chez nous la première femme devient fatigue*" (Here the first woman becomes tired). However, as someone else emphasised, the company did not recognise the other women. It was unclear if the president shared this opinion. But he added that the wife was the one who had the authority; she was the one who was recognised and respected by the company and society.

Another participant declared that it was Mobutu who said that children with someone other than the wife should be recognised by their father. This would have been the time when children from outside began to live in Cité Gécamines and go to school there. I was told that it was the worker's wife who took care of the husband's offspring with other women, which again reinforces women's agency in this context.

The window of opportunity opened for me to ask about health issues in relation to relationships with women outside Cité Gécamines. Again, the president took the stand. At that time HIV was not an issue, there was syphilis, but once you were affected, the president said, it was not a problem because there was treatment at the hospital and people were discreet; nobody knew about a sexually transmitted disease. The only disease that became public knowledge was leprosy, because if you were infected you were isolated and therefore everyone knew about it.

During this *baraza* I tried again and again to motivate other participants to share their thoughts, mainly through nonverbal signs, so as to not interrupt the president while he was speaking. However, generally everybody nodded in agreement, and only once in a while did someone else further specify a point. I realised that this *baraza* was the president's *baraza*. He had assumed the role of explaining to me, the researcher, how things had been and would be today, while the others took on the role of supporting his statements.

We then talked about health issues in relation to housing in Cité Gécamines. Here too, the president took the lead and presented a chronicle of housing there. He started by describing the Cité in the beginning, although it was unclear to which period exactly he was referring. But he said it was what he could remember, and his description probably started around the mid-1950s. At that time, water was provided at public water pumps; the toilets were therefore not indoors but outdoors. He explained that there were different types of houses: those for bachelors, those for a married man without children and those for a married man with children. There were also modern and older houses, with access to the more modern houses dependent on employment classification. Furthermore, in the beginning, Cité Gécamines was not electrified; electrical power started in the years between 1963 and 1965. At that time – here there is a link to health – there was generally malaria and typhoid, and occasional cholera epidemics. The occupational disease silicosis was also present. As in the discussion during an earlier *baraza,* the ODVs present on this day did not demonise this disease but accepted it as possible collateral damage to the work in the mine. However, what was criticised during this *baraza* was the environment in which they lived now: the soil and air were contaminated as a result of the mining company's activities. Nobody had spoken about this before, not even during the interviews. The mining business was usually presented to me as a positive concept of *kazi,* with all the benefits that were sorely missed today.

We also talked about accidents at work. To put this topic in the right context, the president first explained the pension system for those workers who became disabled as a result of a work-related accident. The pension received was determined by the percentage of the disability, and one was entitled, as the president specified, to all "benefits" except the amount for transport to the job, which was otherwise added to the salary. Depending on the degree of disability, people could then either remain in their previous position or were assigned a new job that corresponded to their remaining physical abilities. There was also, the president stressed, a service for prostheses. This statement immediately triggered another reference to the overall good situation at that time: "*On avait tout*" (We had everything).

However, at this point, one member of the Waza Arts Centre stated: "You did get everything, except a decent salary! You got everything, except a future, what kind of emancipation was then possible for a worker?" At first there was some uncertainty among the group about how to react. The president essentially agreed, adding that workers at that time had everything: housing, education, healthcare, food, and so on, and that this therefore would have been a kind of emancipation because workers felt respected by being provided with these benefits. The person from the Arts Centre approached the president and wanted to know if this relationship [between employer and employee] should be a model for the future. The president answered in the affirmative.

On further questioning, he specified that he hoped that in future there would be regular payments, because this would prevent thievery in Cité Gécamines.

Another participant added that the *prime mobilier* (furniture allowance) was a good system, and someone else listed all the benefits the company provided in the good times as the model for the future. And then he declared: "*Vous êtes notre interprète!*" (You are our interpreter!) to summarise his thoughts. So, I was again pushed into the role of the one who gets information and, above all, receives an assignment. At that moment, I was not a participant in the conversation but a recipient.

The president took up the issue again and explained that in the good times, the UMHK and Gécamines employed the workers' children after they had been educated at their schools. Today, however, the few remaining jobs were no longer automatically given to children of former workers. In this context, I was also told that at that time if the husband died during his employment the wife was automatically employed by the mining company, a system that saved the family. All statements referring to the future started with "*Dans le temps ...*" (At that time ...) and thus referred to one phase: a time when the situation was perceived as good. The present was considered miserable.

When I initiated the closing phase of this *baraza*, everybody was invited to express concluding remarks. Again, the president rose to speak. He stressed the importance of the wages, described today's catastrophic situation again and, in short, retold the history of the 10,655 members of the ODV, and mentioned that every week some of them would die. Moreover, their children would leave home. Generally, the community was characterised by precarity, divorce and death, an echo of the master narrative.

2.4 *Baraza Four*

Planned to talk about health and hygiene.[11]

Setting: Nine men (one of them the secretary of the ODV*), Carl-Philipp, Gulda, myself, Patrick Mudekereza and Sari Middernacht of Waza Arts Centre, the last two taking notes.*

As soon as everyone was seated, a participant announced that we would pray. We all stood up. His words were difficult to comprehend and spoken very fast. However, I understood that he referred to the ODVs' very difficult situation. Reference to a divine force accompanied the opening of this *baraza*. As it

11 There were two *baraza* on this topic, because so many signed up for it.

turned out, the gentleman was a lay preacher. The secretary suggested, as in earlier *baraza*, that everyone should introduce themselves and mention why they chose to join the *baraza* on this topic. The initial prayer and the presence of the lay preacher was probably the trigger for all participants to first thank God before making their opening statement. But the opening prayer also influenced the opening statements in other ways.

Every introduction centred around the ODVs' current situation, in line with the lay preacher's words during the prayer. Some participants specified their difficulties, stating for example: "Since 2003 we have had no more access to the hospital; there is nothing and we are living very badly". The master narrative dominated the content of each statement, with slight variation. One speaker cried out: "*Tuko abandonné depuis 2003. Quel crime avons-nous commis? Tunakufa! Hatuna chakula. Haina bien*" (We have been abandoned since 2003. What crime have we committed? We are dying! We have no food. It is not good). He repeated "What crime have we committed?" several times; he was shouting and crying. I wept. Silence followed. Finally, one participant took the floor and repeated the master narrative "*C'était bien à l'époque!*"; so did the following speaker, who added that he was very ill.

The next speaker also restated the master narrative, and said that he had worked for the mining company from 1961 to 2003. He emphasised today's problems of poor healthcare provision, relating that there was not even any malaria treatment available. He concluded his statement with "*Asante, mama, kutuvisiter, tunakufa*" (Thank you, Daniela, for visiting us, we are dying). What exactly did he mean by this sentence? Gratitude that I was there, but *visiter* means to visit, not to support. Was it clear that I had no political or economic influence and that there was no expectation of me, although I had been given the role of the interpreter in an earlier *baraza*? In this moment, it became clearer to me that listening to them had helped them. They appreciated me for coming several times. Creating the opportunity for them to share their thoughts and feelings brought them some relief. They opened their hearts and expressed their hope that my book would open new doors to them. The last person to introduce themselves was the secretary. However, as was the case during the previous *baraza* he had attended, he did not speak about himself but stated that he was there to assist me.

I started by raising the issue of occupational illness. I asked them, as with the previous group discussing health issues, if they felt any anger towards the mining company because silicosis was a consequence of working in the mine. I also asked because I knew that some of the participants suffered from this disease. Again, I was not able to elicit a reply. Rather, the participants preferred to emphasise that the company had taken good care of them. I was told about the medical examinations workers attended in the good old times, and that the company would care for them if they became ill. There was nothing to criticise, I was told, but nowadays, yes, they were abandoned.

As in the other *baraza* on the same subject, I touched on the fact that I had read in the archives that workers underwent the medical examinations for statistical and scientific purposes. One participant reacted by saying that all was good at the time of the UMHK; they were well taken care of. None of the other participants expressed anything different. I then asked if they felt that they were treated as well as the senior staff in Makomeno in terms of medical care. One person confirmed that they received the same medical care, with the only difference being that the senior staff had a *docteur de famille* (a family doctor).

The discussion then shifted back to occupational accidents. Several of those present reported that they had had an accident at work. One participant had lost a finger, another had a serious problem with his foot, and another had broken his leg. They all asserted that they had received excellent medical care after the accidents, that they had been able to return to their former jobs and that it had not been necessary to transfer them to another job because of the permanent damage. Once again, someone cited "*njo baba njo mama*" and underscored that the company took care of them.

As we began to gather conclusions from this *baraza*, one speaker voiced a qualified criticism, saying that they had worked a lot for a small wage but that they also got everything. The secretary then spoke up for the first time and vehemently claimed that they were exploited. This was the first time he had uttered a criticism during a *baraza*. Up to that point I had felt that he was protecting the master narrative, that in his function as secretary he was also respected by the others, and that this hierarchy did not allow any criticism of the master narrative. Since the president was not present this time, the secretary was the one there with the highest status, which may be one of the reasons why he made this statement. This was one of the few occasions when the master narrative broke open, and as before, it was in the context of the level of pay.

Again, it was a member of the Waza Arts Centre who asked from the back: "What should the work look like for the next generation?" The answer from one participant corresponded to what we were told at an earlier *baraza*. He explained how it was in the good old days and that children were very well educated both at school and in the workplace; as a result, they were employed. The idea of the future seemed to be the desire to renew the past.

2.5 *Baraza Five*

Planned to talk about identity.

Setting: Eight men, Carl-Philipp, Gulda, myself, Patrick Mudekereza and Sari Middernacht of the Waza Arts Centre, the last two taking notes.

The introductory round was similar to the other *baraza*. In the opening statement, each speaker spoke about the drastic change in his life when he lost his job. Several of them used the expression "*être gécaminois*" (to be a member of Gécamines) as the reason they chose this *baraza* on identity. In summary, the participants mentioned points that were often raised with me. They stressed that although the work was hard, they were treated well, they received their salary regularly on the 15th of every month, they received a property bonus, they received healthcare, and so on.

Since the participants referred to themselves as "*agent*" (agent) and "*travailleurs*" (worker), I wanted to understand the difference. They explained that an *agent* was superior to the workers and that this function existed among the senior staff and blue-collar workers. A long explanation ensued about the different classes among the workers of the mining company, the kind of benefits associated with each class according to which class one was promoted, and so on. I was amazed at how well everyone could remember the different classes and exact benefits associated with each category of job. This included, for example, the details of the food rations.

My desire was to understand how the participants saw and described themselves. But I realised that this question about identity was too academic; I had to rephrase it several times to make myself understood. One speaker then said that he understood what I meant, but that identity was not something one would use for oneself; rather it was something used by others to describe a person. He explained to me that he had chosen his wife and his religion himself, and now lived in Lubumbashi, but that he was originally from the Kasai region, so you could say he was a Kasai. Nevertheless, what he really felt was that he was a *gécaminois*, which means that the job of mineworker was more prominent in his identity than categories such as origin, gender and marital status. This was strengthened by his new group identity as an ODV.

The discussion then moved on to what it means when people come from different regions and all work for the same company. I asked if there were occasional disputes owing to different origins. One participant stated that there were only small fights. The "*tshanga tshanga qui était notre patron*" (the *tshanga tshanga* who was our boss) took care of these little disputes. Back in the good times, that would have been the case. Today, on the other hand, there was a risk of serious violence, but there was no one left to deal with it. This argument was directly related to politics and was the trigger for the next speaker's statement. He said that nowadays politicians would try to use the former workers in their favour and destroy the sense of community. This would not work, he stressed, at least not among the ODVs, because they were all *gécaminois* and stuck together.

Shortly afterwards, I asked what would happen if the ODVs were successful in their fight for compensation and received the money from the World Bank. They would no longer be united in the common struggle, I argued, so what would be left? One participant immediately replied that even then they would still be ODVs, that this would never change and that they would stand together to move forward and make progress. But, he added, they would need someone to hold them together, as the president of the ODVs was currently doing. He then concluded: "*Baba Gécamines nous a gardé, Baba Kabemba [the president] nous garde*" (Father Gécamines was watching over us, Father Kabemba is watching over us). Then someone added that they would need a new father if life were to change.

I followed up and asked if they could not exist without a father. The answer was that every group needs a leader: "*On a besoin d'un conducteur*". Besides, he confessed, they were tired because they had been fighting for a long time and more than 4,000 of them had already died. Another participant added that he would not be able to look for another father because the time for another father was already over in financial terms, because "*Nous tous sommes déjà à la fin*" (We are all at the end). He concluded: "*Watulipe faranga yetu – huyu ni baba*" (The one who should pay us – that is the (new) father).

2.6 *Baraza Six*

Planned to talk about surveillance and control.[12]

Setting: Seven men, one of them the secretary, one ODV woman, Carl-Philipp, Gulda, myself, Patrick Mudekereza and Sari Middernacht of Waza Arts Centre, the last two taking notes.

In the round of introductions, it turned out that three of the men used to have a job that involved surveillance and control, which is why they wanted to participate in this discussion. The secretary, as in earlier *baraza*, was present, but did not want to introduce himself. He emphasised once again: "*Je suis là pour l'assistance*" (I am here to assist).

As in the previous *baraza* dedicated to the same theme, I wanted to reproduce some quotations from the interviews in which people stressed the importance of the *tshanga tshanga* system and its benefit for the overall organisation of life in Cité Gécamines. Just as in the other group, all the participants nodded in agreement and I was told, as before, that the *malonda* was the eye and ear

12 There were two *baraza* on this issue, because so many signed up for it.

of the *tshanga tshanga*. With the *tshanga tshanga* and the *malonda* they were even free, added someone. There were rules, as in any family that has to function well. "*Hapana kuiba, biote salama*" (There was no thievery, all was peaceful), emphasised a speaker.

Peace and order applied not only to working life but also to private life. There were, I was told, *les fiches disciplinaires* (disciplinary files), which were a good system because they controlled people and were in line with *la convention collective* (the collective agreement) on how life should be organised and be. One speaker added: "*La surveillance était bien, cela allait jusqu'aux jeux des enfants*" (Supervision was good, it went as far as children's games). Someone added that they were happy to comply with the UMHK/Gécamines regulations back in the good old days because wages were paid on time, and meals and healthcare were available. Today, however, there was nothing. Then another person stated that they had suffered in the three years before 2003 when they were not paid, and since then "*Nous sommes dirigés par les gens sans âme qui ne pensent pas aux autres. Il n'y a pas de surveillance, nous sommes abandonnés à nous-mêmes*" (We are led by soulless people who do not think about others. There is no surveillance, we are left to ourselves). One person said that they were in a way doomed. Another participant described themselves as follows: "*Nous sommes des victimes pour rien*" (We are victims for nothing). The reference to victim linked the past with the present.

I quoted a statement from an interview I remembered at this moment: "*Peut-être on était mal préparé pour le future*" (Maybe we were not prepared well enough for the future). How would the ODVs in this *baraza* evaluate this statement? A speaker then started talking about Mobutu and said that Mobutu had indeed been pro-Gécamines, that he had not closed his eyes, that in Mobutu's time everyone was paid on the same day, at the same hour, everywhere. Another participant answered: "*Pour quelqu'un qui a bien mangé on est distrait, personne n'a pensé à s'organiser parce que tout venait*" (For someone who has eaten well you are distracted, no one thought of getting organised because everything came to us).

The following points were then mentioned in connection with the future: pessimism about healthcare, because today only incompetent nurses were working in the health centres – this was not the case in the good old times; and difficulties for the younger generation to find employment today. One speaker said that his sons would have no work and therefore they, their wives and children would live with him and his wife on the same property, all around *un petit rien* (a little nothing).

The future depends on the World Bank's willingness to pay compensation – that is the understanding of the ODVs. They are waiting for the World Bank representative, as the uproar on the occasion of my first visit demonstrated. One participant related the question about the future to the behaviour of the World Bank. He noted that there would be no litigation with mining companies in Zambia. Only they (the ODVs) would suffer, "*si nous étions comme des Arabes* (as if we were like Arabs). *La Banque Mondiale ametuuwa*" (The World Bank killed us). Nobody was speaking about the ODVs anymore, neither on the radio nor on TV, complained another participant. The ODVs not only felt neglected but also forgotten by the world.

Our discussion about the future became a description of today's situation, which was dire in comparison to the glorious past. For the ODVs, talking about the future seemed possible only in reference to the past. The master narrative plays an important, if not the most important, role in reflecting on the future and highlighting the change they have experienced. In their current situation, nostalgic references seem to be the only strategy to cope with the present. One participant concluded in this *baraza*: "*Tunateswa sana, haina bien*" (We suffer a lot, it is not good). Another nodded in agreement and added, looking at me: "*Vous êtes notre ambassadeur, notre espoir*" (You [referring to me] are our ambassador, our hope).

As I mentioned in an earlier chapter, my role in the solution to their problem was a recurring theme, and in the preparation of the *baraza*, during the trigger event and during many individual conversations I made it clear that I could not change the situation. My contribution would be the book. And each time they assured me that they understood and that the book was a good thing. But during the *baraza*, every now and then I was put into the role of the *conducteur* they were hoping for, the *papa* they had lost. After all, I was the researcher from the global North who obviously had enough money to fly to Lubumbashi several times by plane. I cannot blame those who expressed their hope that I would become their *conducteur*.

3 Feeling Lost, but Productively

I often felt lost about how to describe the ODVs' situation, how to deal with this master narrative that seemed non-negotiable and how to handle the feeling that I could not live up to the expectation of being the leader.

The answer came at the moment I realised that I would not find a solution, but that this feeling of being lost could be success enough, because it stopped me from imposing categories I was not satisfied with. And I was constantly reflecting on my positionality as a white, female, free and privileged researcher to whom ODVs opened their doors, their private archives, their thoughts and their pains. Van de Port describes this sensation in academia where knowledge is created successfully only if clear categories can be found:

> We write about what we know, not about what we don't know. And we thus seek to temper that uncomfortable suspicion that "the world itself lies largely beyond our linguistic and intellectual grasp" (Jackson 2012: 29). Subjecting the world to our orderly aesthetic of straight lines, clear categories, coherent narratives, transparent methods, neat schemes and learnt vocabularies, we provide our readers with a sense of being in control. The people we study may be lost. We are not.[13]

In the context of this research, the ODVs felt neglected but not lost. I was the one who regularly felt lost. It was they who had a stringent and coherent master narrative, which they pursued with admirable consistency. Being nostalgic is a strategy for survival, though they are criticised for this by their children's generation. Their compliance to a strict master narrative is more than understandable. Sometimes they did this by violating the usual rules of co-operation at a communicative event, namely in not answering a question, or with an answer containing a reference to the master narrative when I had hoped for other information, all to return to the master narrative that was understandably of utmost importance to them.

It is therefore most interesting to reflect on "the contrast between the routine and deviant"[14] in communication during the *baraza*. In this sense, the most meaningful statements were those that deviated from the master narrative. The question that then arises is whose voice was raised, and whose heard? Whose voice was valuable? And what strategies were used to silence voices? I consider two elements central to understanding how these voices were weighted during the *baraza* by the ODVs: hierarchies and place.

Differences in hierarchy between the participants were clearly visible, which reflected that the ODV organisation is hierarchical in its structure. As the discussion of the extracts of the *baraza* showed, hierarchies were evident between the ordinary members of the ODV and the executive board, especially the president and up to a certain point the secretary and the teacher. But the lay priest also influenced the other participants, as was shown. In retrospect, it comes as no surprise that the secretary criticised the low salaries of the

13 Mattijs van de Port, "Baroque as Tension: Introducing Turmoil and Turbulence in the Academic Text", in *Modes of Knowing: Resources from the Baroque*, eds. John Law and Evelyn Ruppert, 1st ed (Manchester: Mattering Press, 2016), 167.

14 Paul ten Have, *Doing Conversation Analysis*, 2nd ed., Introducing qualitative methods (Los Angeles, CA: Sage, 2007), 145.

workers during the *baraza* when the president was absent. At all other times, he was the observer and secretary taking notes.

The ODVs' hierarchy levels influenced not only the participating ODVs, but me as well. I didn't dare interrupt the president, and the video recordings show that I – like the others – always waited until there was a break that allowed me to take my turn. Perhaps the most insightful *baraza* in terms of turn-taking was the one in which the teacher and the women negotiated the roles of women, the issue of "other women" and especially the access to wages. When the women brought up issues, the image that the master narrative had given me until then crumbled a bit. Strategies to silence the women's voices were mainly on a linguistic level. The teacher chose not to translate everything for them, or assessed their statements. The secretary objected several times to topics that were not pleasant (in the sense that they did not support the master narrative), saying that discussing them was not the issue now. Having the power to insist on issues or change them as needed is a sign of power.

4 Entanglements

The *baraza* took place in the house that is the command centre of the ODVs' activities. It is therefore a place that, because of its history, cannot allow anything other than retaining the glorious past and the present plight, which is the ODVs' core message in the struggle for compensation. If I consider the ODV board members as the elites of the ODV, and their meeting house as the space which exists unchanged in its materiality, but the function of which transformed from a mere residence to a command centre of their fights for compensation, then Goodman's finding of nostalgia in Mombasa fits very well:

> I interpret nostalgia for places that are no longer there (or are no longer what they once were) as a tactic by which older elites attempt to define Mombasa as "theirs", as a city they have more rights to than others.[15]

The master narrative belongs to the ODVs, not to me. Their insistence on the master narrative, and their strategy during the *baraza* to repeatedly steer the topics towards it, is therefore more than understandable.

During the *baraza* we collected and discussed fragments of knowledge. This assemblage, to use Law's terminology,

15 Zoe Goodman, "Tales of the Everyday City: Geography and Chronology in Postcolonial Mombasa" (PhD dissertation: SOAS University of London, 2018), 220.

> is a process of bundling, of assembling or better of recursive self-assembling in which the elements put together are not fixed in shape, do not belong to a larger pre-given list but are constructed at least in part as they are entangled together.[16]

From the *baraza* I learned many lessons about knowledge co-production and sharing. Co-production of knowledge is constantly challenged by different interests at a given moment. Take, for example, the comment "*Elle a bien répondu*" (she responded well) made by the teacher. He defined what was the "right" answer at that moment from a woman whose voice he thought he could assess and who was addressing me. The main interest at that moment was to provide support for an argument that upheld the master narrative. At the same time, however, all participants were accompanied by the desire to show a common interest in sharing. The *baraza* were therefore characterised by respectful co-operation even in the case of differences of opinion and resultant communication strategies, such as silence or changing the subject. As described in the introduction, discourse theory assumes that certain people or groups of people are able to influence the body of knowledge much more easily than others. This was demonstrated in the *baraza*. People in (perceived) positions of power define what is considered "true", change it and influence it. Various factors affect the perceived power of a person, such as the teacher, the secretary, the president, the researcher. But positions can always change and are always renegotiated in the *barazaweb*.

I also learned about the need for more sensitive and context-relevant methodology, the place of empathy in research, the need to keep rethinking our vocabulary, the ever-pressing question of our positionality, the beneficiaries of our research projects, the silenced voices (both in the archives and in the *baraza*), and the need to recalibrate theoretical groundings. The starting point of the research group's journey was the umbrella topic "housing". I return to this concept in summarising my part of this journey

16 Law, *After Method*, 42.

CHAPTER 6

Conclusions

1 The House as a Trigger of Nostalgia

I will use the metaphor of the journey to recap how this book project has unfolded. The journey started when I joined an interdisciplinary research project on employment-tied housing in (post)colonial Africa. The overall objective of this research was to explore how employment-tied housing served as a "tool of empire to exercise absolute control over private, social, and sexual relations of inhabitants and dwellers".[1] Coming in as a linguist, there was a need to figure out how my contribution would enrich the research project and allow me to learn from methodologies in other disciplines. This is where research in the archives featured prominently. The first step of the journey initially took me to the archives in Brussels in 2013. I spent three weeks there digging into the files to look for the material to help me apply for project funding.[2]

My first findings in the UMHK archives revealed that the provision of housing served to accommodate the workforce and as the main measure to control workers. Surveillance of workers manifested in a paternalistic approach that provided not only housing but also healthcare, education, leisure activities, food rations and other benefits. The materialised object, the house, was used by the colonial and postcolonial state and the company to define "home", which included most of all the imposition of the Belgian and company's conception of the nuclear family, the role of women and the role of men, among other aspects. These conceptualisations and the paternalistic experience in general left long-term traces among the target group for my project and the ODV organisation that represents the 10,655 workers who lost their jobs in 2003 after they started work there in the 1950s.

Interviews and the *baraza* were the second and most important step of the journey. During this phase, beyond asking my research collaborators questions, I could LISTEN and LEARN from ODVs about objects of loss, individually and in group discussions, during which the main mantra kept being repeated: "*C'était bien à l'époque mais l'avenir iko sombre*". This repetition explains my choice to use this rallying cry as the title of the book in order to announce the deep nostalgia the ODVs have been suffering from since 2003.

1 Martina Barker-Ciganikova, "Introduction", 4.
2 I later returned to the archives in Brussels several times.

Challenged by the dissonance between a historical record of labour exploitation (on the one hand) and a widely invoked contemporary nostalgia for this historical labour regime, especially in relation to the provision of social benefits in general and housing in particular, the interviews, the *baraza*, and the texts on the everyday life of the ODVs allowed me to explain this nostalgia beyond structural and socioeconomic terms.

For the ODVs, 2003 was the turning point, not national independence in 1960. The ex-workers talked with great nostalgia about the time before 2003, when work offered wages, healthcare, food and leisure, and when they were able to meet the expectations they had set for themselves as fathers, heads of family, husbands, men, colleagues, and so on. During their former employment, a certain amount of money was deducted from their wages, which guaranteed that they became the owners of the houses built by the UMHK/Gécamines. The house as such was therefore not part of the objects of loss in their nostalgic narratives, because it was the only materialised object left from the past. However, the house serves two purposes nowadays. First, it is a resource to deal with a precarious economic situation, in that they rent it out (and move to the *boyerie* or an annex), or adapt it to use it as a store or place for manufacture. Second, the house constantly triggers the beautiful memories of the past: the only thing left which evokes all that is no longer there and is still longed for.

2 Continued Insistence – the Function of the Master Narrative

This monograph also pays particular attention to the research process and the production of knowledge in a context where the researcher and the members of the communities being researched constantly navigated between different roles in a web of shared and differing interests. This research taught me to pay more attention to framing, methodologies, theories and vocabularies developed beyond the context of research, and to frequently interrogate my place as a white privileged woman in the research setting, especially my expectations, which were not necessarily those of my research partners. For example, while the ODVs were negotiating their identity, I was negotiating my changing roles depending on the setting, the topic of the *baraza*, the degree of emotions involved in the narratives, open or subtle requests to me and hopes placed in me. Whether these hopes were right or wrong is not the point. What matters is the legitimate fact that opening their wounds to me came with the anticipation of my own agency in improving their situation, which was characterised by nostalgia and the feeling of being abandoned and no longer having a father who cared for them. As one participant stated, the new father would be the one who paid them.

"Whatever its object, nostalgia serves as a negotiation between continuity and discontinuity: it insists on the bond between our present selves and a certain fragment of the past, but also on the force of our separation from what we have lost."[3] In chapter four, I discussed objects of loss: stability, *kazi*, leisure, space, the privilege to confine women to domesticity, and *heshima*. Respect for oneself and being respected by society thanks to the status as mineworker, and even now in a restricted sense as *ex-gécaminois,* was central to my interlocutors.

During the journey, I understood the emotional impact of the word *heshima*, which went together with the masculinity they saw themselves as being deprived of. *Heshima* covered aspects such as being the breadwinner, being a member of the Gécamines family, having time and money for leisure, assigning one's wife to domesticity and being able to entertain an extramarital relationship. The hierarchy in the relationship between a man (the breadwinner) and the wife (the one expected to care for the family) was and still is obvious, as the section on gender and identity has shown. I found it interesting to see that this hierarchy still holds as it manifested in the new framework of the *baraza*, moments during which women were once more silenced by the teacher, who did not translate for them or did not translate statements of theirs that he considered unnecessary or challenging performed masculinity. Ending the book with the notes on the *baraza* highlights what I could cover during the journey and the remaining questions that I may take up in a future project in order to further develop this new scheme, which centres on knowledge co-production.

3 The *barazaweb* as a New Framework

One major gain of the book project was the *barazaweb*, which shows how a field-based methodology can be of use for sociolinguistics, history, archive research and even the question of the economy of knowledge production, knowledge circulation and knowledge validation. What I call the *barazaweb* is an attempt to provide a forum for sharing thoughts and worries on a complicated situation. It succeeded in many ways, but I also discovered points that need to be critically accessed. The *barazaweb* council as a method was fruitful in the following ways:

- Providing an open social format;
- Sharing with the ODVs knowledge in the archives that was not accessible to them;

3 Atia and Davies, "Nostalgia", 184.

- Providing the ex-mineworkers with a forum for sharing their collective memories while granting their voices the status of alternative archives;
- Creating a space for knowledge co-production/participatory scholarship where all voices were given prominence;
- Testing co-operation with other organisations, for example, the Waza Arts Centre, which led to an exhibition;
- Creating a space for sharing one's wounds (remember the man who showed his scars to me);
- Opening up moments of talking as healing, hoping for a change;
- Offering space for trust.

The *barazaweb* council as an approach raised the following questions:

- How to deal with unexpected emotions?
- How to keep my balance when my "human" identity conflicted with my "researcher" identity?
- How to respond to expectations I could not fulfil?
- How to react to women being silenced once again?
- Would a women-only *baraza* generate meaningfully different results?
- How to manage silence after the outburst of emotions?
- How to navigate through the languages?
- How to address the recurrent plea for money?

Despite these challenges, I am convinced that this shared space generated a differentiated knowledge on the situation of the ODVs. Their factual and emotional solidarity, group knowledge and private archives add to (dry) knowledge in the archives by making the ODVs' voices heard: "*Vous êtes notre ambassadeur, notre espoir*" (You [referring to me] are our ambassador, our hope). My response to their rightful expectation was that the best I could do would be to channel their narratives in a book. At this step of the journey, which is surely not the last – here it is! "Mama Daniela", as they kindly and culturally referred to me, is not from the World Bank, as some ODVs thought at our first encounter, a moment that could have given a very different orientation to the journey, but which gladly took another turn after my position was clarified. I gained their trust and I made them the only promise I could make. I hope to have kept my little promise, to have reawakened their voices and reminded them of their cry since 2003. "*C'était bien à l'époque mais l'avenir iko sombre*" is the master narrative, the contours of which I, together with the ODVs, have explored in this book in the spirit of shared authority. I opened the book with this question: Do the words and voices from the archives still matter when the one you are talking to you is crying? Shedding but also sharing tears was another key moment of the *baraza*. I close the book with another question: Will the tears of the ODVs be seen, will their voices be heard and will some light be brought into their future, in the end?

Extensive Summary in French/Resume Detaille En Français

Cette monographie est le résultat d'une recherche qui associe les données dans les archives à Bruxelles et les données empiriques collectées à Lubumbashi. D'une part, je m'intéresse aux récits d'anciens mineurs de l'un des principaux acteurs du secteur minier au Katanga, l'Union Minière du Haut-Katanga (UMHK). Ces anciens travailleurs ont évoqué un passé glorieux et leurs espoirs pour l'avenir. La pertinence de leurs références nostalgiques pour faire face à la vie actuelle, les éléments déclencheurs de la nostalgie et les choses perdues auxquelles ils aspirent sont au cœur de l'analyse. D'autre part, je me concentre sur l'approche méthodologique, car les questions relatives à la production de connaissances et aux processus communicatifs impliqués ont été cruciales pour l'analyse du thème susmentionné. Le langage utilisé reproduit les inégalités en favorisant les uns tout en marginalisant les autres. Cependant, dans un processus de communication, les rôles des dominants et des dominés sont soumis à un processus de négociation constant, qui dépend des objectifs spécifiques des participants à un moment donné.

J'aborde la nostalgie des anciens mineurs comme une stratégie pour supporter leur situation de vie actuelle, et en plus, je considère leur « politique » de communication dans le cadre de la recherche comme leur possibilité d'exprimer leurs désirs et leurs préoccupations. Il était pour moi important non seulement d'examiner de près l'interaction entre mon rôle de chercheuse et le rôle des partenaires de recherche et leur influence sur la collecte et l'interprétation des données, mais aussi de montrer que les relations de pouvoir dans un cadre de recherche doivent être constamment remises en question. Le lien entre la chercheuse et les partenaires de recherche a donc également été exploré sous l'angle de la positionnalité.

Le processus de recherche a été caractérisé par des changements et des adaptations à de nouvelles questions. L'objectif du projet global interdisciplinaire dans le cadre duquel j'ai mené cette recherche était d'explorer comment le logement lié à l'emploi servait de mesure de contrôle sur les questions et les relations privées et sociales des employés et des résidents. Le logement a servi comme un point important à l'exercice du pouvoir et de la domination sur les sociétés, afin de discipliner les « sujets coloniaux » et, plus tard, les citoyens. L'accent a été mis sur ce que l'on appelle « l'ère du développement », des années 1940 aux années 1970, dans trois contextes différents : Livingstone en Zambie, Thika au Kenya et Lubumbashi (RD Congo).

 | DOI:10.1163/9789004724907_008

Le long chemin entre l'idée de recherche initiale et le résultat du sous-projet que je présente ici a commencé dans les archives. Après les premières recherches d'archives à Bruxelles, il est rapidement apparu que l'histoire entremêlée de Lubumbashi avec l'UMHK et son successeur, la Gécamines, la société minière qui a fourni des logements à sa main-d'œuvre dès le début, constituait des piliers importants pour aborder les questions de logement. En outre, la question du logement était l'une des principales mesures prises par l'État (post)colonial et la société minière pour contrôler la main-d'œuvre. J'étais donc convaincue que les tentatives de la société de façonner et de contrôler l'humeur des travailleurs – tant pendant la période coloniale qu'après – avaient dû laisser des traces. Le ressentiment des travailleurs envers l'entreprise était donc raisonnablement compréhensible. Parler avec d'anciens ouvriers qui ont vécu dans les maisons fournies par l'entreprise ou qui ont grandi dans ces maisons en tant qu'enfants d'ouvriers semblait donc tout à fait approprié.

L'attention s'est donc portée sur les ODV, ceux qui ont été concernés par le programme l'opération Départ Volontaire (ODV) lancé par la Banque Mondiale. Après que l'activité minière ait connu un fort déclin depuis les années 1990s deux raisons urgentes amènent la RD Congo et la Banque Mondiale à coopérer à nouveau. D'abord, pour soutenir le processus de paix et ensuite, pour répondre au besoin urgent de la RD Congo de relancer l'économie nationale. Dans ce contexte, la libéralisation du secteur minier était cruciale pour la Banque Mondiale. Donc le programme de réforme (l'opération Départ Volontaire) a été développé. Cette opération visait à réduire le nombre d'employés d'environ 24 000 à 14 000. Puisque les travailleurs n'avaient pas reçu de salaire depuis octobre 2001, ils étaient financièrement épuisés à ce moment-là et 10 655 travailleurs ont donc accepté de « partir volontairement ». Dans le contexte de cette opération, les anciens employés ont créé le Collectif des ex-agents de la Gécamines dans le but d'exiger le paiement intégral de tous les arriérés de salaire et autres avantages en nature. Le Collectif des ex-agents de la Gécamines est organisé en plusieurs sous-groupes, celui qui est au centre de cette étude est le groupe de Lubumbashi. Les membres du collectif de Lubumbashi sont devenus non seulement le nœud du projet de recherche mais aussi des partenaires de recherche.

Comme ma position a influencé et potentiellement biaisé ma compréhension et ma vision du monde, je me suis également penchée sur la manière dont j'ai influencé mon environnement de recherche. Je décris donc également l'histoire de notre communauté de recherche, depuis le moment où nous nous sommes rencontrés jusqu'à la manière dont la relation a évolué, passant d'une prudence compréhensible à une confiance mutuelle.

D'un point de vue méthodologique, j'ai d'abord travaillé dans les archives et mené des entretiens avec d'anciens mineurs lors de mon premier et de mon deuxième séjour de recherche à Lubumbashi. Je me suis toutefois demandé comment approcher une recherche qui remet en question ses propres interprétations et qui est réflexive sur sa propre production de connaissances.

Les réflexions sur l'approche de l'autorité partagée et le développement du *barazaweb* comme méthode pour répondre aux réalités du contexte étaient centrales. Le *barazaweb* s'appuie sur l'idée du conseil, du regroupement, la notion de s'asseoir et d'apprendre ensemble, un espace respectueux de confrontation des discours, de co-construction du savoir, d'autorité partagée et de démocratisation de la connaissance. Je décris également pourquoi et comment les langues impliquées dans le processus de recherche sont importantes. Ces étapes ont préparé le terrain pour que je puisse m'engager dans le contexte conceptuel auquel je me réfère pour analyser ce à quoi aspirent les anciens mineurs dans leurs souvenirs nostalgiques.

Partager une partie des archives ainsi que mes premiers résultats de recherche préliminaire et ma lecture des questions abordées dans les entretiens avec les membres d'ODV était une idée qui a émergé des discussions avec Sari Middernacht et Patrick Mudekereza du Centre d'Art Waza à Lubumbashi, qui ont commencé en 2018. Pour le projet Mitaani #mapping Moments en juillet 2019, le Waza Art Centre et moi-même avons donc décidé d'organiser des *baraza*. Les discussions entre les membres de l'ODV et moi-même devraient aboutir à une analyse commune de l'évolution des conceptualisations de ces thèmes, dont les questions sont basées sur mes réflexions après la recherche dans les archives.

Sur la base du principe de l'autorité partagée, de nouvelles idées et des connaissances sociétales supplémentaires auxquelles j'aurais pu être aveugle autrement devraient être permises. En outre, le *baraza* documenté devrait servir de données pour l'analyse du processus de négociation sur la nostalgie. Il faut souligner que la voix des ex-travailleurs est vitale dans un processus d'analyse collaborative. Alors que dans les entretiens, leurs voix étaient des sources individuelles, c'est dans les négociations collectives des concepts que les anciens travailleurs contribueront sur un pied d'égalité aux différentes couches, changements et significations des concepts. Ainsi, cette approche devrait démocratiser la production de connaissances. Il s'agit d'une co-création de connaissances scientifiques. En plus, le processus de négociation lui-même et les objets qui y sont liés (les sessions filmées et les bandes dessinées de ces discussions) serviront de matériel de conservation pour le Centre d'Art Waza (et seront donc publics et à nouveau accessibles aux ex-travailleurs). Il permettra un examen critique des résultats de la recherche par les participants et le grand public.

Les interconnexions entre les participants du *barazaweb* sont visibles dans la présentation parfois différente des discussions que nous avons eues. J'ai ainsi pu avoir un aperçu de la manière dont le savoir était produit à ces moments précis.

Je discute du récit principal des ODV « *C'était bien à l'époque !* » et de leur rappel constant de ce qu'ils ont reçu, dans le contexte du paternalisme et de l'approche industrielle paternaliste de l'UMHK, visible dans les documents d'archives et les déclarations des ODV comme « être bien soigné ». En outre, je soutiens qu'il existe une interdépendance entre les personnes et la matérialité. Je considère les objets spatiaux, en particulier les maisons, qui sont le seul objet matérialisé qui reste après que les ODV ont tout perdu, comme des déclencheurs de nostalgie.

Le slogan récurrent d'ODV « *C'était bien à l'époque !* » est compris comme l'étendue des expériences quotidiennes auxquelles les anciens mineurs se réfèrent. Ainsi, j'explore leurs objets sociaux et émotionnels de perte selon trois catégories : stabilité, respect (*heshima*) et identités. J'aborde ces points sur la base de biographies sélectionnées et je les mets en conversation avec les résultats des recherches dans les archives.

Le premier concept que j'associe à la stabilité est le concept de *kazi* (travail). C'était la condition pour qu'ils deviennent des ODV, c'est la base de ce à quoi ils s'identifient. La nostalgie des travailleurs pour *kazi* se réfère à une époque où l'emploi était synonyme de prospérité, qui se reflétait dans des choses matérielles telles que le logement, la nourriture, le salaire, l'offre de soins de santé, l'éducation et les loisirs, ainsi que le prestige. Il n'y a pas eu une seule conversation où l'on ne m'a pas rappelé ces avantages qui accompagnaient *kazi* dans « le bon vieux temps ». Les loisirs sont liés à *kazi* et constituent donc également un élément de stabilité. Ils n'existent pas en tant qu'activité en soi, mais comme partie intégrante du concept de vie professionnelle et privée. Ainsi, j'utilise l'imbrication du travail et des loisirs comme lentille pour étudier le paternalisme dans les entreprises. Un autre thème lié à la stabilité sur lequel je travaille est l'espace car plusieurs aspects y sont liés : l'histoire spatiale de Lubumbashi, avec la ségrégation des citadins et ses effets jusqu'à aujourd'hui, les mesures prises par l'UMHK pour contrôler la main-d'œuvre en définissant son mode de vie, et les organes de contrôle de l'espace *malonda* et *tshanga tshanga*, qui avaient assuré une sécurité qui fait cruellement défaut aux ODV aujourd'hui.

La deuxième catégorie est le respect. Le sentiment de manque de *heshima* (respect) depuis 2003 parmi les membres des ODV s'est exprimé sous la forme de différents problèmes, indépendamment du sexe. Les participants ont associé le respect à des questions différentes, mais étroitement liées. Premièrement, la reconnaissance du travail fourni par l'entreprise sous forme de salaires et d'avantages sociaux tels que les soins de santé, les rations alimentaires, etc. Deuxièmement, l'appréciation par les familles des ODV, car le travail a permis de satisfaire leurs besoins – et peut-être plus encore. Troisièmement, l'estime de l'environnement social sous forme de prestige, car ils étaient membres de la « famille UMHK » et accomplissaient un travail important et apprécié. Ce sont surtout les membres de l'ODV qui occupaient un poste de direction qui ont soulevé ce dernier point, tandis que les ouvriers et les cadres ont exprimé leur appréciation en termes de salaire et d'avantages sociaux. Quatre cas individuels (deux hommes et deux femmes) sont examinés de plus près sous l'angle de la question du respect.

La troisième catégorie concerne les rôles des sexes et l'identité. *Être gécaminois* est le résumé de tout ce qui unit les ODV, la vie professionnelle qu'ils ont eue, la vie qu'ils ont perdue et les expériences et souvenirs qu'ils partagent. Cela vaut pour tous les sexes. Comme des concepts liés au sexe sont apparus à plusieurs reprises, tant dans les archives que dans les entretiens et les discussions, je m'appesantis sur les concepts de masculinité et de féminité et des attentes qui leur sont attribuées. Les participants au *baraza* ont souligné que l'on attendait des hommes qu'ils s'occupent financièrement de la famille. La perte de revenus a donc radicalement changé la relation entre les hommes et les femmes. Les hommes ne pouvaient plus remplir leur rôle de soutien de famille. Ils étaient soumis à des normes morales, mais ils étaient surtout responsables de la vie saine de leurs maris afin de préserver leur force de travail productive.

L'objectif d'ODV – pour le formuler de manière provocante – était de maintenir leur récit et de me convaincre constamment de leur situation économique précaire. Ils devaient donc d'abord créer leur groupe, leur communauté. Je considère que les membres des ODV sont conduits par le temps, car le tournant de 2003 a radicalement changé leur vie. L'association des ODV a été créée à ce moment. Les membres partagent une histoire en tant qu'employés de l'UMHK/Gécamines et l'expérience d'un temps présent secoué, alors qu'un avenir incertain les attend.

Pendant les *baraza*, nous avons collecté et discuté des fragments de connaissance. J'ai tiré des *baraza* de nombreuses leçons sur la coproduction et le partage de la connaissance, sur la nécessité d'une méthodologie plus sensible et contextuelle, sur la place de l'empathie dans la recherche, sur la nécessité de repenser sans cesse notre vocabulaire, sur la question toujours pressante de notre positionnalité, sur les bénéficiaires de nos projets de recherche, sur les voix qui sont réduites au silence tant dans les archives que dans les *baraza*, et sur la nécessité de recalibrer les bases théoriques.

Les résultats du projet de recherche ont permis de dégager trois éléments importants:

Les premières découvertes dans les archives de l'UMHK ont révélé que les logements servaient non seulement à donner un toit à la main-d'œuvre, mais aussi à contrôler les travailleurs. La surveillance des travailleurs se manifestait par une approche paternaliste qui fournissait non seulement le logement, mais aussi les soins de santé, l'éducation, les activités de loisirs, les rations alimentaires, etc. L'objet matérialisé, la maison, était utilisé par l'État colonial et postcolonial et l'entreprise pour définir le « domicile », ce qui incluait surtout l'imposition de la conception belge et de l'entreprise de la famille nucléaire, du rôle des femmes, du rôle des hommes, etc. Ces conceptualisations et l'expérience paternaliste en général ont laissé des traces à long terme parmi le groupe cible des entretiens et de la *baraza*, l'association des ODV.

Les entretiens et les *baraza* ont constitué une étape très importante de la recherche. En plus de poser des questions à mes partenaires de recherche, j'ai pu ÉCOUTER et APPRENDRE des ODV sur les objets de perte, à la fois individuellement et dans des discussions de groupe au cours desquelles un mantra principal était répété : « *C'était bien à l'époque mais l'avenir est sombre* ».

Pour les ODV, 2003 a été le point tournant (et non l'indépendance de 1960). Les anciens travailleurs ont parlé avec une grande nostalgie de l'époque d'avant 2003, où le travail offrait un salaire, des soins de santé, de la nourriture, des loisirs et où ils pouvaient répondre aux attentes qu'ils avaient placées en eux en tant que pères, chefs de famille, maris, hommes, collègues, etc. Quand les ODV étaient employés, une certaine somme d'argent était déduite de leur salaire, ce qui leur garantissait de devenir propriétaires des maisons construites par l'UMHK/Gécamines. La maison en tant que telle ne fait donc pas partie des objets de perte dans leurs récits nostalgiques car elle est le seul objet matérialisé qui reste du passé. Cependant, la maison a deux fonctions aujourd'hui : Premièrement, elle est la source permettant de faire face à une situation économique précaire puisqu'ils louent la maison ou l'adaptent pour l'utiliser comme magasin ou site de production. Deuxièmement, la maison déclenche constamment les beaux souvenirs du passé : la seule chose qui reste évoque tout ce qui n'est plus là et qui est encore désiré.

Au final, cette recherche m'a appris à prêter plus d'attention aux méthodologies, aux théories, aux vocabulaires développés en dehors des contextes de recherche, et à interroger fréquemment ma position de femme blanche privilégiée dans le cadre de la recherche, notamment mes attentes qui ne sont pas forcément celles de mes partenaires de recherche. Par exemple, alors que les ODV négociaient leur identité, je négociais mes rôles qui changeaient en fonction du cadre, du sujet du *baraza*, des émotions impliquées dans les narrations, des demandes ouvertes ou subtiles qui m'étaient adressées et des espoirs placés en moi. L'idée de *barazaweb* comme lieu de co-production de la connaissance est née de cette interrogation de ma positionnalité.

Ce que j'appelle le *barazaweb* est une tentative d'établir un forum pour partager des pensées et des inquiétudes sur une situation compliquée. Le *barazaweb* a réussi à bien des égards, mais j'ai également découvert des points qui doivent être examinés d'un œil critique. Malgré de nombreux défis, il est très visible que cet espace partagé pendant les *baraza* a généré une connaissance différenciée de la situation des ODV. Leurs connaissances factuelles, émotionnelles, solidaires, de groupe et leurs archives privées s'ajoutent aux connaissances des archives en faisant mieux entendre la voix des ODV : « Vous êtes notre ambassadeur, notre espoir ». Ma réponse à cette attente légitime était que le mieux que je pouvais faire était de faire entendre leurs voix dans ce livre.

Appendices

Appendix 1

Report of the ODVs on the research stay July 2020.

RAPPORT SYNTHESE DU SEJOUR DE Mlle
DANIELA WALDBURGER

POINT DE VUE

- CONNAÎTRE LA VIE SOCIALE DES TRAVAILLEURS – EX-AGENTS DE LA GECAMINES (SURNOMÉ DEPART VOLONTAIRES),
- AVANT – PENDANT – APRES LA FIN DE SERVICE.

LE PRESIDENT [redacted] DANS UNE DES REUNIONS IL AVAIT INFORME LE CONTACT AU TELEPHONE AVEC MONSIEUR PATRICK LE DIRECTEUR DU CENTRE SOCIO CULTUREL WAZA ANNONÇANT L'ARRIVÉE EN RDC DE Mlle DANIELA WALDBURGER DANS CES PROGRAMMES ELLE AURAIT SOUHAITER VOIR ET PARLER AVEC LES-EX-TRAVAILLEURS DE LA GECAMINE.

- EN DATE DU 12 JUILLET 2019, LE VENDREDI ON TENAIT LA REUNION HEBDOMADAIRE SUPERVISER PAR LE PRESIDENT [redacted]

LA DELEGATION DU CENTRE SOCIO-CULTUREL WAZA PILOTÉ PAR Mr PATRICK LE DIRECTEUR, ACCOMPAGNÉ DE MONSIEUR [redacted] MADAME SARI, MADEMOISELLE DANIELA WALDBURGE ET MONSIEUR CARL PHILIPP BORNSDEIN LA DELEGATION ETAIT VENU PRENDRE DE CONTACT AVEC LE COMITE DES ANTENNES REPRESENTANT TOUS LES EX-TRAVAILLEURS DE LA GECAMINES ET TRACER LES PROGRAMMES DES INTERVIEWS LE MARDI 16 JUILLET 2019, LE BUREAU OU SE TENAIT LES REUNIONS HEBDOMADAIRES DES ANTENN

FIGURE A1 Report of the ODVs on the research stay July 2020, page 1

ETAIT DE LOCALISER A LA RESIDENCE DE L'ANTENNE
MAYELE MAMPOKO SE TROUVANT DANS L'ENCEINTE
DE L'INTERNAT DE LA GECAMINES POUR METTRE
L'EQUIPE DE WAZA A MIEUX FAIRE LE PROGRAMME.
A CET EFFET, ON AVAIT INVITER TOUS LES CAMARADES
DANS LA SALLE DE FETE DE L'EGLISE CATHOLIQUE
NOTRE DAME DE LA PAIX POUR UNE RENCONTRE.
ARRIVEE DANS LA SALLE IL Y AVAIT EU LES
PROJECTIONS DES FILMS DES TRAVAILLEURS DE
L'UNION MINIERE DU HAUT-KATANGA (UMHK)
PENDANT L'EPOQUE COLONIALE; LA VIE DES
TRAVAILLEURS ETAIT TRES BONNE.
APRES L'INDEPENDANCE, L'UNION MINIERE
AVAIT CHANGE LE NOM DE LA GECOMINES;
LA VIE SOCIALE DES TRAVAILLEURS ETAIT BONNE,
LES SALAIRES ETAIENT PAYES CHAQUE
QUINZAINE DU MOIS ET LES RAVITAILLEMENTS
ETAIENT REGULIERS, LES ECOLES FONCTIONNER
NORMALEMENT ET LES SOINS MEDICAUX
ETAIENT AU RENDEZ-VOUS

APRES LA RUPTURE DU TRAVAIL:

LES EX-TRAVAILLEURS DE LA GECAMINES
VIVENT ACTUELLEMENT DANS LA PRECARITE
QUI N'A PAS DE NOM; LA VIE SOCIALE NE
SE JUSTIFIE PAS TOUT A ETE JETER DANS
L'EAU.
- AVANT DE METTRE FIN A LA CARRIERE, L'EX-
TRAVAILLEURS DE LA GECAMINES ONT FAIT

FIGURE A2 Report of the ODVs on the research stay July 2020, page 2

TRENTE-SIX MOIS D'ARRIERES DES SALAIRES,
ENSUITES LES MIETTES PAYES A COMPTE GOUTTE ONT
DUREE SIX MOIS, ON PAYER CENT PERSONNES PAR
JOUR.
DEBUTE AU MOIS D'AOÛT 2003 POUR CLOTURER EN
JANVIER 2004.

EVALUATION:

APRES LES PROJECTIONS DES FILMS DANS LA
SALLE DE L'EGLISE CATHOLIQUE NOTRE DAME DE
LA PAIX ET LE PARTAGE DES BOISSONS (BIERES,
SUCRE ET DES GATEAUX) MLLE DANIELA AVAIT
DEMANDER A NOS CAMARADES DE SE FAIRE
ENREGISTRER POUR LES INTERVIEUVS ET LES
PRISES DES PHOTOS.
LES ENREGISTREMENTS ONT PRIS AU MOINS
CINQUANTES CAMARADES REPARTIS EN DEUX
GROUPES: L'AVANT-MIDI ET L'APRES-MIDI
SELON LES DIRECTIVES DES CHOIX DE MLLE
DANIELA WALDBURGER.
CONCERNE: LE TRAVAIL – LA SANTE – LA SECURITE –
– LE MARIAGE – LE DIVORCE – L'HYGIENE
– LE GARDINAGE ETC...
LES PRISES DES PHOTOS PAR LES DEUX CAMERAMENS
L'UN DE WAZA GUILDA ELMAGAMBO ET
MONSIEUR CARL PHILIPP VENU D'AUTRICHE
AVEC MLLE DANIELA.
ENSUITE LES CAMARADES INTERVIEUVÉS A LA
FIN, ILS ONT EU CHACUN UNE INVITATION
DE SE RENDRE AU CENTRE SOCIO-CULTUREL

FIGURE A3 Report of the ODVs on the research stay July 2020, page 3

WAZA. ARRIVEE A CE LIEUX LE DIRECTEUR
MONSIEUR PATRICK NOUS AVAIT CONDUIT DANS
LA SALLE OU IL YAVAIT LA PRESENTATION
DES TABLEAUX DESSINES ET LES ECRITS DES
INTERVIEUWS DES ODV PAR Mlle DANIELA.
NOUS ETIONS SORTIS ASSEOIR DEVANT LE STANDING
DANS L'ENCLO DE WAZA SUIVRE LES PROJECTION
DES FILMS DES INTERVIEUWS DE Mlle DANIELA
AUX ODV; POUR FINIR NOUS PARTAGER LES
BOISSONS (BIERES ET SUCRES) SIGNE DAUTEUR
DE Mlle DANIELA ET MONSIEUR CARL-PHILIPP.

NB. LES INVITES ONT EU CHACUN UNE ENVELLOPA
CONTENANT L'ARGENT POUR LE TRANSPORT.
EN GROS-MODO, VOILA L'ARRIVEE ET LE RETOUR
DE Mlle DANIELA WALDBURGER ET MONSIEUR
CARL PHILIPP BORNSDEIN PARMI LES-EX
TRAVAILLEURS DE LA GECAMINES (SURNOMME
ODV) LICENCIE ABUSIVEMET.

LE SECRETAIRE RAPPORTEUR

FIGURE A4 Report of the ODVs on the research stay July 2020, page 4

Appendix 2

Cartoons by Colby

FIGURE A5 Illustrations by Colby in the Waza Arts Centre

FIGURE A6 Illustrations by Colby in the Waza Arts Centre

Bibliography

Aiello, Flavia, and Roberto Gaudioso, eds. *Lubumbashi aujourd'hui: Langues, arts et société*. Mémoires lieux de savoir. Paris: L'Harmattan, 2021.

Akyeampong, Emmanuel, and Charles Ambler. "Leisure in African History: An Introduction". *International Journal of African Historical Studies* 35, no. 1 (2002): 1–16.

Alexander, Ben. "Excluding Archival Silences: Oral History and Historical Absence". *Archival Science* 6, no. 1 (2006): 1–11. https://doi.org/10.1007/s10502-006-9020-8.

Amuri Mpala-Lutebele, Maurice, ed. *Lubumbashi, cent ans d'histoire*. Comptes rendus. Paris: L'Harmattan, 2013.

Angé, Olivia, and David Berliner, eds. *Anthropology and Nostalgia*. 1st ed. New York, Oxford: Berghahn Books, 2015.

Atia, Nadia, and Jeremy Davies. "Nostalgia and the Shapes of History". *Memory Studies* 3, no. 3 (2010): 181–86. https://doi.org/10.1177/1750698010364806.

Atieno Odhiambo, Eisha S. "Kula Raha: Gendered Discourses and the Contours of Leisure in Nairobi, 1946–63". *AZANIA: Journal of the British Institute in Eastern Africa* 36–37, no. 1 (2001): 254–64.

Banywesize, Emmanuel M. "Placide Tempels et le destin de la pensée africaine contemporaine". In *Lubumbashi, cent ans d'histoire*, edited by Maurice Amuri Mpala-Lutebele, 275–88. Paris: L'Harmattan, 2013.

Barker-Ciganikova, Martina. "Introduction". In *The Politics of Housing in (Post-) Colonial Africa: Accommodating Workers and Urban Residents*, edited by Kirsten Rüther, Martina Barker-Ciganikova, and Daniela Waldburger, 1–30. Berlin, Boston: De Gruyter Oldenbourg, 2020.

Battley, Belinda. "Authenticity in Places of Belonging: Community Collective Memory as a Complex, Adaptive Recordkeeping System". *Archives and Manuscripts* 48, no. 1 (2020): 59–79. https://doi.org/10.1080/01576895.2019.1628649.

Bennett, Julia. "Gifted Places: The Inalienable Nature of Belonging in Place". *Environment and Planning D: Society and Space* 32, no. 4 (2014): 658–71. https://doi.org/10.1068/d4913p.

Bennett, Julia. "Narrating Family Histories: Negotiating Identity and Belonging Through Tropes of Nostalgia and Authenticity". *Current Sociology* 66, no. 3 (2018): 449–65. https://doi.org/10.1177/0011392115578984.

Bhattacharya, Kakali. "Othering Research, Researching the Other: De/Colonizing Approaches to Qualitative Inquiry". In *Higher Education: Handbook of Theory and Research*. Vol. 24, edited by John C. Smart, 105–50. Dordrecht: Springer Netherlands, 2009.

Bissell, William Cunningham. "Engaging Colonial Nostalgia". *Cultural Anthropology* 20, no. 2 (2005): 215–48.

Bissell, William Cunningham. *Urban Design, Chaos, and Colonial Power in Zanzibar*. Bloomington, IN: Indiana University Press, 2011.

Blaser, Mario, and Marisol de la Cadena. "Pluriverse: Proposals for a World of Many Worlds". In *A World of Many Worlds*, edited by Marisol de la Cadena, and Mario Blaser, 1–22. Durham, NC: Duke University Press, 2018.

Blokland, Talja. "Bricks, Mortar, Memories: Neighbourhood and Networks in Collective Acts of Remembering". *International Journal of Urban and Regional Research* 25, no. 2 (2001): 268–283.

Bodenstein, Carl-Philipp, and Daniela Waldburger. ""There Is a Fault Here!" – A Report on a More Inclusive Research Method in a Project in Lubumbashi (DR Congo)". *FIELD: A Journal of Socially-Engaged Art Criticism*, no. 17 (2021). http://field-journal.com/.

Botombele, Bokonga Ekanga. *Cultural Policy in the Republic of Zaire*. Paris: The UNESCO Press, 1976.

Bouchard, Vincent. "Commentary and Orality in African Film Reception". In *Viewing African Cinema in the 21st Century: Art Films and the Nollywood Video Revolution*, edited by Saul Mahir and Ralph Austen, 95–107. Athens, OH: Ohio University Press, 2010.

Boym, Svetlana. *The Future of Nostalgia*. New York: Basic Books, 2001.

Brichet, Nathalia. *An Anthropology of Common Ground: Awkward Encounters in Heritage Work*. Manchester: Mattering Press, 2018. https://doi.org/10.28938/9780995527799.

Bruner, Jerome. "The Narrative Construction of Reality". *Critical Inquiry* 18, no. 1 (1991): 1–21.

Bucholtz, Mary, and Kira Hall. "Language and Identity". In *A Companion to Linguistic Anthropology*, edited by Alessandro Duranti, 269–94. Oxford: Basil Blackwell, 2004.

Bucholtz, Mary, and Kira Hall. "Identity and Interaction: A Sociocultural Linguistic Approach". *Discourse Studies* 7, nos. 4–5 (2005): 585–614.

Busse, Dietrich. "Diskurslinguistik als Kontextualisierung – Sprachwissenschaftliche Überlegungen zur Analyse Gesellschaftlichen Wissens". In *Diskurslinguistik nach Foucault*, edited by Ingo H. Warnke, 81–106. Berlin, Boston: De Gruyter, 2007.

Callaci, Emily. *Street Archives and City Life: Popular Intellectuals in Postcolonial Tanzania*. Radical Perspectives. Durham, NC: Duke University Press, 2017.

Chapelier, Alice. *Elisabethville – Essai de géographie urbaine*. Brussels: Academie royale des sciences coloniales, 1957.

Chipande, Hikabwa D. "Football on the Zambian and Katangese Copperbelts: Leisure and Fan Culture from the 1930s to the Present". In *Across the Copperbelt: Urban & Social Change in Central Africa's Borderland Communities*, edited by Miles Larmer, Enid Guene and Benoît Henriet, 101–21. Suffolk and Rochester, NY: James Currey, 2021.

Chow, Rey. *Writing Diaspora: Tactics of Intervention in Contemporary Cultural Studies*. Bloomington, IN: Indiana University Press, 1993.

Clement, Piet. “Une expérience ambiguë d’autogestion: Le centre extra-coutumier d’Elisabethville, 1932–1957”. In *Lubumbashi, cent ans d’histoire*, edited by Maurice Amuri Mpala-Lutebele, 117–31. Paris: L’Harmattan, 2013.

Coghlan, David. “What Will I Do? Toward an Existential Ethics for First Person Action Research Practice”. *International Journal of Action Research* 9, no. 3 (2013): 333–52. DOI 10.1688/1861-9916_IJAR_2013_03_Coghlan.

Cooper, Frederick. *Decolonization and African Society: The Labor Question in French and British Africa*. Cambridge: Cambridge University Press, 1996.

Coquery-Vidrovitch, Catherine. “The Process of Urbanization in Africa (From the Origins to the Beginning of Independence)”. *African Studies Review* 34, no. 1 (1991): 1–98.

Couldry, Nick. *Why Voice Matters: Culture and Politics After Neoliberalism*. 1st ed. Los Angeles, CA: Sage, 2010.

Cuvelier, Jeroen. “Men, Mines and Masculinities: The Lives and Practices of Artisanal Miners in Lwambo (Katanga Province, DR Congo)”. Ghent: Instituut voor Antropologie in Afrika, Ghent University, 2011.

Cuvelier, Jeroen. “Work and Masculinity in Katanga’s Artisanal Mines”. *Africa Spectrum* 49, no. 2 (2014): 3–26.

De la Cadena, Marisol, and Mario Blaser, eds. *A World of Many Worlds*. Durham, NC: Duke University Press, 2018.

Deppermann, Arnulf, Helmuth Feilke, and Angelika Linke. “Sprachliche und kommunikative Praktiken: Eine Annäherung aus linguistischer Sicht”. In *Sprachliche und kommunikative Praktiken*, edited by Arnulf Deppermann, Angelika Linke, and Helmuth Feilke, 1–23. Jahrbuch des Instituts für Deutsche Sprache. Berlin and Boston, MA: De Gruyter Mouton, 2016.

De Rooij, Vincent A. “Letters to the Editor from the Section Habari Za Kwetu in Mwana Shaba (Journal d’entreprise de L’U.M.H.K)”. *Archives of Popular Swahili* 1 (1998). http://lpca.socsci.uva.nl/aps/mwanashabaApril1958letters.html.

Dibwe dia Mwembu, Donatien. *Bana Shaba abandonnés par leur père: Structures de l’autorité et histoire sociale de la famille ouvrière au Katanga, 1910–1997*. Mémoires lieux de savoir. Archive congolaise. Paris: L’Harmattan, 2001.

Dibwe dia Mwembu, Donatien. *Histoire des conditions de vie de travailleurs de l’Union minière du Haut-Katanga/Gécamines (1910–1999)*. Lubumbashi: Presses universitaires de Lubumbashi, 2001.

Dibwe dia Mwembu, Donatien. “Lubumbashi: Histoire et mémoire d’une ville industrielle”. In *Villes d’Afrique: Explorations en histoire urbaine*, edited by Jean-Luc Vellut, 131–44. Cahiers africains. Paris: L’Harmattan, 2007.

Dibwe dia Mwembu, Donatien. *Faire de l’histoire orale dans une ville africaine: La méthode de Jan Vansina appliquée à Lubumbashi, R-D Congo*. Mémoires lieux de savoir, Archive congolaise. Paris: L’Harmattan, 2008.

Dibwe dia Mwembu, Donatien, ed. *Les identités urbaines en Afrique. Le cas de Lubumbashi (R.D. Congo)*. Mémoires lieux de savoir. Paris: L'Harmattan, 2009.

Dibwe dia Mwembu, Donatien. "La structure de la famille ouvrière de Lubumbashi (1910–2010)". In *Lubumbashi, cent ans d'histoire*, edited by Maurice Amuri Mpala-Lutebele, 167–81. Paris: L'Harmattan, 2013.

Dibwe dia Mwembu, Donatien. "A History of the Gécamines Labour Camp, Lubumbashi, 1912 to Present Day". In *Revolution Room*, edited by VANSA/Centre d'Art Waza, 22–25, 2017.

Dibwe dia Mwembu, Donatien. "La perception du kazi (travail salarié) par les travailleurs de la Gécamines (1910–2010)". In *La société congolaise face à la modernité (1700–2010): Mélanges eurafricains offerts à Jean-Luc Vellut*, edited by Mabiala Mantuba-Ngoma, and Mathieu Zana Etambala, 161–76. Cahiers africains No 89. Paris: L'Harmattan, 2017.

Dibwe dia Mwembu, Donatien, Olivier Kahola, Mutete Sapato, and Aimée Kasandji. "Les communes et leurs habitants". In *Les identités urbaines en Afrique. Le cas de Lubumbashi (R.D. Congo)*, edited by Donatien Dibwe dia Mwembu, 83–109. coll. Mémoires lieux de savoir. Paris: L'Harmattan, 2009.

Dibwe dia Mwembu, Donatien, and Matthieu Kayembe wa Kayembe. "La ville de Lubumbashi, population et consommation de l'espace, 2000 à 2017". In *Lubumbashi aujourd'hui: Langues, arts et société*, edited by Gaudioso Aiello, 135–59. Mémoires lieux de savoir. Paris: L'Harmattan, 2021.

Dlamini, Jacob. *Native Nostalgia*. Johannesburg: Jacana, 2009.

Down, Simon, Karin Garrety, and Richard Badham. "Fear and Loathing in the Field: Emotional Dissonance and Identity Work in Ethnographic Research". *M@n@gement* 9, no. 3 (2006): 95. https://doi.org/10.3917/mana.093.0095.

Dumett, Raymond E. "Africa's Strategic Minerals During the Second World War". *The Journal of African History* 26, no. 4 (1985): 381–408.

Dunn, Kevin C. "Imagining Mobutu's Zaïre: The Production and Consumption of Identity in International Relations". *Millennium – Journal of International Studies* 30 (2001): 235–58.

Editions du Bureau de l'Information pour Indigènes (INFIND) Service des A.I.M.O. du Gouvernement Général. *À chacun sa maison* 4. Kalina, 1953.

Fabian, Johannes. "Kazi: Conceptualizations of Labor in a Charismatic Movement Among Swahili-Speaking Workers". *Cahiers d'études africaines* 50 (1973): 293–325. https://doi.org/10.3406/cea.1973.2713.

Fabian, Johannes. "Missions and the Colonization of African Languages: Developments in the Former Belgian Congo". *Canadian Journal of African Studies / Revue Canadienne des Études Africaines* 17, no. 2 (1983): 165–87. https://doi.org/10.2307/484212.

Fabian, Johannes. *Language and Colonial Power: The Appropriation of Swahili in the Former Belgian Congo 1880–1938*. African studies series 48. London, New York and Melbourne: Cambridge University Press, 1986.

Fabian, Johannes. "Simplicity on Command: On Pidginization of Swahili in Shaba (Zaïre)". In *The Fergusonian Impact, in Honor of Charles A. Ferguson on the Occasion of His 65th Birthday. Vol. 1: From Phonology to Society*, edited by Joshua A. Fishman et al., 377–85. Berlin: Mouton de Gruyter, 1986.

Fabian, Johannes, ed. *History from Below: The "Vocabulary of Elisabethville" by André Yav, Text, Translations, and Interpretive Essay*. Amsterdam and Philadelphia, PA: John Benjamins Publishing Company, 1990.

Fabian, Johannes. *Power and Performance: Ethnographic Explorations Through Proverbial Wisdom and Theater in Shaba, Zaire/Johannes Fabian*. New directions in anthropological writing. Madison, WI and London: University of Wisconsin Press, 1990.

Fairclough, Norman. *Language and Power*. London: Longman, 1989.

Ferguson, James. *Expectations of Modernity: Myths and Meanings of Urban Life on the Zambian Copperbelt*. Perspectives on Southern Africa 57. Berkeley, CA: University of California Press, 1999.

Ferguson, James. *Global Shadows: Africa in the Neoliberal World Order*. Durham, NC: Duke University Press, 2006.

Ferrari, Aurélia, Marcel Kalunga, and Georges Mulumbwa. *Le Swahili de Lubumbashi: Grammaire, textes, lexique*. Dictionnaires et langues. Paris: Éditions Karthala, 2014.

Fetter, Bruce. *L'Union minière du Haut Katanga, 1920–1940. La naissance d'une sousculture totalitaire*. Brussels: Centre d'études et de documentation africaines, 1973.

Fetter, Bruce. *The Creation of Elisabethville, 1910–1940*. Stanford, CA: Hoover Institution Press, 1976.

Foucault, Michel. *Dispositive der Macht: Über Sexualität, Wissen und Wahrheit*. Berlin: Merve Verlag, 1978.

Foucault, Michel. *Die Ordnung des Diskurses*. Frankfurt am Main: Fischer-Taschenbuch Verlag, 1991.

Foucault, Michel, and Daniel Defert. *Analytik der Macht*. Frankfurt am Main: Suhrkamp, 2005.

Frisch, Michael H. *A Shared Authority: Essays on the Craft and Meaning of Oral and Public History*. SUNY series in oral and public history. Albany, NY: State University of New York Press, 1990.

Frisch, Michael H. "Commentary – Sharing Authority: Oral History and the Collaborative Process". *The Oral History Review* 30, no. 1 (2003): 111–13.

Gabriel, Yiannis. "Organizational Nostalgia: Reflections on "The Golden Age". In *Emotion in Organizations*, edited by Stephen Fineman, 118–41. London: SAGE Publications, 1993.

Gardt, Andreas. "Diskursanalyse – Aktueller Theoretischer Ort und Methodische Möglichkeiten". In *Diskurslinguistik nach Foucault*, edited by Ingo H. Warnke, 27–52. Berlin and Boston, MA: De Gruyter, 2007.

Gebeye, Berihun A. "Decoding Legal Pluralism in Africa". *The Journal of Legal Pluralism and Unofficial Law* 49, no. 2 (2017): 228–49. https://doi.org/10.1080/07329113.2017.1351746.

Geenen, Kristien. "Categorizing Colonial Patients: Segregated Medical Care, Space and Decolonization in a Congolese City, 1931–62". *Africa* 89, no. 1 (2019): 100–124. https://doi.org/10.1017/S0001972018000724.

Gertenbach, Lars. "Die Droge als Aktant: Akteur-Netzwerk-Theorie". In *Handbuch Drogen in sozial- und kulturwissenschaftlicher Perspektive*, edited by Robert Feustel, Henning Schmidt-Semisch and Ulrich Bröckling, 263–77. Wiesbaden: Springer VS, 2019.

Goodman, Zoe. "Tales of the Everyday City: Geography and Chronology in Postcolonial Mombasa". PhD dissertation: SOAS University of London, 2018.

Grévisse, Ferdinand. *Le centre extra-coutumier d'Elisabethville: Quelques aspects de la politique indigène du Haut-Katanga industriel*. Brussels: Institut Royal Colonial Belge, 1951.

Gysels, Marjolein. "French in Urban Lubumbashi Swahili: Codeswitching, Borrowing, or Both". *Journal of Multilingual and Multicultural Development* 13, nos. 1–2 (1992): 41–55.

Harris, Verne. "Hauntology, Archivy and Banditry: An Engagement with Derrida and Zapiro". *Critical Arts* 29, sup1 (2015): 13–27. https://doi.org/10.1080/02560046.2015.1102239.

Harris, Verne. *Ghosts of Archive*. Abingdon, New York: Routledge, 2020. https://doi.org/10.4324/9780429343827.

Have, Paul ten. *Doing Conversation Analysis*. 2nd ed. Introducing qualitative methods. Los Angeles, CA: Sage, 2007.

Hertz, Rosanna. *Reflexivity & Voice*. Thousand Oaks, CA: Sage, 1997.

Higginson, John. "Bringing the Workers Back in: Worker Protest and Popular Intervention in Katanga, 1931–1941". *Canadian Journal of African Studies / Revue Canadienne des Études Africaines* 22, no. 2 (1988): 199–223.

Higginson, John. "Steam Without a Piston Box: Strikes and Popular Unrest in Katanga, 1943–1945". *The International Journal of African Historical Studies* 21, no. 1 (1988): 97–117.

Higginson, John. *A Working Class in the Making. Belgian Colonial Labor Policy, Private Enterprise, and the African Mineworker, 1907–1951*. Madison, WI: University of Wisconsin Press, 1989.

High, Steven. "Sharing Authority: An Introduction". *Journal of Canadian Studies/Revue d'*études canadiennes 43, no. 1 (2009): 12–34.

Hönke, Jana. "New Political Topographies. Mining Companies and Indirect Discharge in Southern Katanga (DRC)". *Politique Africaine* 120, no. 4 (2010): 105–27.

Hunt, Nancy Rose. "Domesticity and Colonialism in Belgian Africa: Usumbura's Foyer Social, 1946– 1960". *Signs: Journal of Women in Culture and Society* 15, no. 31 (1990): 447–74.

Hymes, Dell. *Ethnography, Linguistics, Narrative Inequality: Toward an Understanding of Voice*. London, Bristol, PA: Taylor & Francis, 1996.

Jahn, Thomas, Matthias Bergmann, and Florian Keil. "Transdisciplinarity: Between Mainstreaming and Marginalization". *Ecological Economics* 79 (2012): 1–10. https://doi.org/10.1016/j.ecolecon.2012.04.017.

Jewsiewicki, Bogumil. "Peintures de cases, imagiers et savants populaires du Congo, 1900–1960". *Cahiers d'études africaines* XXXI, 3, no. 123 (1991): 307–26.

Jewsiewicki, Bogumil. *Mami Wata. La peinture urbaine au Congo*. Paris: Gallimard, 2003.

Jewsiewicki, Bogumil. "Imaginaire collectif des katangais au temps de la désindustrialisation. Regard du dedans et regard d'en dehors". *Cahiers d'études africaines* 50, 198-199–200 (2010): 1–33. https://doi.org/10.4000/etudesafricaines.16493.

Jewsiewicki, Bogumil. "Leaving Ruins: Explorations of Present Pasts by Sammy Baloji, Freddy Tsimba, and Steve Bandoma". *African Arts* 49, no. 1 (2016): 6–25. https://doi.org/10.1162/AFAR_a_00267.

Jewsiewicki, Bogumil, Donatien Dibwe dia Mwembu, and Rosario Giordano, eds. *Lubumbashi 1910–2010. Mémoire d'une ville industrielle – Ukumbusho Wa Mukini Wa Komponi.* Paris: L'Harmattan, 2010.

Jiménez, Alberto Corsín. "Spiderweb Anthropologies: Ecologies, Infrastructures, Entanglements". In *A World of Many Worlds*, edited by Marisol de la Cadena and Mario Blaser, 53–82. Durham, NC: Duke University Press.

Kadima-Tshimanga, Bajana. "La société sous le vocabulaire blancs, noirs et evolués dans l'ancien Congo belge (1955–1959)". *Mots* 5, no. 1 (1982): 25–49. https://doi.org/10.3406/mots.1982.1073.

Kasombo Tshibanda, Michaël. "'Vocabulaire de ville de Elisabethville': Commentaire d'un point de vue sociolinguistique". In *Lubumbashi 1910–2010. Mémoire d'une ville industrielle – Ukumbusho Wa Mukini Wa Komponi*, edited by Bogumil Jewsiewicki, Donatien Dibwe dia Mwembu and Rosario Giordano, 92–106. Paris: L'Harmattan, 2010.

Kasombo Tshibanda, Michaël, Agnès Mwamba Chomba, and Diane Kabedy' a Sombw. «Traces du kiswahili dans l'exploitation minière au Katanga». In *La société de la copperbelt katangaise. Une autopsie de la situation socio-économique, politique et culturelle,* edited by Donatien Dibwe dia Mwembu, 213–237. Paris: L'Harmattan, 2021.

Kerr, Daniel. "'We Know What the Problem Is': Using Oral History to Develop a Collaborative Analysis of Homelessness from the Bottom up". *Oral History Review* 30, no. 1 (2003): 27–45. https://doi.org/10.1525/ohr.2003.30.1.27.

Ketelaar, Eric. “Archives as Spaces of Memory”. *Journal of the Society of Archivists* 29, no. 1 (2008): 9–27. https://doi.org/10.1080/00379810802499678.

Lagae, Johan. “In Search of a ‘Comme Chez Soi’. The Ideal Colonial House in Congo, 1885–1960”. In *Itinéraires croisés de la modernité Congo belge (1920–1950)*, edited by Jean-Luc Vellut, 239– 82. Paris and Tervuren: L’Harmattan and l’Institut Africain – Cedaf / Afrika Instituut-Asdoc, 2001.

Lagae, Johan. “Modern Living in the Congo: The 1958 Colonial Housing Exhibit and Postwar Domestic Practices in the Belgian Colony”. *The Journal of Architecture* 9, no. 4 (2004): 477– 94. https://doi.org/10.1080/1360236042000320332.

Lagae, Johan. “Rewriting Congo’s Colonial Past: History, Memory, and Colonial Built Heritage in Lubumbashi, Democratic Republic of the Congo”. In *Repenser les limites: L’architecture à travers l’espace, le temps et les disciplines*, edited by Alice Thomine-Berrada and Barry Bergdol. Paris: Publications de l’Institut national d’histoire de l’art, 2005.

Lagae, Johan, and Sofie Boonen. “A City Constructed by ‘Des Gens D’ailleurs’: Urban Development and Migration Policies in Colonial Lubumbashi, 1910–1930”. *Comparativ: Zeitschrift für Globalgeschichte und vergleichende Gesellschaftsforschung,* 25, no. 4 (2015): 51–69.

Lagae, Johan, and Sofie Boonen. “Scenes from a Changing Colonial ‘Far West’: Picturing the Early Urban Landscape and Colonial Society of Cosmopolitan Lubumbashi, 1910–1931”. *Stichproben* 28 (2015): 11–54.

Lagae, Johan, and Sofie Boonen. “Ruashi, a Pessac in Congo? On the Design, Inhabitation, and Transformation of a 1950s Neighborhood in Lubumbashi, Democratic Republic of the Congo”. In *The Politics of Housing in (Post)Colonial Africa*, edited by Kirsten Rüther, Martina Barker-Ciganikova and Daniela Waldburger, 66–97. Berlin: De Gruyter Oldenbourg, 2020.

Lagae, Johan, Sofie Boonen, and Donatien Dibwe dia Mwembu. “M(G)R. De Hemptin(N)E, I Presume? Transforming Local Memory Through Toponymy in Colonial/Post-Colonial Lubumbashi, DR Congo”. In *Place Names in Africa: Colonial Urban Legacies, Entangled Histories*, edited by Liora Bigon, 177–94. Cham: Springer International Publishing, 2016.

Lambertz, Peter. *Seekers and Things: Spiritual Movements and Aesthetic Difference in Kinshasa*. New York and Oxford: Berghahn, 2018.

Larmer, Miles. *Living for the City*. Cambridge: Cambridge University Press, 2021. https://doi.org/10.1017/9781108973120.

Larmer, Miles, Enid Guene, and Benoît Henriet, eds. *Across the Copperbelt: Urban & Social Change in Central Africa’s Borderland Communities*. Suffolk and Rochester, NY: James Currey, 2021.

Latour, Bruno. *Reassembling the Social: An Introduction to Actor-Network-Theory.* Clarendon lectures in management studies. Oxford: Oxford University Press, 2007.

Law, John. "On the Methods of Long-Distance Control: Vessels, Navigation and the Portuguese Route to India". *The Sociological Review* 32, 1_suppl (1984): 234–63. https://doi.org/10.1111/j.1467-954X.1984.tb00114.x.

Law, John. *After Method: Mess in Social Science Research.* International Library of Sociology. Hoboken, NJ: Taylor and Francis, 2004.

Law, John, and Vicky Singleton. "ANT and Politics: Working in and on the World". *Qualitative Sociology* 36, no. 4 (2013): 485–502. https://doi.org/10.1007/s11133-013-9263-7.

Lazure Vieria, Daviel. "Precolonial Imaginaries and Colonial Legacies in Mobutu's 'Authentic' Zaïre". In *Exploitation and Misrule in Colonial and Postcolonial Africa*, 1st ed., edited by Kenneth Kalu and Toyin Falola, 165–90. African Histories and Modernities. Cham: Springer International Publishing, 2019.

Lepore, Jill. "Historians Who Love Too Much: Reflections on Microhistory and Biography". *The Journal of American History* 88, no. 1 (2001): 129–44. https://doi.org/10.2307/2674921.

Lerum, Kari. "Subjects of Desire: Academic Armor, Intimate Ethnography, and the Production of Critical Knowledge". *Qualitative Inquiry* 4, no. 7 (2001): 466–483.

Lindsay, Lisa, and Stephen Miescher. *Men and Masculinities in Modern Africa.* Portsmouth: Heinemann, 2003.

Makori, Timothy Mwangeka. "Artisanal Mines, Governance and Historical Generations in the Congo Copperbelt". PhD dissertation: University of Toronto, 2019.

Malevez, Apolline. "'Les Douceurs De L'intimité': Men and the Making of Domesticity in Belgian Architecture Magazines (1890–1914)". *Dix-Neuf*, 2021, 1–15. https://doi.org/10.1080/14787318.2021.1926874.

Mantuba-Ngoma, Mabiala, and Mathieu Zana Etambala, eds. *La société congolaise face à la modernité (1700–2010): Mélanges eurafricains offerts à Jean-Luc Vellut.* With the assistance of Jean-Luc Vellut. Cahiers africains No 89. Paris: L'Harmattan, 2017.

Martin, Phyllis. *Leisure and Society in Colonial Brazzaville.* Cambridge: Cambridge University Press, 2009. https://doi.org/10.1017/CBO9780511584756.

Masandi, Pierre Kita. "L'éducation féminine au Congo belge". *Paedagogica Historica* 40, no. 4 (2004): 479–508. https://doi.org/10.1080/0030923042000250018.

Meeuwis, Michael. "Bilingual Inequality: Linguistic Rights and Disenfranchisement in Late Belgian Colonization". *Journal of Pragmatics* 43, no. 5 (2011): 1279–87. https://doi.org/10.1016/j.pragma.2010.10.009.

Meeuwis, Michael. "The Origins of Belgian Colonial Language Policies in the Congo". *Language Matters: Studies in the Languages of Africa* 42, no 2 (2011): 190–206. https://doi.org/10.1080/10228195.2011.571704

Meizoz, Jérôme. *Postures Littéraires: Mises En Scène Modernes De L'auteur.* Geneva: Slatkine Érudition, 2007.

Meizoz, Jérôme. "Sociocritique, ethnologie et sociologie de la littérature". *Romantisme* 145, no. 3 (2009): 97–110.

Middernacht, Sari. *From Collective Curating to Sharing Curatorial Authority: Collaborative Practices as Strategies of Democratisation in Exhibition Making in Lubumbashi, Democratic Republic of Congo*. Unpublished Master's thesis: University of the Witwatersrand, Johannesburg, 2018.

Ministère des Colonies. *Plan décennal pour le développement économique et social du Congo belge*. Brussels: Editions de Visscher, 1949.

Mobjörk, Malin. "Consulting Versus Participatory Transdisciplinarity: A Refined Classification of Transdisciplinary Research". *Futures* 42, no. 8 (2010): 866–73. https://doi.org/10.1016/j.futures.2010.03.003.

Monaville, Pedro A. G. "Decolonizing the University: Postal Politics, the Student Movement, and Global 1968 in the Congo". PhD dissertation: University of Michigan, 2013.

Mukendi, Luc. "Cité Gécamines and Operation Voluntary Departure". In *Revolution Room*, edited by VANSA/Centre d'Art Waza, 30–32, 2017.

Mulumbwa Mutambwa, Georges. "Kiswahili Kya Mu Lubumbashi, un dialecte ou une langue ? Une contribution au débat". In *Lubumbashi aujourd'hui: Langues, arts et société*, edited by Flavia Aiello and Roberto Gaudioso, 15–54. Paris: L'Harmattan, 2021.

Mutamba Makombo, Jean-Marie. *Du Congo belge au Congo indépendant, 1940– 1960: Émergence des évolués et genèse du nationalisme*. Kinshasa: Ifep, 1998.

Mutongi, Kenda. "'Worries of the Heart': Widowed Mothers, Daughters and Masculinities in Maragoli, Western Kenya, 1940–60". *The Journal of African History* 40, no. 1 (1999): 67–86.

Ngalasso, M. M. "Etat des langues et langues de l'état au Zaire". *Politique Africaine* 23 (1986): 7–27.

Ochs, Elinor. "Constructing Social Identity: A Language Socialization Perspective". *Research on Language and Social Interaction* 26, no. 3 (1993): 287–306.

Ochs, Elinor, and Lisa Capps. "Narrating the Self". *Annual Review of Anthropology* 25 (1996): 19–43.

Odhiambo, E. S. Atieno. "Kula Raha: Gendered Discourses and the Contours of Leisure in Nairobi, 1946–63". *Azania: Archaeological Research in Africa* 36–37, no. 1 (2001): 254–64. https://doi.org/10.1080/00672700109511711.

Ogundipe-Leslie, Molara. "Literature and Development: Writing and Audience in Africa". In *African Literature and Africa's Development: Mapping Intersections*, edited by Anne V. Adams and Janis A. Mayers, 27–36. Trenton, NJ: Africa World Press, 1998.

Patai, Daphne. "(Response) When Method Becomes Power". In *Power and Method: Political Activism and Educational Research*, edited by Andrew D. Gitlin, 61–73. Critical social thought. New York: Routledge, 1994.

Pauni, Pierre Kasongo, and Donatien. Dibwe dia Mwembu. "Vocabulaire de ville de Elisabethville, rédigé par André Yav, traduit et commenté". In *Lubumbashi 1910–2010. Mémoire d'une ville industrielle – Ukumbusho Wa Mukini Wa Komponi*, edited by

Bogumil Jewsiewicki, Donatien Dibwe dia Mwembu and Rosario Giordano, 33–71. Paris: L'Harmattan, 2010.

Perrings, Charles. *Black Mineworkers in Central Africa: Industrial Strategies and the Evolution of an African Proletariat in the Copperbelt, 1911–1941*. New York: Africana Publishing Corp., 1979.

Petit, Pierre, and Georges Mulumbwa Mutambwa. "'LA CRISE': Lexicon and the Ethos of the Second Economy in Lubumbashi". *Africa* 75, no. 4 (2005): 467–87.

Pickering, Michael, and Emily Keightley. "The Modalities of Nostalgia". *Current Sociology* 54, no. 6 (2006): 919–41. https://doi.org/10.1177/0011392106068458.

Pillow, Wanda. "Confession, Catharsis, or Cure? Rethinking the Uses of Reflexivity as Methodological Power in Qualitative Research". *International Journal of Qualitative Studies in Education* 16, no. 2 (2003): 175–96. https://doi.org/10.1080/0951839032000060635.

Piot, Charles. *Nostalgia for the Future*. Chicago, IL: University of Chicago Press, 2010. https://doi.org/10.7208/chicago/9780226669663.001.0001.

Portelli, Alessandro. "Living Voices: The Oral History Interview as Dialogue and Experience". *The Oral History Review* 45, no. 2 (2018): 239–48. https://doi.org/10.1093/ohr/ohy030.

Quaretta, Edoardo. "Apprendre à 'prendre la bière'. Masculinité, distinction sociale et rapports de couple dans la Lubumbashi contemporaine". In *Lubumbashi aujourd'hui: Langues, arts et société*, edited by Flavia Aiello and Roberto Gaudioso, 177–224. Paris: L'Harmattan, 2021.

Rettová, Alena. *Chanter L'existence: La poésie de Sando Marteau et ses horizons philosophiques*. Středokluky: Zdeněk Susa, 2013.

Rettová, Alena. "Swahili and Swahili Poetry in Lubumbashi: The Language and Lyrics of Sando Marteau". *Archív Orientální* 86, no. 3 (2018): 333–62.

Rice, Tom. *Films for the Colonies: Cinema and the Preservation of the British Empire*. Oakland, CA: University of California Press, 2019.

Rosaldo, Renato. "Imperialist Nostalgia". *Representations* 26 (1989): 107–22; Special Issue: Memory and Counter-Memory.

Rouverol, Alicia J. "Collaborative Oral History in a Correctional Setting: Promise and Pitfalls". *Oral History Review* 30, no. 1 (2003): 61–85. https://doi.org/10.1525/ohr.2003.30.1.61.

Rubbers, Benjamin. "Au temps béni de la colonie. Le Congo belge dans la mémoire des anciens coloniaux et des anciens colonisés". In *Autour de la mémoire. La Belgique, le Congo et le passé colonial*, edited by Rosario Giordano, 121–30. Paris, Turin: L'Harmattan, 2008.

Rubbers, Benjamin. "The Story of a Tragedy: How People in Haut-Katanga Interpret the Post-Colonial History of Congo". *The Journal of Modern African Studies* 47, no. 2 (2009): 267–89. https://doi.org/10.1017/S0022278X09003838.

Rubbers, Benjamin. "Claiming Workers' Rights in the Democratic Republic of Congo: The Case of the Collectif Des Ex-Agents De La Gécamines". *Review of African Political Economy* 37, no. 125 (2010): 329–44. https://doi.org/10.1080/03056244.2010.510629.

Rubbers, Benjamin. *Le paternalisme en question: Les anciens ouvriers de la Gécamines face à la libéralisation du secteur minier katangais (RD Congo)*. Cahiers africains. Paris: L'Harmattan, 2013.

Rubbers, Benjamin. "When Women Support the Patriarchal Family: The Dynamics of Marriage in a Gécamines Mining Camp (Katanga Province, DR Congo)". *Journal of Historical Sociology* 28, no. 2 (2015): 213–34. https://doi.org/10.1111/johs.12050.

Rubbers, Benjamin. "Towards a Life of Poverty and Uncertainty? The Livelihood Strategies of Gécamines Workers After Retrenchment in the DRC". *Review of African Political Economy* 44, no. 152 (2017): 189–203. https://doi.org/10.1080/03056244.2016.1273827.

Rubbers, Benjamin. "Mining Towns, Enclaves and Spaces: A Genealogy of Worker Camps in the Congolese Copperbelt". *Geoforum* 98 (2019): 88–96. https://doi.org/10.1016/j.geoforum.2018.10.005.

Rüther, Kirsten. "Asking Appropriate Questions, Reconsidering Research Agendas: Moving between London and Lusaka, in- and outside the Archive". *Administory*, no. 4 (2019): 110–24.

Rüther, Kirsten, Martina Barker-Ciganikova, and Daniela Waldburger, eds. *The Politics of Housing in (Post)Colonial Africa: Accommodating Workers and Urban Residents*. Berlin: De Gruyter Oldenbourg, 2020.

Sampson, Helen. "'Fluid Fields' and the Dynamics of Risk in Social Research". *Qualitative Research* 19, no. 2 (2019): 131–47. https://doi.org/10.1177/1468794117746085.

Savage, Mike. "Histories, Belongings, Communities". *International Journal of Social Research Methodology* 11, no. 2 (2008): 151–62. https://doi.org/10.1080/13645570801940863.

Schicho, Walter. *Le groupe Mufwankolo. Textes enregistrés et édités par Walter Schicho en collaboration avec Mbayabo Ndala*. Vienna: Afro Pub, 1981.

Schicho, Walter. "Linguistic Notes on the 'Vocabulary of Elisabethville'". In *History from Below: The 'Vocabulary of Elisabethville' by André Yav, Text, Translations, and Interpretive Essay*, edited by Johannes Fabian, 33–54. Amsterdam, Philadelphia, PA: John Benjamins Publishing Company, 1990.

Schicho, Walter. "Non-acceptance and Negation in the Swahili of Lubumbashi". *African Languages and Cultures* 5, no. 1 (1992): 75–89. https://doi.org/10.1080/09544169208717745.

Segall, Avner. "Critical Ethnography and the Invocation of Voice: From the Field/in the Field – Single Exposure, Double Standard?" *International Journal of Qualitative Studies in Education* 14, no. 4 (2001): 579–92. https://doi.org/10.1080/09518390110047084.

Seibert, Julia. "'Wind of Change': Worker's Unrest and the Transformation of Colonial Capital in Katanga – Belgian Kongo". In *Work and Culture in a Globalized World. From Africa to Latin Americ*, edited by Babacar Fall, Ineke Phaf-Rheinberger and Andreas Eckert, 253–72. Berlin and Paris: Editions Karthala, 2015.

Seibert, Julia. *In die Globale Wirtschaft Gezwungen: Arbeit und Kolonialer Kapitalismus im Kongo (1885–1960)*. Frankfurt and New York: Campus Verlag, 2016.

Shopes, Linda. "Commentary – Shared Authority". *The Oral History Review* 30, no. 1 (2003): 103–10.

Sitzia, Lorraine. "A Shared Authority: An Impossible Goal?" *Oral History Review* 30, no. 1 (2003): 87–101. https://doi.org/10.1525/ohr.2003.30.1.87.

Smith, Linda Tuhiwai. *Decolonizing Methodologies: Research and Indigenous Peoples*. 2nd ed. London and New York: Zed Books, 2012.

Strangleman, Tim. "The Nostalgia of Organisations and the Organisation of Nostalgia: Past and Present in the Contemporary Railway Industry". *Sociology* 33, no. 4 (1999): 725–46. https://doi.org/10.1177/S0038038599000462.

Strangleman, Tim. "Networks, Place and Identities in Post- Industrial Mining Communities". *International Journal of Urban and Regional Research* 25, no. 2 (2001): 253–67.

Stråth, Bo. "Ujamaa – the Evasive Translation of an Elusive Concept". In *Doing Conceptual History in Africa*, edited by Axel Fleisch and Rhiannon Stephens, 185–212. Making sense of history 25. New York: Berghahn Books, 2016.

Strathern, Marilyn. "Opening up Relations". In *A World of Many Worlds*, edited by Marisol de la Cadena and Mario Blaser, 23–52. Durham, NC: Duke University Press, 2018.

Tchokothe, Rémi Armand. "Archiving Collective Memories and (Dis)Owning: Special Issue, Ed. Daniela Merolla on Behalf of the International Society for the Oral Literatures of Africa". *Afrika Focus* 32, no. 1 (2019): 171–81. https://doi.org/10.21825/af.v32i1.11792.

Tchokothe, Rémi Armand. *«'Entré en tant que cousin, sorti en tant que gendarme': Visa Balladur, Kwassa Kwassa, (im)mobilité et géopoét(h)ique relationnelle aux Comores»*. Africa Multiple 2. Leiden: Brill, 2023.

Thomas, Keith. "Work and Leisure". *Past & Present* 29 (1964): 50–66.

Thompson, E. P. "Time, Work-Discipline, and Industrial Capitalism". *Past & Present* 38 (1967): 56–97.

Thomson, Alistair. "Introduction – Sharing Authority: Oral History and the Collaborative Process". *Oral History Review* 30, no. 1 (2003): 23–26. https://doi.org/10.1525/ohr.2003.30.1.23.

Trinh, Minh-Ha. *When the Moon Waxes Red: Representation, Gender and Cultural Politics*. New York: Routledge, 1991.

Van Beurden, Sarah. *Authentically African: Arts and the Transnational Politics of Congolese Culture*. Athens, OH: Ohio University Press, 2015.

Van de Port, Mattijs. "Baroque as Tension: Introducing Turmoil and Turbulence in the Academic Text". In *Modes of Knowing: Resources from the Baroque*, 1st ed., edited by John Law and Evelyn Ruppert, 165–96. Manchester: Mattering Press, 2016.

VANSA/Centre d'Art Waza, ed. *Revolution Room.* Johannesburg: Visual Art Network of South Africa/ Lubumbashi: Waza Centre d'Art de Lubumbashi, 2017.

Vanthemsche, Guy. *Belgium and the Congo, 1885–1980.* New York: Cambridge University Press, 2012.

Vellut, Jean-Luc. *Les bassins miniers de l'ancien Congo belge. Essai d'histoire économique et sociale (1900–1960).* Brussels: CEDAF, 1981.

Vellut, Jean-Luc. "Mining in the Belgian Congo". In *History of Central Africa*, 4th imp., edited by David Birmingham and Phyllis M. Martin, 126–62. London, New York: Longman, 1993.

Vellut, Jean-Luc, ed. *Itinéraires croisés de la modernité Congo belge (1920–1950).* Cahiers africains / Afrika Studies. Paris and Tervuren: L'Harmattan and l'Institut Africain – Cedaf / Afrika Instituut-Asdoc, 2001.

Vellut, Jean-Luc, ed. *Villes d'Afrique: Explorations en histoire urbaine.* Cahiers africains. Paris: L'Harmattan, 2007.

Visweswaran, Kamala. *Fictions of Feminist Ethnography.* Minneapolis, MN: University of Minnesota Press, 1994.

Waldburger, Daniela. *Komorisch im Transnationalen Kontext.* Grazer Plurilingualismus-Studien 3. Graz: Karl-Franzens-Univ. Graz Treffpunkt Sprachen Forschungsbereich Plurilingualismus, 2015.

Waldburger, Daniela. "Swahili in Eastern Congo – From a Dominated to a Dominant Language or Vice Versa?" In *Pluricentric Languages and Non-Dominant Varieties Worldwide: Volume 1: Pluricentric Languages Across Continents – Features and Usage*, edited by Rudolf Muhr, 149–63. Frankfurt and Vienna: Peter Lang, 2016.

Waldburger, Daniela, "Social identity/identities among plurilingual Comorians in Marseille (France)". In *Mobility and Minorities in Africa – Nova Collectanea Africana*, edited by Michele Carboni, 193–214. Cagliari: Nova Collectanea Africana Collana del Centro di Studi Africani in Sardegna, 2018.

Waldburger, Daniela. "House, Home, Health and Hygiene – Social Engineering of Workers in Elisabethville / Lubumbashi (1940s to 1960s) Through the Lens of Language Usage". In *The Politics of Housing in (Post)Colonial Africa*, edited by Kirsten Rüther, Martina Barker-Ciganikova, and Daniela Waldburger, 141–166. Berlin: De Gruyter Oldenbourg, 2020.

Waldburger, Daniela. "'Il y a une erreur ici !' Rapport sur une méthode de recherche plus inclusive dans le cadre d'un projet impliquant d'anciens mineurs à Lubumbashi". In *Lubumbashi aujourd'hui: Langues, arts et société*, edited by Flavia Aiello and Roberto Gaudioso, 161–77. Paris: L'Harmattan, 2021.

Waldburger, Daniela. "'C'était bien à l'époque': Work and Leisure Among Retrenched Mineworkers in the Democratic Republic of the Congo". *African Studies* 82, no. 1 (2023): 24– 42. https://doi.org/10.1080/00020184.2023.2195358.

Warnke, Ingo H., ed. *Diskurslinguistik nach Foucault*. Berlin and Boston, MA: De Gruyter, 2007.

White, Luise. *Speaking with Vampires*. Stanford, CA: University of California Press, 2000. https://doi.org/10.1525/9780520922297.

Worby, Eric, and Shireen Ally. "The Disappointment of Nostalgia: Conceptualising Cultures of Memory in Contemporary South Africa". *Social Dynamics: A Journal of African Studies* 39, no. 3 (2013): 457–80.

Yékú, James, and Ayobami Ojebode. "From Google Doodles to Facebook: Nostalgia and Visual Reconstructions of the Past in Nigeria". *African Studies Review* 64, no. 3 (2021): 498–522. https://doi.org/10.1017/asr.2020.118.

Young, Crawford. *Politics in the Congo: Decolonisation and Independence*. Princeton, NJ: Princeton University Press, 1965.

Archival Sources

State Archives in Brussels, Belgium, Archives générales du Royaume 2 – Dépôt Joseph Cuvelier, Première série (AGR 2)

654-03037, 1937, Union Minière du Haut Katanga – Services d'Afrique, Departement M.O.I., Rapport Annuel 1937.

654-03038, 1939, Union Minière du Haut Katanga – Services d'Afrique, Departement M.O.I., Rapport Annuel 1938.

654-03042, 1947, Union Minière du Haut-Katanga – Services d'Afrique, Département M.O.I., Rapport 1940–1946.

654-03042, 1948, Union Minière du Haut-Katanga – Services d'Afrique, Département M.O.I., Rapport Annuel 1947.

654-03043, 1948, Union Minière du Haut-Katanga – Services d'Afrique, Département M.O.I., Rapport Annuel.

655-03045, 1949, Union Minière du Haut-Katanga – Services d'Afrique, Département M.O.I., Rapport Annuel.

655-03046, 1950, Union Minière du Haut-Katanga – Services d'Afrique, Département M.O.I., Rapport Annuel.

655-03047, 1951, Union Minière du Haut Katanga – Services d'Afrique, Département M.O.I., Rapport Annuel.

656-03049, 1952, Union Minière du Haut-Katanga – Services d'Afrique, Département M.O.I., Rapport Annuel.

656-03050, 1953, Union Minière du Haut-Katanga – Services d'Afrique, Département M.O.I., Rapport Annuel.

657-03051, 1954, Union Minière du Haut-Katanga – Services d'Afrique, Département M.O.I., Rapport Annuel.

2424, 24.11.1955, Union Minière du Haut-Katanga – Réunions du conseil d'administration.

657-03052, 1955, Union Minière du Haut-Katanga – Services d'Afrique, Département M.O.I., Rapport Annuel.

657-03053, 1956, Union Minière du Haut-Katanga – Services d'Afrique, Département M.O.I., Rapport Annuel.

657-03054, 1957, Union Minière du Haut-Katanga – Services d'Afrique, Département M.O.I., Rapport Annuel.

634, 1958, Union Minière du Haut-Katanga – Services d'Afrique, Département M.O.I., Rapport Annuel.

635, 1959, Union Minière du Haut-Katanga – Services d'Afrique, Département M.O.I., Rapport Annuel.

636, 1960, Union Minière du Haut-Katanga – Services d'Afrique, Département M.O.I., Rapport Annuel.
637, 1961, Union Minière du Haut-Katanga – Services d'Afrique, Département M.O.I., Rapport Annuel.
638, 1962, Union Minière du Haut-Katanga – Services d'Afrique, Département M.O.I., Rapport Annuel.
639, 1963, Union Minière du Haut-Katanga – Services d'Afrique, Département M.O.I., Rapport Annuel.
640, 1964, Union Minière du Haut-Katanga – Services d'Afrique, Département M.O.I., Rapport Annuel.

Library of Contemporary History, Royal Museum for Central Africa, Tervuren, Belgium

Mwana Shaba, No. 11, October 1964.
Mwana Shaba, No. 12, November 1964.
Mwana Shaba, No. 13, December 1964.
Mwana Shaba, No. 123, 15 April 1966.
Mwana Shaba, No. 125, 15 May 1966.
Mwana Shaba, No. 126, 1 June 1966.
Mwana Shaba, No. 127, 15 June 1966.

ANOM (Archives Nationales d'Outre-Mer), Aix-en-Provence, France

Territoire du Sénégal, Cercle Linguère Rapport politique, Commandant du Cercle Gienger, Sénégal 1952, FR ANOM 14 MIOM 2738, AOF 2G52/214.

Index

Printed in the United States
by Baker & Taylor Publisher Services